EDIBLE
WILD MUSHROOMS
OF NORTH AMERICA

Merry christmas Rick!
Love, Leslie & Dave
( - practice your cooking for
our next visit (!:) )
- 1998 -

# Edible Wild Mushrooms of North America

A FIELD-TO-KITCHEN GUIDE
BY DAVID W. FISCHER AND ALAN E. BESSETTE

University of Texas Press, Austin

Second paperback
printing, 1996

Requests for permission
to reproduce material
from this work should be
sent to Permissions,
University of Texas Press,
Box 7819,
Austin, Texas 78713-7819

♾ The paper used in this publication
meets the minimum requirements of
American National Standard for
Information Sciences—Permanence of
Paper for Printed Library Materials,
ANSI Z39.48-1984.

LIBRARY OF CONGRESS CATALOGING-IN-PUBLICATION DATA

Fischer, David W. (David William), 1959–
    Edible wild mushrooms of North America : a field-to-kitchen guide / by
David W. Fischer and Alan E. Bessette. — 1st ed.
        p.     cm.
    Includes bibliographical references and index.
    ISBN 0-292-72079-3 (alk. paper). — ISBN 0-292-72080-7 (alk. paper)
        1. Mushrooms, Edible—North America—Identification.   2. Mushrooms,
Poisonous—North America—Identification.   3. Cookery (Mushrooms)
I. Bessette, Alan.   II. Title.
QK617.F53   1992
589.2′2204632′097—dc20                                                91-24351
                                                                              CIP

All photographs are
by Alan E. Bessette except
where indicated with initials
at bottom of the photograph.

DA   David Arora
TB   Timothy J. Baroni
JB   Jack Billman
JC   John F. Connor, Jr.
WG   Warren Greene
EJ   Emily Johnson
GL   Gary H. Lincoff
OM   Orson K. Miller, Jr.
SM   Susan Mitchell
ARB  Arleen Rainis Bessette
KS   Kit Scates-Barnhart
JS   Joy Spurr
WS   Walter J. Sundberg
ST   Steve Trudell

All black-and-white drawings
are by Philippa Brown.

Design and typography
by George Lenox

Frontispiece: Tree Volvariella (*Volvariella bombycina*)

# Contents

# Recipes

TO
DR. ORSON K. MILLER, JR.,
in recognition of his many years
of encouraging mycologists,
both amateur and professional,
and in acknowledgment
of his work, which first sparked
and kindled our fascination
with fungi

# Preface

Throughout North America, people gather and eat certain species of edible wild mushrooms with which they are familiar. In many cases, such knowledge of edible fungi is a folk phenomenon, based upon information handed down from generation to generation. European and Asian ancestry is especially responsible for this practical familiarity.

Most mycophagists, or people who eat wild mushrooms, are familiar with only a few edible species. Some people know about morels, others collect boletes, and some enjoy the Giant Puffball. But this folk knowledge is very limiting. Most people are skeptical of the idea that a large number of mushroom species can be easily identified and safely eaten. They have, in the great melting pot of the New World, inherited mycophobia—the fear of mushrooms—that is typical of Anglo-Saxon heritage. Wild mushrooms have a reputation for being mostly poisonous, and the common perception is that the edibles are nearly impossible to safely identify.

To some extent, these perspectives are valid. There are many poisonous species of mushrooms, and some are potentially life-threatening. It is also true that many mushrooms are difficult to correctly identify. Beyond these facts, though, is an important point: dozens of common delicious edible wild mushrooms can be identified very easily, even by beginners. That is the reason for this book.

Fear of mushrooms must be waning somewhat because the number of people interested in edible wild fungi is soaring. Local and regional mushroom clubs' membership rosters are swelling with novices whose primary interest is in identifying edible wild mushrooms. The information explosion of the last decade made many people aware of such wild gourmet mushrooms as chanterelles, morels, boletes, and puffballs.

Ironically, some experienced mycologists—people who study fungi—are nervous about encouraging beginners. Many novices are too self-confident, too dependent upon color pictures for identifying species, simply too anxious to pick something and eat it. In the face of carelessness, accidents happen, and no one wants to be blamed.

The rule governing edibility of any food you identify is simple: eat nothing unless you're absolutely sure it is safe. When people find out about our interest in eating wild mushrooms, they invariably ask, "How can you tell which are edible and which are poisonous?" The answer is a simple analogy. How do we know that frog legs are edible and toad legs aren't? We read, we learn, we study; in short, we educate ourselves about such things, thereby gaining cumulative knowledge of the subject. There is usually a follow-up question: "Aren't you afraid of making a mistake and poisoning yourself?" The answer is no, and the frog-and-toad analogy works again: until you can tell a frog from a toad, don't catch your own frogs for dinner.

Opposite page:
Sulphur Shelf (*Laetiporus sulphureus*)
WG

For the person who wishes to learn how to identify and prepare edible wild mushrooms, starting out can be difficult. The problem is that most field guides are not primarily oriented toward edible mushrooms. They present long, detailed descriptions of mushrooms, often using an extensive vocabulary of terms peculiar to botany or mycology. This book is intentionally different. It is specifically designed to help the beginner identify and prepare the most commonly eaten wild mushrooms of North America. Experienced mycophagists can also use this book to increase the number of edible species they can identify with confidence.

## Acknowledgments

This book is the product of a great deal of work by many people besides the authors. Our special thanks go to Arleen Rainis Bessette, who spent months collecting wild mushrooms and using them to create dozens of wonderful new recipes for this book. She also arranged and composed most of the recipe photographs, contributed several photographs, and read the manuscript and made numerous helpful suggestions. Dr. Barry L. Wulff, Dr. Paul F. Lehmann, and Stephen Rains also reviewed the manuscript; their comments, suggestions, and criticisms improved this work immeasurably. Dr. Joseph F. Ammirati critiqued the section on mushroom toxins; we are grateful for his expert assistance. Several individuals contributed photographs: we thank David Arora; Dr. Timothy J. Baroni; Jack Billman; John F. Connor, Jr.; Warren Greene; Emily Johnson; Gary H. Lincoff; Dr. Orson K. Miller, Jr.; Susan Mitchell; Kit Scates-Barnhart; Joy Spurr; Dr. Walter J. Sundberg; and Steve Trudell. The outstanding illustrations throughout this book were created by Philippa Brown. We greatly appreciate the many wonderful recipes contributed by numerous fungal gourmets. Joe and Laura Bess, Leisa Fischer, George and Rose Fischer, Maura G. Howe, Richard and Jean Howe, and Marian Martin deserve special thanks for their support and encouragement. Both of us are grateful to the members of the Mid York and Central New York Mycological societies and the North American and Rochester Area Mycological associations for their support and enthusiasm. Bill Chapman and Sally Reymers kindly helped in the selection of specimen photographs. Finally, we thank the entire staff at the University of Texas Press. The quality of design and photographic reproduction evident in this book are only the most visible characteristics attesting to their high standards.

# PART ONE

# DISCOVERING
# MYCOPHAGY

*Fungi ben mussheroms; there be two manners of them, one maner is deedley and slayeth them that eateth them and be called tode stoles, and the other doeth not.* —THE "GRETE HERBAL" (1526)

*Some of the finest foods in the world are free for the picking, and the truly poisonous ones are few, but one must learn to be discriminating.* —DR. JAMES J. WORRALL (1990)

# 1.

## An Introduction to the Mushroom

### *What Is a Mushroom?*

For many years, mushrooms and other fungi were classified as members of the Plant Kingdom. More recently, they have been placed in their own kingdom, the Fungi Kingdom. This seems only fair: mushrooms and other fungi lack chlorophyll, and their reproductive systems are wholly different from those of plants.

It is important to understand that mushrooms are simply the equivalent of fruit, bearing the microscopic spores that are the fungal equivalent of seeds. In other words, mushrooms are the reproductive structures of fungi. The fungus "body" is called the mycelium. It consists of a network of microscopic threads called hyphae. The mycelium is typically hidden in the food source (the substrate) from which it absorbs nutrients.

In terms of nutritional requirements there are three groups of mushroom-producing fungi. The first group is the saprobes, those fungi that receive nourishment by breaking down dead organic matter such as leaves, wood, feces, or humus. The second group is the parasites, which steal nutrients from living trees, plants, animals, or other fungi, weakening or killing their hosts in the process. The third group is the mycorrhizal fungi. These are essentially symbiotic fungi that receive much of their nourishment from the roots of trees or other plants. They benefit their host species by breaking down some nutrients into forms that are more easily utilized by the hosts and by increasing water and mineral absorption.

When conditions are favorable, a fundamental change occurs in the mycelium. It greatly increases its absorption of water and begins to form the complex structure we call a mushroom. Each mushroom grows rapidly, pushing its way out from the substrate to produce and release spores, thus perpetuating the species.

Some fungi require highly specialized habitats in order to exist— for example, the roots of a certain kind of tree, a certain climate, a certain type of soil. Others are more adaptable and, as a rule, more common. Some are short-lived, deriving nourishment from their substrates for only a few months. Others are perennial, some living for as long as several centuries.

### *Mushrooms and Taste*

Those who are unacquainted with the tremendous variety of edible mushrooms often ask, "Don't they all taste pretty much the same? If I don't like the store-bought variety of mushrooms, why bother with the others?"

The answer takes the form of an analogy. Just because someone dislikes figs and beets doesn't mean he or she dislikes all fruits and vegetables. Different mushrooms have different flavors, different textures, and different aromas. It can be said that most mushrooms have

Opposite page:
Young, tender Dryad's Saddles lurk in the shadows of fallen logs.

a "mushroomy" flavor, but it can also be said that most fruits taste fruity and that most meats taste meaty.

Because most people aren't used to eating a variety of mushrooms, they tend to be more aware of the common flavor components of mushrooms than is the case with meats, fruits, vegetables, or other kinds of food. Most mushroom fanciers are convinced that there isn't anyone who wouldn't like at least some kinds of mushrooms, if only the opportunity existed to try a variety of different ones.

This belief has been corroborated by personal experience. Those of us who have opened the minds—and mouths—of some of our most skeptical friends and relatives have enjoyed their surprised smiles when they tasted their first morel or their first slice of a puffball. Of course, not everyone likes every kind of mushroom. Even between enthusiasts there are differences of opinion on the culinary value of some of the edible mushrooms covered by this book. Taste is perhaps the most individual of the five senses. Therefore, in addition to our own preferences, we have considered opinions from a number of print and personal sources before deciding which species to include. Some people don't like sushi, or peanut butter, or prunes; some people won't like chanterelles, or morels, or puffballs. You will have to find out for yourself which edible wild mushrooms you like and which, if any, you don't.

Mycophobia remains a problem as a psychological factor: it is very difficult to enjoy anything you fear. Many people are profoundly afraid of eating wild mushrooms. Do not press the issue with such individuals.

Mushrooms may never play as big a dietary role in North America as they do in other parts of the world, but for those who enjoy trying different kinds of food, the Fungi Kingdom holds a vast array of gastronomic delights. For many, wild mushrooms are a whole new kind of food, and—with few exceptions—they won't be found in the produce section of the supermarket. They're free, lying scattered across the North American landscape. Find them, and enjoy them.

## Mushrooms and Nutrition

For those who are trying to control their weight, mushrooms are an ideal food. They please the palate while minimizing calories. It has been suggested that we can eat all the mushrooms we want and still lose weight, because it takes more calories to digest mushrooms than they provide. Mushrooms are truly low-calorie delights: the common cultivated *Agaricus* button mushroom has only thirty calories per one hundred grams, mostly in the form of protein! Mushrooms' fat and carbohydrate levels are negligible, and they contain no cholesterol.

These nutritional benefits become insignificant, of course, if the mushrooms are fried in butter or oil and then served with cheese or other fattening foods. Preserving the "light" nature of the mushroom requires simple cooking techniques, such as baking or broiling.

Almost no information is available on the nutritional value of various kinds of *wild* mushrooms. We can only presume that there is at least some variation from species to species. As a rule, though, mushrooms are composed of about 90 percent water. They contribute some protein; B, C, and D vitamins; and several minerals. They are low in fat, carbohydrates, and calories.

Use of wild mushrooms as food likely dates back to prehistoric man. Hunter-gatherer societies probably tried various kinds of wild mushrooms and, through trial and error, learned which kinds to eat and which to avoid. One of the earliest documentations of the use of wild mushrooms as food dates back to the Greek and Roman cultures of about 400 B.C. Classical Roman literature contains many references to mycophagy. Ancient Romans considered some species to be such wonderful delicacies that they dubbed them food for the gods. One edible *Amanita* species is still commonly called Caesar's Mushroom.

Mushrooms hold out no hope as a solution to the world's hunger problems, but they do provide promise to those who want to enjoy a variety of delicious, healthy, natural foods.

Fresh Golden Chanterelles and White Matsutakes displayed alongside cultivated mushrooms at Pike Place Market in Seattle. ARB

# 2.

## Fundamentals of the Hunt

### What to Take

Experienced mushroom foragers use a variety of tools and supplies, depending on what kind of mushrooms they hope to find, the terrain, weather, and other factors. The following is a list of the items that are most often helpful:

**A sharp knife** for cutting mushrooms free from wood, and for slicing specimens to check for insect larvae. Some mushroom hunters prefer a jackknife; others a hunting knife with a sheath. A good knife can also be used for field dressing species you already know. Morels and chanterelles, for example, usually need no further trimming at home.

**A soft-bristled brush** for brushing away any insects, soil, or plant debris from your mushrooms. You can buy a mushroom brush, but a pastry brush is a suitable substitute.

**A large flat-bottomed wicker basket with an arc-shaped handle** to help prevent specimens from being crushed.

**Waxed paper** for wrapping different species to keep them separated in the basket. Waxed paper sandwich bags are ideal. Leave them open to permit some air circulation. Plastic bags should not be used because they contribute to rapid spoilage. Small brown paper lunch bags will suffice.

**A note pad or index cards, and a pencil.** When you collect a new kind of mushroom, make notes about its habitat and growth habit—what are nearby tree or plant species? Is it growing on wood or on the ground? Are specimens clustered or scattered?— and use them to double-check your identification when you get home. Keep each note with the corresponding specimens. Also, don't use a pen. Pencils are far more reliable in damp weather.

**A walking stick.** Always a good idea for the hiker, a sturdy walking stick is also useful for discreetly poking around in fallen leaves.

**A field guide to trees.** Many edible mushrooms are associated with specific kinds of trees. Knowing how to identify trees is a definite advantage for the mushroom hunter.

**Bug repellant.** Habitat and season are often the same for mushroom and mosquito. There are many other little pests, including blackflies, deer flies, and ticks. Be careful not to get any repellant from your hands onto the mushrooms you're collecting for the table.

**A compass and topographic maps.** Especially when you're gathering mushrooms in unfamiliar territory, it's all too easy to lose your sense of direction in the woods. A reliable compass and the pertinent topographic map can be a great help.

**Waterproof gear and emergency food.** Waterproof matches in a waterproof container, rainwear, candy bars or other high-energy foods, and an extra jacket or coat can be a great comfort in case you discover you don't know the area or don't read topo maps well.

## *Where to Look, When to Go, and How to Pick*

### CHOOSING A COLLECTING AREA

When planning a mushroom hunting expedition, or foray (the term enthusiasts favor), pick a place with the greatest diversity. At the top of the list would be an area with several types of coniferous and deciduous woods; with steep and gentle hills, flat plains, and swampy spots; with rocky soils and sandy patches. Most mushrooms are specific to a certain type of habitat. The more kinds of habitats you can explore, the more kinds of mushrooms you'll find.

Remember also that many popular edible mushrooms grow on lawns and on the big old trees that are common near older houses and farms. Some of the most productive mushroom forays are conducted on four wheels. Be sure to knock on the door and ask permission first. Don't get arrested for puffball pilferage.

Many parks and other public lands have strict regulations against disturbing virtually anything. Check with the appropriate authorities before gathering mushrooms in parks. State and county forests generally have more tolerant policies, but find out first. Private lands—even those posted against trespassing—are often the best bet for mushroom hunters. Most landowners will allow access for mushroom picking if you simply ask. Do not pick mushrooms from along nature trails or popular hiking trails. Leave them there to be admired by others.

Season and weather should be considered when you're deciding where to look for mushrooms. During the dry days of summer, open, sunny areas and south-facing slopes are inferior to shady north-facing slopes, swamps, bogs, and other wet places. Save lawns and other open areas for the days following rain. If the weather is dry, look for mushrooms that grow on wood, focusing your search on forests with abundant logs and tree stumps (decayed wood retains moisture far better than soil). Swamps and bogs are usually the best—or *only*—bet during extended droughts, usually producing mushrooms when other habitats appear devoid of fungi.

During spring, conifer forests in many areas on the East Coast are poor places to look for mushrooms. You'll have better luck in deciduous woods. On the West Coast, though, morels and other species are often most abundant under conifer trees. In mountainous areas in the north, the mushroom season is short—typically May through September—but the fungi fruit abundantly except during the driest days of summer.

When your hunt is successful, take note of the date, the place, and recent weather conditions. Most mushrooms will appear year after year in the same place until the fungi have exhausted their food supplies. Some avid mushroom hunters keep journals, which are valuable tools for predicting when and where specific kinds of mushrooms will fruit in subsequent mushroom seasons. Enviable indeed is the mycophagist who can head confidently for the woods on a bright spring morning and return in the afternoon with a basketful of morels—proof of the wisdom that can come only from experience.

## MUSHROOM FRUITING PATTERNS

Complex combinations of several factors, including temperature, humidity, precipitation, and day length, govern mushroom fruiting patterns. They are not, as a rule, well understood. It is difficult to predict precisely when and where a given fungus will fruit; however, some principles are useful for planning a mushroom foray. Most experienced mushroom hunters develop some facility for knowing when and where to find their favorite wild mushrooms.

Generally, wet periods following dry periods lead to the greatest number and variety of mushrooms. Wind is often essential for spore dispersal, but has a negative effect on mushroom fruiting because it increases evaporation of the moisture that mushrooms need to grow. Freezing temperatures and droughts are the only factors that will halt fruiting in most mushrooms.

Mushroom hunters are a rare breed: They like rain. Some of them pray for it; some curse when the weather forecaster calls for "beautiful sunny weather through the weekend." The best time to look for mushrooms is two or three days after a significant rainfall. One inch of rain accumulated over twenty-four hours is better than two inches of torrential rain overnight. Water from a quick downpour has little time to saturate the ground before draining off into streams and rivers. In very flat areas, of course, this is less applicable. But don't restrict yourself solely to mushroom forays after rain or during cooler weather, or you may miss some species altogether. Some fungi fruit in drier weather and in warmer temperatures.

In most places, late summer and early fall to midfall are the best times of year for collecting wild mushrooms. When the nights get cooler and the rains come every few days, the woods and fields are sometimes so filled with mushrooms that it's hard to avoid stepping on them. Yet autumn doesn't deserve all the glory. Spring and summer provide a different variety of mushrooms, including many delicious edibles that won't be around in the fall. Most species have limited fruiting seasons. Morels, for example, can only be found for six weeks or so during springtime. Some excellent chanterelles and boletes are most frequent during summer. It is true, though, that many mushroom species are rarely found before late summer or early fall.

A few edibles, such as the Shaggy Mane and the Sulphur Shelf, have split seasons in some parts of North America: they fruit mostly in spring and fall, but are scarce at other times. Other species, including the Oyster Mushroom and the Wine-cap Stropharia, may appear almost year-round. Very few mushrooms prefer cold winter weather—the Velvet Foot, or Winter Mushroom, is the notable exception.

Mushroom fruiting patterns are affected more by unusual weather than are, for example, the blooming seasons of wildflowers. For instance, a particularly long warm spring followed by an unusually cold wet period in early summer may induce some fall mushrooms to appear two months earlier than normal.

Southern regions are blessed with longer foraging seasons, but mushrooms are generally less abundant at any given time. In many parts of California, some mushrooms that have limited seasons in other regions are gathered nearly year-round, and many typically autumn species fruit during winter, as they often do in Texas and along the Gulf Coast.

In desert areas, the only time you're likely to find many mushrooms is during and immediately after the rainy season. In northern climes where the snow flies fast and furiously, winter is frustrating for the mushroom hunter; few species can be gathered, even during the warmest winter thaws.

The *best* information on when and where to find mushrooms is *local* information. Join your area's mushroom club, and you'll avoid a lot of trial-and-error foraging.

## HOW TO PICK WILD MUSHROOMS

Picking mushrooms is like picking berries, apples, or other fruits in that it doesn't harm the organism itself unless it is done carelessly. Conduct yourself in the way that disturbs the environment the least. When you pick mushrooms, don't rip them free. Be gentle, disturbing their habitat as little as possible. When you find a mushroom you can't identify immediately, be extra careful about how you pick it. Use a knife to carefully dig or pry specimens from wherever they're growing; otherwise, you may leave behind structures that are necessary for accurate identification. The absence of a cuplike structure called a volva around the base of the stalk is a key identifying characteristic for most of the edible gilled mushrooms covered by this book; the presence of a volva is characteristic of several fatally poisonous mushroom species.

Note whether the mushroom stalks are clustered (growing from a common point) and whether there is a partial veil (fungal tissue covering the undersurface of the cap) or a ring (a veil that remains attached to the stalk). These characteristics might not be so apparent when you get home with the specimens. Make notes about these characteristics, and write down a brief description of the habitat, for example, "Found on moss-covered log in pine woods." These notes will be helpful when you try to identify the mushroom at home. Be sure not to get confused about which notes apply to which specimens.

Whenever possible, collect specimens in various stages of development, including small buttons, or immature mushrooms, and specimens with fully opened caps. Don't overpick, though. Take only a few specimens unless you're gathering edible mushrooms with which you're already familiar. And always leave some for "seed." This is to your own advantage: it will help ensure successful forays next season.

When you have selected your specimens, either place them gently in a waxed paper bag or wrap them carefully in waxed paper. Place the specimens in your basket, and keep them separated from other species. In hot weather, mushrooms can deteriorate rapidly after being picked, so keep your collection cool and out of direct sunlight.

Mushrooms are most easily identified soon after picking. When this is not possible, refrigerate your specimens. Many experienced mushroom hunters keep ice-filled picnic coolers in their vehicles during summertime expeditions.

**If for any reason you are unable to conclude with absolute certainty whether a mushroom specimen conforms to all the key identifying characteristics for the species you think you've found, don't eat it. The enjoyment of edible wild mushrooms leaves no room for gambling.**

### INEDIBLE EDIBLES: YUCKY BUGS AND CONTAMINANTS

Like most living things, mushrooms are composed primarily of water. The fungal fruiting process—the rapid, seemingly overnight development of each mushroom—requires a lot of moisture, either in the substrate or in the form of rain or humidity. Some mushrooms, when dried, weigh as little as one-sixteenth of what they weigh fresh.

This factor presents a need for some caution in terms of *where* one collects edible mushrooms. Unfortunately, our environment is inundated by a plethora of chemical contaminants. Probably every living thing on Earth, including every kind of food, contains at least trace amounts of toxic chemicals such as heavy metals, pesticides, and miscellaneous carcinogens. For the mycophagist, there are several types of areas that should be avoided.

Probably no one would knowingly gather edible mushrooms near a landfill or toxic dump site, but some of the other areas to avoid are less obvious. Lawns, especially the healthiest-looking ones, are often treated with various chemicals. Before picking mushrooms found on lawns, especially golf courses and other well-kept grounds, investigate whether any chemicals have been applied there. Picking mushrooms in such locations requires asking permission anyway, so inquire about lawn treatments when you request permission.

Second, avoid picking mushrooms on or adjacent to crop fields, where similar chemicals might be used. Even if chemicals sprayed on food crops are presumed safe, their concentration in mushrooms may be much higher than in the food crops themselves.

Third, avoid picking mushrooms along roadsides. Motor vehicle exhaust contains a number of toxic substances, especially heavy metals. Stay at least one hundred yards away from major interstate highways, one hundred feet away from secondary highways, fifty feet away from paved secondary roads, and ten feet away from one-lane dirt roads. These "safety-zone" distances can be reduced, depending on the ground cover. A thick spruce plantation, for example, will absorb a lot of exhaust fumes within thirty feet of a secondary highway. It is also wise to consider prevailing wind directions, especially in open areas.

When harvesting mushrooms found growing on a tree, except in the woods or forest, make sure that the tree isn't being treated. Many fungi that grow on wood are parasitic. If the tree is valued by the landowner, it could be receiving treatment with fungicides or insecticides in an attempt to save its life.

Areas near power lines, railroads, and firebreaks should also be carefully avoided, because herbicides are often used to limit the growth of nearby vegetation. Don't pick mushrooms near industrial areas or near buildings, especially older ones. The ground around them may be contaminated with lead or other poisonous or carcinogenic chemicals from old paint that has been scraped off.

Once you've located safe terrain and conclusively identified some mushrooms for the table, there is another matter to consider: insects and their larvae. The largest, most mature specimens are more likely to be infested by insects or larvae, but dissection is the only way to determine infestation. Mushrooms, large and small, are enjoyed by many animals, including deer, squirrels, and other mammals. Slugs are particularly fond of fungi. Edible mushrooms that have been partially eaten by slugs or other animals are perfectly fine for the table. Just rinse them lightly or wipe them clean with a damp cloth. Insects and their larvae—flies and gnats in particular—are a special problem. Few of these pests, if any, are potentially harmful if ingested by humans, especially if the mushrooms are thoroughly cooked; however, there is also the aesthetic aspect to consider.

When you get your edible mushrooms home, use a sharp knife to cut off the base of each stalk. Frequently, this will reveal insect larvae tunnels. In most fleshy mushrooms, the larvae start at the bottom, eventually working their way up through the stalk and into the cap. Sometimes the stalk will be infested, while the cap remains undamaged. In some large-capped mushrooms, it may even be possible to salvage most of the cap by removing its core, where it's attached to the stalk. Remember: one worm doesn't spoil the whole apple.

## A Different Kind of Hunt: The Ritual of the Mushroom Foray

—Enter the woods quietly. Watch your step to avoid twigs that might snap and dry leaves that might crackle. You must be silent—not to avoid alarming the quarry, but to avoid distracting yourself from the ritual. Keep your nose to the wind, bearing in mind that some quarry is more easily detected by scent than by sight.

—Meticulously scan the forest floor, keeping in mind that some of the choicest quarry is also the best camouflaged. Forsake no possible terrestrial hiding places; but scour the piles of last autumn's fallen leaves, and examine the carpets of green moss. Inspect the upturned roots of windfallen trees, and observe the rotting logs, for some wonderful delight may be hiding anywhere.

—Walk not erect, nor in a straight line, but, rather, stay low and wander aimlessly and in circles. Remember perspective is everything, and what cannot be seen from here must be seen from there. Steal glances above, too, into the trees and at their trunks; for often the object of your quest will be hiding there, counting on your eyes to be too earthbound to spot it in its arboreal sanctuary.

—**Look, look again, look even once more, and, finally, look again, never counting how many times, for it is the rule of the mushroom hunt that they who have not found any mushrooms have not looked closely enough, nor long enough, nor at enough places, nor from enough different angles.**

While this may seem exaggerated, it is not. Mushrooms are notoriously good at eluding even those who know them well. You know what you're looking for—mushrooms. But unless you're after a certain species, it is impossible to say what they look like. Mushrooms are so varied in shape, color, size, and habitat, that you face a real challenge when searching for mushrooms, especially at the most mushroom-less times of the year.

Keep in mind that foraging for mushrooms is an especially likely way to become lost in the woods. When you're busy examining the forest floor—especially if you're gleefully filling your basket with edible mushrooms—it is fairly easy to lose your sense of direction and wander too far from the trail. Especially when foraging in an unfamiliar area, let someone know where you're going and when you expect to return. Carry a compass, a topographic map, and—just in case—such emergency supplies as waterproof matches, rainwear, and candy bars. A basketful of gourmet mushrooms is of little solace to someone who's spending an unplanned night in the woods.

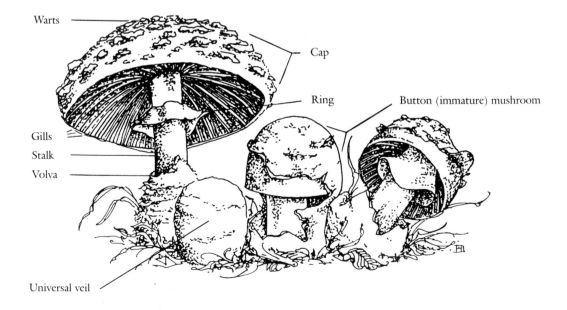

Warts

Cap

Gills

Stalk

Volva

Ring

Button (immature) mushroom

Universal veil

# 3.

# *What Have You Found?*

### *Examining a Mushroom: An Exercise for Beginners*

This book uses key identifying characteristics as the primary means of conclusively identifying a mushroom as edible. Most of the characteristics are fairly simple, but a few do require brief explanation. Examine the illustrations, and learn those terms that are unfamiliar.

A great way to begin is by buying fresh white button mushrooms from the grocery store. Select these from the bulk section, if your store has one. Get the biggest specimen you can find, plus several others of various sizes. Take a good look at them.

The **cap** surface is rounded and smooth. There are no **"warts"**—patches of fungal tissue that can be removed without tearing the cap surface—present on the mushroom cap, and there are no **scales**. Likewise, the cap is neither **depressed** nor topped with a knoblike **umbo**. It is white to light tan, perhaps with a faint pinkish tint. Press down firmly on it with your fingernail. Observe that within a couple of minutes, it has bruised a light tan or pinkish color.

Examine the **stalk**. It is white to light tan, possibly with a pinkish tint. It is neither scaly nor hairy, and it is not noticeably tapered. Some wild mushrooms have a cuplike **volva** around the **base** of the stalk; this species does not. (A volva is a remnant of a **universal veil**, a layer of tissue that completely encloses certain mushrooms in the **button** stage.)

Look beneath the cap. A feltlike tissue called a **partial veil** completely or partially obscures the gills. The veil is white to light tan or, again, it may have a pinkish tint. On an older and larger specimen, the veil may have separated from the edge of the cap and may remain as a membranous **ring** on the stalk.

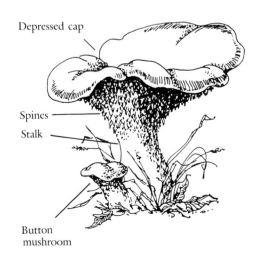

Depressed cap

Spines

Stalk

Button mushroom

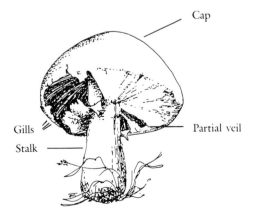

Cap

Gills

Stalk

Partial veil

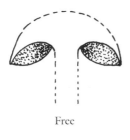

Free

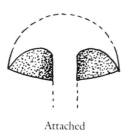

Attached

Descending

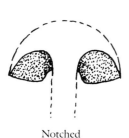

Notched

Hold the mushroom upside down, and using a sharp, thin-bladed, nonserrate knife, cut straight down through the stalk and cap. This is called a longitudinal section. Note the color of the **gills**: they are off-white to light pink in newer specimens, brown in older specimens. The gills do not descend the stalk, and they are not indented, or notched, before attaching to the stalk. In fact, the gills are not attached directly to the stalk at all; rather, they are free from it. Also, the gills are very close to each other, almost touching, and none is forked. Their edges are more or less straight, not serrate. (Not all mushrooms have gills. Many species of wild mushrooms have layers of **tubes** or downward-pointing **spines** on the cap's undersurface. On mushrooms with tubes instead of gills, under the cap you would find a **pore surface** made up of the open ends of the tubes.)

Note that since cutting the mushroom, the **flesh** has changed from whitish to light tan, perhaps with a pinkish tint. This is a bruising, or staining, effect. Bite off a small piece of the cap. Chew it, taste it, and then spit it out. It tastes mild, not bitter or acrid (peppery). Make a spore print, as instructed in the next section. Note the color: the spore print is brown or reddish brown. (Because the commonly cultivated *Agaricus* mushroom is usually harvested in an immature stage—as a **button mushroom**—this part of the exercise may require a wild mushroom specimen.)

This exercise provides a valuable means of familiarizing yourself with many of the characteristics you must observe in order to use this book to identify edible wild mushrooms. Take the exercise seriously, and you are well on your way.

## How to Make a Spore Print

Making a spore print, a deposit on paper of a mushroom's spores, revealing their color, is essential to the safe identification of many edible wild mushrooms, especially those with gills. It's fairly simple and requires only a little patience.

Choose one of the larger, more mature specimens from your collection of each species. Using a sharp knife, cut off the stalk as close to the cap as possible. Gently remove the veil, if present, to expose the gills. Place the cap, gills facing down, on a piece of white paper. In case the mushroom might produce a white spore print, place a smaller piece of black paper under part of the cap. Cover the cap and paper with a jar, glass, or bowl to prevent interference from circulating air.

Most species will deposit enough spores within a few hours to allow you to see the color of the spore print. If, when you check it, there is no spore print visible, it may be that the mushroom had already discharged most of its spores before you started. It may also be that you haven't waited long enough. Let it sit overnight, covered and undisturbed, and check it again in the morning.

There are two shortcuts that can sometimes be used to speed up the process of determining spore print color. The first is to wrap the mushroom cap snugly in white paper. This can be done in the field when you're putting the mushrooms in your collecting basket, but be careful to keep track of which mushrooms go with which wrapped caps. Carry the little packages so they remain gill side down during the rest of your foray. By the time you get home, you likely will find ready-made spore prints when you unwrap the mushroom caps. The second shortcut is possible when mushrooms grow in clusters. A spore print may be visible on the top of a cap that is situated directly beneath the gills of another cap. Trust the color of such a spore print *only* if the print's pattern clearly reflects the arrangement of the gills.

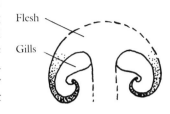

Flesh
Gills

Inrolled cap

Never presume that a specimen's spore print will be the same color as its gills. Although this is sometimes true, it is just as often misleading. Some mushroom gills are initially one color, then mature to another, and the spore print is a different color entirely. **Always keep in mind that when a spore print color—or any other characteristic—is listed as a key identifying characteristic, it *must* be verified before accurate identification is possible.**

Incurved cap

## Avoiding Amanitas

In North America, Europe, and many other parts of the world, the vast majority of fatal and seriously debilitating mushroom poisoning cases—90 percent, according to some estimates—are caused by *Amanita* species such as the Destroying Angel and the Death Cap. The victims often describe themselves as experienced mushroom hunters, but they cannot be called knowledgeable. With rare exception, they are unaware of such basic features as gill attachment and spore print color.

Ironically, the Amanitas can be easily identified to genus. If the mushroom hunter recognizes and avoids them, the likelihood of tragic error is greatly reduced.

All North American and European Amanitas share five key field characteristics. First, the gills are either free from the stalk or barely attached to it. Second, the gills are white or nearly so (some stain yellowish, pinkish, reddish, or brownish, and some have yellow gill edges). Third, they produce white spore prints. Fourth, they are found on the ground. Fifth, they are initially enclosed in a universal veil.

The universal veil ruptures or disintegrates as the mushroom expands, but it leaves remnants which provide clues that the mushroom is, in fact, an *Amanita*. Each of the notoriously deadly species has a white cuplike or saclike volva enclosing the base of the stalk, but the specimen must often be carefully excavated from soil or humus to find it. Many species' universal veils leave warts, which can be gently removed without tearing the cap's "skin" or cuticle, on the upper surface of the cap. Most Amanitas also have membranous partial veils, but some do not.

Every mycophagist should get to know the genus *Amanita*, and give it a wide berth. These beautiful mushrooms serve as extraordinary photographic subjects—but *keep them out of your kitchen*!

"If you can't eat it, what good is it?"

This question was posed to me by an over-enthusiastic novice mycophagist at a local mushroom foray. Setting aside my temptation to chastise her for her disinterest in the other life forms with which we share our marvelous planet, I politely expressed the perspective that all mushrooms can be appreciated for their beauty, form, and ecological role.

"Why not make some spore prints?" I asked. "Then, you can begin to identify fungi which are critical decomposers of organic matter or important mycorrhizal symbionts with various trees."

"Oh," she replied, "I haven't got time for that sort of thing. Just tell me if I can eat it or not!"

"Every mushroom is edible," I said, "at least once!" The din of laughter from the crowd around the table seemed to be poetic justice, but the woman's attitude didn't seem to be affected by it.

A few weeks later, she came to my office to have me verify her identifications of several mushroom species. She had correctly identified such distinctive edibles as the Golden Chanterelle, the Lobster Mushroom, and the King Bolete.

"What do you think of these Blewits?" she asked, proudly holding out a collection of lilac-colored mushrooms. She wasn't looking for verification of her identification of these specimens.

"Did you make a spore print?" I asked, examining the undersurface of one of her specimens.

"Why bother?" she responded. "What else could I mistake them for?"

"Blewits have pale pink spore prints," I told her. "These mushrooms have a cortina—a cobwebby partial veil—and would produce rusty brown spore prints. This is a *Cortinarius,* and many species of this genus are poisonous. Some have even caused fatalities."

"Oh, no!" she exclaimed. "I gave some of these to a couple of my friends, and told them that they were Blewits!"

Two hasty and embarrassing phone calls were made from my office in the next several minutes. Fortunately, the recipients of this "gift" hadn't eaten the mushrooms.

*Cortinarius* is a remarkable genus of mushrooms, having several hundred species, most of which are of unknown edibility. This incident could have had far more serious ramifications, and the whole situation would never have occurred if she had simply made a spore print.

—ALAN BESSETTE

Scales

Cap

Gills

Stalk

Ring

# 4.

## The Mycophagist's Ten Commandments

1. **Never eat a mushroom unless it is positively identified as edible.** Mistakes can result in toxic reactions ranging from mild gastric upset to death. If in doubt, throw it out!

2. **Eat only fresh mushrooms that are free from infestation by insects or larvae.** Mushrooms can spoil, and eating any spoiled food can cause food poisoning or other adverse reactions.

3. **Thoroughly cook all mushrooms unless they are specifically known to be edible raw.** Some mushrooms contain toxins or gastrointestinal irritants that must be destroyed by cooking.

4. **Eat mushrooms only in moderate quantities.** Mushrooms are not easily digested; overeating them is an easy way to get sick.

5. **When trying a mushroom for the first time, eat only a small portion, and don't try any other new kinds for forty-eight hours.** As with many kinds of food, some people are sensitive or allergic to mushrooms commonly eaten by other people. Individuals with known food allergies or sensitivities should be extra careful when trying mushrooms new to them, especially those species known to present problems for some individuals.

6. **Don't pick mushrooms from contaminated habitats.** These include polluted areas, chemically treated lawns, ornamental trees, and places close to highways, landfills, toxic waste sites, crop fields, power lines, railroads, buildings, industrial areas, or firebreaks. Contaminants may accumulate in wild mushrooms.

7. **Never assume that a wild mushroom you find overseas is the same edible species you know from North America** or vice versa. Too many serious cases of mushroom poisoning occur because vacationers and immigrants unwittingly gather dangerous look-alike species not found in their native lands.

8. **Be conservative about feeding wild mushrooms to children, the elderly, and the infirm.** Avoid edible species known to cause adverse reactions in some people, and don't let children, the elderly, or persons in poor health try an unfamiliar kind of wild mushroom until you and other friends or relatives have identified and eaten it without any adverse reactions. Limit portion sizes for children, the elderly, and the sick because they're generally more susceptible to toxins than other people are.

9. **When trying a mushroom for the first time, save a few intact, uncooked specimens in the refrigerator for forty-eight hours.** If someone develops an illness within two days after trying an unfamiliar mushroom, the physician may want expert identification to rule out the mushroom as the culprit.

10. **Examine every specimen in every collection of mushrooms to avoid inadvertent mixing of different species.** Even experienced mushroom hunters can err if they become careless and fill their baskets too hurriedly.

# 5.

## How to Use This Guide and Beyond

Although detailed descriptions are presented for each species of edible wild mushroom covered in this book, the focus is on key identifying characteristics. For each edible species, there is a brief checklist of the features that are most essential for ruling out other species or groups. In many cases, closely related edible species are covered by the same list of key identifying characteristics. In these cases, the characteristics used to distinguish one species from another are presented in the section titled "Description."

As far as possible, this book avoids technical terms and uses characteristics that are easily observed by the novice. The few botanical and mycological terms used are explained either in the text or in the glossary. The only characteristic that complicates the identification process for some species is spore print color. Making a spore print is a simple procedure, but it may take as long as twenty-four hours; therefore, some patience is in order (see "How to Make a Spore Print," p. 14).

Using this book to identify edible mushrooms is fairly simple. First, examine the color plates of edible species. When you find a mushroom that looks strikingly similar, check the corresponding key identifying characteristics to make sure your specimen matches them. If it does, make sure your specimen is consistent with the full description given under the list of key identifying characteristics. Read the section on fruiting, and be suspicious of any specimens that contradict the habitat, range, or fruiting patterns cited there. If any poisonous mushrooms are listed under "Similar Species," note the characteristics that distinguish them from the edible species. Read the section titled "Edibility," and observe any further advice given there.

As a practical matter, the key identifying characteristics should be confirmed *in the field*. The exception to this is spore print color, which usually can't be confirmed immediately.

Two types of field characteristics—odor and taste—warrant special attention. These may seem subjective, open to interpretation according to individual olfactory sensitivity; however, in practice, taste and odor characteristics are essential to proper identification and classification of many kinds of mushrooms. For the purposes of this book, we are only concerned with three kinds of tastes, and they are used as key identifying characteristics for only a handful of species. If you can distinguish things that taste bitter and acrid (peppery hot) from things that do not (things that taste mild), you will have no difficulty confirming taste characteristics listed as key identifying characteristics.

A word of caution: some poisonous and inedible mushrooms that must be ruled out by taste are *very* peppery (this is especially true of the latex, or fluid obtained from the gills, of some *Lactarius* species), yet the sensation of such tastes is usually delayed for several seconds.

Taste a tiny bit of the flesh or the latex for only a few seconds, and then spit it out; the taste will likely be more apparent *after* spitting. If it tastes mild, not bitter or peppery, double-check it by tasting a second tiny bit, this time holding it in your mouth for fifteen seconds before spitting. There is no significant risk involved in tasting raw mushrooms unless you swallow the flesh.

Odor characteristics are slightly more troublesome. Especially if your sense of smell is limited by sinus problems, tobacco smoking, or other factors, you should get an extra opinion or two on any odor used as a key identifying characteristic. This is especially important in the case of edible *Agaricus* species—the Meadow Mushroom, the Horse Mushroom, and the Prince.

Finally, observe the precautions outlined in "Inedible Edibles" on page 10, and *always* obey "The Mycophagist's Ten Commandments" on page 17. If you follow this plan, the risk of unexpected adverse reactions will be virtually nil.

## Beyond This Guide: Further Study of Mushrooms

The scope of this book is mostly limited to common, easily identified species of mushrooms. In North America there are nearly a hundred other wild mushroom species that are known to be edible, plus thousands of species that are either poisonous, inedible, or of unknown edibility.

The field of mycology is perhaps the most fascinating of the natural sciences. Whether you're only interested in eating wild mushrooms, studying the whole kingdom, or challenging your photographic skills, there are innumerable resources that can help. There are dozens of mushroom field guides for North America, including many regional ones. There are also a number of wild mushroom cookbooks. The "Recommended Reading" section on page 245 lists many of these books.

If you develop a real passion for mushrooms, you'll learn as much from professional and other amateur mycologists as you will from a dozen books. There are an increasing number of regional mushroom clubs. Most call themselves mycological associations or societies. To track them down, contact the North American Mycological Association (NAMA), which will direct you to a club in your area. NAMA's address is listed in directories of organizations, which can be found in the reference departments of most libraries.

Once you track down the nearest mushroom club, you'll be delighted by the number of people who are interested in and knowledgeable about wild fungi. In addition to organized group forays, mushroom clubs sponsor lectures and workshops, slide presentations, and much more. For the mushroom fancier, membership and participation in at least one such organization is very close to Nirvana.

I spent many years studying mushrooms, particularly the edible species, before I finally found and joined a mushroom club. I will never forget my first introduction to the local association. Members held a mushroom fair, aptly named "Mushroom Mania," at a local museum.

I was absolutely thrilled. There were dozens of display tables loaded with fresh specimens of nearly as many species as are covered by most field guides. There were several microscopy tables, examination of microscopic characteristics being essential to the accurate identification of many mushrooms. There were tables devoted to cultivation. There were others devoted to toxic and hallucinogenic mushrooms. There was a table with mushroom books, mushroom T-shirts, mushroom bumper stickers ("WARNING: I Brake for Mushrooms" is popular), and other mushroom paraphernalia. There were large color photographs of mushrooms. There were mushroom sculptures, mushroom coffee mugs, mushroom everything! Best of all, there were tables with electric frying pans, where devoted mycophagists were cooking Giant Puffballs, Shaggy Parasols, Sulphur Shelves, and other delicious wild mushrooms.

This, I knew from the instant I walked into the spacious yet cramped room, was mushroom heaven. I had been a mushroom fanatic for a long time, learning what I could from books, with only one friend who shared my passion. But finally, there I was, in a room with dozens of other people, each as single-minded as I was.

"No," I told myself at last, "I'm *not* crazy. I'm just a mycology orphan who has just been reunited with his family."
—DAVID FISCHER

# PART TWO

# FORGOTTEN FRUIT: EDIBLE WILD MUSHROOMS OF NORTH AMERICA

Opposite page: Oyster Mushrooms

# 6.

# *Chanterelles and Similar Mushrooms*

The Golden Chanterelle, usually just called "the Chanterelle," is one of the world's most highly prized mushrooms. To the novice, it and other members of the genus *Cantharellus* look pretty much like gilled mushrooms; however, the chanterelles lack true gills. They have, at most, gill-like folds or wrinkles beneath their caps, but they lack the true platelike gills (technically called "lamellae") characteristic of the mushroom typically found at the grocery store and its thousands of kindred species. True gills are formed before a mushroom cap expands; in the chanterelles, the gill-like folds develop only as the mushroom expands.

Without exception, members of the genus *Cantharellus* are edible, and most are quite delicious. Related species of the genera *Craterellus* and *Polyozellus* are also wonderful edibles. Only the genus *Gomphus,* exemplified by the Scaly Vase Chanterelle (*G. floccosus;* see p. 148), includes known poisonous species that produce unpleasant gastrointestinal symptoms in some people.

One species, the Lobster Mushroom (*Hypomyces lactifluorum*), included in this section is not technically in the Chanterelle family. It is included here for the convenience of the novice because of its similarity to the Golden Chanterelle. Besides, it doesn't even begin to fit elsewhere in this book—you'll have to read its description (p. 34) to understand why.

Opposite page: Hoh Rainforest of the Olympic Peninsula, Washington state
ARB

# GOLDEN, WHITE, SMOOTH, AND CINNABAR-RED CHANTERELLES

*Cantharellus cibarius*
*C. subalbidus*
*C. lateritius*
*C. cinnabarinus*

Golden Chanterelle (*Cantharellus cibarius*)

## KEY IDENTIFYING CHARACTERISTICS

1. Whitish, yellow, orange, or reddish orange mushroom
2. Cap edge inrolled, lobed, or wavy; cap surface smooth to minutely hairy but lacking coarse scales
3. True gills absent and undersurface with blunt, forked, gill-like ridges; *or* true gills absent and undersurface yellow and smooth or slightly wrinkled
4. Found on the ground in woods

**DESCRIPTION:** The Golden Chanterelle (*Cantharellus cibarius*) is usually described as "egg yolk yellow," but it is sometimes more yellowish orange, especially when immature. The mushroom is two to six inches wide and two to six inches high. It has a smooth-surfaced, round top with an inrolled edge that becomes lobed or wavy at maturity. In age, the top of the cap is usually somewhat sunken at the center and sometimes a bit roughened or slightly cracked. The undersurface of the cap is yellow to orange, usually paler than the upper surface. Characteristic of the genus *Cantharellus*, the cap undersurface lacks true gills; instead, there are blunt, forked, gill-like ridges, which are typically cross veined, extending from the edge of the cap onto the stalk. Near the edge of the cap, these ridges may have fairly thin edges, like true gills; however, they are always very blunt at the stalk. The stalk is solid, colored like the cap or paler; it tapers toward the base. The cap flesh is yellow; the stalk flesh is white to pale yellow. The cap, stalk, or both will often slowly stain deeper orange where cut or bruised. The Golden Chanterelle has a distinct, apricotlike odor.

The Smooth Chanterelle (*C. lateritius*) is nearly identical to the Golden Chanterelle but has a smooth to only slightly wrinkled undersurface. The other two species differ from the Golden Chanterelle mostly in color. The White Chanterelle (*C. subalbidus*) is almost white, bruising orangish. The Cinnabar-red Chanterelle (*C. cinna-*

White Chanterelle (*Cantharellus subalbidus*)

Smooth Chanterelle (*Cantharellus lateritius*)

*barinus*) is reddish orange, fading to pinkish. It is also much smaller than the others—less than two inches wide or high.

The spore print colors are as follows: pale yellow (Golden Chanterelle), white (White Chanterelle), pale yellowish orange (Smooth Chanterelle), and pinkish white (Cinnabar-red Chanterelle).

**FRUITING:** These chanterelles are all mycorrhizal, associated especially with oaks and various conifers. The Golden Chanterelle is found throughout much of North America, fruiting from midsummer through early fall; it is found later—even as late as February—in California. *C. subalbidus* is found in the Pacific Northwest under oaks and various conifers, fruiting in autumn. *C. cinnabarinus* is found in eastern North America, fruiting from midsummer through midfall. It is associated primarily with oaks. *C. lateritius* is also usually found in

It was late spring, 1974. A friend and I were practicing archery in my backyard. Some of the arrows missed the target, missed the bales of hay behind the target, and flew into the nearby woods. As we searched for the arrows, our curiosity was piqued by the variety of mushrooms scattered about the woods. We collected several specimens. I took them to a local mycologist, who identified them for me and loaned me a field guide that described many of those I had found.

Over the course of several weeks, I collected more and more mushrooms, tried to identify them with the field guide as best I could, and then took them to the mycologist for confirmation. I was correctly identifying most of my specimens and became increasingly confident about my ability to correctly name species that were new to me. During this period of time, I cooked and ate many of the species that my friend, the mycologist, had confirmed were edible.

Then, when I was collecting more mushrooms in my favorite woods on a muggy July afternoon, I discovered the mother lode: an enormous number of egg-yolk yellow mushrooms, growing singly and in groups on the ground. I had no idea what they were, but I picked a number of them in case they proved to be edible.

Back at home, I keyed them out with the field guide, Orson K. Miller, Jr.'s *Mushrooms of North America*. They were *Cantharellus cibarius*, the Golden Chanterelle. I was thrilled that this was a prized edible species. They even *looked* delicious. I cleaned and sliced several robust specimens and then sautéed them. As I finished the last bite, I remember thinking, this is truly food for the gods.

(*continued*)

Cinnabar-red Chanterelle (*Cantharellus cinnabarinus*)

(*continued*)

As I was perusing the field guide a short time later, I came upon a color photograph of what looked to be the same mushroom I had just enjoyed. But, to my great dismay, this picture was labeled *Omphalotus olearius,* the common—and *poisonous*—Jack O'Lantern! Could it be that the delicious mushrooms I had consumed not more than an hour earlier were poisonous?

Soon I became aware of my rapidly increasing pulse. My palms became sweaty, my breathing shallow and quick, my face flushed. These, I was sure, were the symptoms of mushroom poisoning. How could I have made such a careless mistake? I was soon in a state of panic. What now? Should I seek medical attention?

Feeling embarrassed and angry about my error, I was determined to discover how I had made such a mistake. I began to compare the descriptions of the Golden Chanterelle and the Jack O'Lantern in earnest. The more I read, the more I became convinced that what I had eaten was, indeed, the Golden Chanterelle. As the evening progressed, I felt fine and sensed a tremendous feeling of relief.

This story serves to illustrate three very important points. First, be certain of your identification. Second, be aware of poisonous look-alikes. Third, in some cases, panic reactions can cause symptoms characteristic of mushroom poisoning, even when one consumes the finest of edible mushrooms.

—ALAN BESSETTE

oak woods in eastern North America, and fruits mostly in middle and late summer. Each of these species is usually found singly, in small groups, or scattered through the woods. Although it is not typical, the Golden Chanterelle may be found in small clusters.

**SIMILAR SPECIES:** The Jack O'Lantern species (*Omphalotus illudens* and *O. olivascens;* see p. 148) provoke decidedly unpleasant toxic reactions. They can be easily distinguished from the chanterelles, though; they have true gills, not the blunt, forked ridges characteristic of *Cantharellus* species. Also, the Jack O'Lanterns grow on wood (but, sometimes, on buried wood) and are almost always clustered. If your specimen has well-developed unforked gills, you've found the wrong mushroom: don't eat it.

The Scaly Vase Chanterelle (*Gomphus floccosus;* see p. 148) causes gastric disturbance in many people. The sunken upper surface of the cap is distinctly scaly, and the under-outer surface is much paler than the upper-inner surface. There are a number of smaller *Cantharellus* species, none of which are suspected of being poisonous. Several of the smaller chanterelles are commonly collected for the table (see the Trumpet and Yellow-footed chanterelles on p. 27).

The edible False Chanterelle (*Hygrophoropsis aurantiaca;* see photo) is common and abundant throughout most of North America. Its orange gills are repeatedly forked, and they descend the stalk, but they are distinctly thin edged. The False Chanterelle's cap varies tremendously in color—from nearly white to orange or orangish brown—and it fruits on the ground or on decaying wood, typically in conifer forests, during summer and fall. While mistaking it for a true chanterelle only leads to acute culinary disappointment, mistaking the poisonous Jack O'Lantern, which has unforked thin-edged gills, for the False Chanterelle, leads to acute gastrointestinal distress.

**EDIBILITY:** The Golden Chanterelle is on the same short list as the morels and the famous Perigord Truffle. It is prized by gourmet chefs worldwide and commands a very high price both in gourmet specialty shops and at expensive restaurants.

In most parts of North America, chanterelles are fairly common and can often be gathered in large quantity during late summer. Unfortunately, in some areas, chanterelles are also highly susceptible to infestation by insect larvae. Fortunate is the mushroom hunter who finds a large quantity of chanterelles that haven't been thoroughly invaded by nasty little "worms."

If you're less lucky, and the chanterelles you find have been infested by insect larvae, you may be able to salvage part of each mushroom anyway. As in many fungi, the base of the stalk is usually the source of the infestation. The thinner flesh of the cap edges is often spared and can be cut off. This portion is also the most flavorful. This technique does require a good-sized collection to provide enough for most recipes, though.

Many experienced mushroom hunters simply ignore the insect larvae, not giving the added protein a second thought. We cannot recommend this practice, because we don't know much about the edibility of insect larvae. But we have observed that the dried chanterelles that can be purchased—at steep prices—from gourmet shops often show distinct insect larvae tunnels. Buyer, beware!

Chanterelles, as a group, are rich in flavor—it doesn't take much to please the palate. As is the case with most foods, not everyone likes the distinctive taste of chanterelles. But many mushroom hunters prefer chanterelles over every other kind of mushroom. The chanterelle flavor cannot be characterized. They are also aromatic—some species have a wonderfully fruity odor when fresh.

Many gourmets insist that reconstituted chanterelles are superior in flavor to fresh ones. Whatever they may gain in flavor, however, they lose in texture: Chanterelles, like many mushrooms, become chewy when preserved by drying.

False Chanterelle
(*Hygrophoropsis aurantiaca*)

## KEY IDENTIFYING CHARACTERISTICS

1. Trumpet- or funnel-shaped mushroom less than four inches tall, with or without central perforation on top of cap
2. Blunt, forked, or veined, yellow to gray, orangish, or lilac, gill-like ridges under cap, *or* undersurface of cap yellowish tan to orangish yellow or salmon pink, smooth to wrinkled
3. Top surface of cap yellow, yellowish brown, orangish brown, or brown
4. Stalk yellow, especially bright near base; hollow in mature specimens
5. Found in close groups or clusters in moss

**DESCRIPTION:** The Trumpet Chanterelle (*Cantharellus tubaeformis*) is initially yellow to brown, somewhat trumpet shaped, smooth, and slightly rounded on top. The undersurface has blunt, yellow to

# TRUMPET AND YELLOW-FOOTED CHANTERELLES

*Cantharellus tubaeformis*
*C. xanthopus*

Trumpet Chanterelle (*Cantharellus tubaeformis*)

gray or lilac, gill-like ridges that extend onto the stalk. As the mushroom grows, the cap typically darkens and develops tiny fibrous scales. The edge of the cap becomes wavy and lobed, and the ridges on the undersurface become forked, cross veined, and grayish or lilac tinted (sometimes even a rich lilac color). The cap becomes as much as three inches wide, occasionally slightly more. The stalk remains yellow, especially near the base, and becomes hollow; it can grow up to four inches tall. The spore print is white to cream.

The Yellow-footed Chanterelle (*C. xanthopus*) is very similar to the Trumpet Chanterelle in appearance, size, and growth habit. The top of the cap is pale orangish brown to brownish, and it is often perforated at the center in mature specimens. The undersurface is smooth to slightly wrinkled, lacking the Trumpet Chanterelle's more distinct gill-like ridges. It matures to a salmon pink color, rather than the grayish lilac typical of the Trumpet. The cap of the Yellow-footed Chanterelle is distinctly lobed in mature specimens. The spore print is pale orangish tan.

**FRUITING:** Both species grow in moss, particularly at the edge of coniferous bogs. In northeastern North America, where their known ranges overlap, one species will often be found growing quite close to the other. The Trumpet Chanterelle is frequently found on soggy, mossy, well-decayed conifer logs, even in upland areas. Both species fruit from midsummer through midfall. The Trumpet Chanterelle's range extends across northern North America, while the Yellow-footed Chanterelle is primarily an eastern North American species.

**SIMILAR SPECIES:** There are several closely related species of chanterelles; all have been collected and eaten, and none are poisonous. There are no dangerous species for concern here. The only family members to be avoided are the distinctive Scaly Vase Chanterelle (*G. floccosus*), which is poisonous (see p. 148) and its closest relatives. The Yellow-footed Chanterelle is one of several nearly identical species

Yellow-footed Chanterelle (*Cantharellus xanthopus*)

formerly classified as *C. lutescens*. The Trumpet Chanterelle is also known as *C. infundibuliformis*.

**EDIBILITY:** A few people have reported mild digestive discomfort after eating the Trumpet Chanterelle, but both it and the Yellow-footed Chanterelle are enjoyed by most without any difficulty. Exercise moderation when trying the Trumpet Chanterelle for the first time.

Both species are highly regarded by many mycophagists, not only for their aromatic flavor and delicate texture, but for their almost flowerlike appearance. The Yellow-footed Chanterelle, in particular, is a lovely mushroom whose appearance is reminiscent of some species of lily.

Because of their preference for boggy areas, either species makes a fine substitute for the Golden Chanterelle in dry years when their popular brother is scarce. The brownish coloration of the upper surfaces can be difficult to spot, but the bright yellow stalks are easily noticed.

Both species lend themselves well to drying. Dried specimens can be pulverized and added to various dishes as a flavoring in the same manner as the Black Trumpet (*Craterellus fallax*), which is edible (see p. 32), but a larger quantity is required.

The Trumpet and Yellow-footed Chanterelles are among the few species of mushrooms that can be frozen fresh for about three months without significant loss of taste or texture. Freeze them quickly in an airtight container.

The mycelium of each species is perennial, and can be expected to produce more mushrooms in the same place year after year. Make a note of when and where you find them.

# FRAGRANT CHANTERELLE

*Craterellus odoratus*

Fragrant Chanterelle (*Craterellus odoratus*)

## KEY IDENTIFYING CHARACTERISTICS

1. Orange cluster of thin-fleshed, funnel-shaped "caps" rising from single "stalk"
2. Odor very fragrant and fruity
3. Undersurface of each "cap" smooth to wrinkled; no gills present

**DESCRIPTION:** This mushroom is essentially a cluster of yellowish orange to bright orange, thin-fleshed, funnel-shaped, caplike append-ages that arise from a similarly colored, common, hollow, basal "stalk" that is not clearly differentiated from the "caps." The under-surface of each cap is smooth to slightly wrinkled, similar in color but paler than the smooth upper surface. The flesh of each cap is orange and very thin. The mushroom is three to six inches in both height and width and exhibits a distinctly fragrant, fruity odor. The spore print is pale yellowish orange.

**FRUITING:** This aromatic mushroom is found only in the southeast-ern United States, from North Carolina south to Florida and west to Mississippi. It fruits in late summer and early autumn on the ground in mixed woods.

**SIMILAR SPECIES:** No other mushroom fits the key identifying characteristics listed above.

**EDIBILITY:** This remarkably aromatic and flavorful mushroom is very highly regarded by wild mushroom enthusiasts in its rather lim-ited range. They note, however, that specimens must be gathered and cooked while fairly young and very fresh; otherwise, the aroma and taste become thoroughly disagreeable. Recipes that call for other spe-cies of the Chanterelle family are appropriate for this unusual fungus. It can be preserved by drying, pickling, or canning. It will also hold up well if frozen fresh.

Clustered Blue Chanterelle (*Polyozellus multiplex*)

# CLUSTERED BLUE CHANTERELLE

*Polyozellus multiplex*

## KEY IDENTIFYING CHARACTERISTICS

1. Bluish or purplish cluster of vase-, spoon-, or fan-shaped caps
2. Odor fragrant
3. Undersurface of each cap has veinlike wrinkles; no gills present

**DESCRIPTION:** This mushroom varies in color from grayish purple to bluish gray but becomes nearly black in age. Each cap in the cluster is vase, spoon, or fan shaped and one to four inches wide; the flesh is thick and grayish purple. The caps usually have sunken centers and lobed or wavy edges. The undersurface of each cap is bluish to purplish, with veinlike wrinkles or folds that descend the stalk. The caps grow from a common solid or hollow basal stalk that is often fused with adjacent stalks. The mushroom is usually three to six inches high. The total width of clusters typically ranges from four inches to one foot, but occasionally huge specimens are found that measure well over a foot—or even a yard!—in diameter. This species has a distinctly fragrant odor. The spore print is white.

**FRUITING:** The Clustered Blue Chanterelle is most frequently found in the Rocky Mountains, but it may be found across much of northern North America. It fruits on the ground during summer and fall in conifer woods, especially under spruce and fir trees.

**SIMILAR SPECIES:** No other mushroom closely resembles this very distinctive species.

**EDIBILITY:** Who says there's no blue food? Mushroom hunters in the Rocky Mountains and elsewhere heartily enjoy this fine blue (*sometimes,* at least) mushroom. It can be remarkably gigantic, a trait very much appreciated by its devotees. Like most species of the Chanterelle family, this lone member of the genus *Polyozellus* is a sight for the sore eyes of any mycophagist lucky enough to come upon it. Like its relatives, it can be easily preserved by drying.

# BLACK TRUMPET, HORN OF PLENTY, AND FRAGRANT BLACK TRUMPET

*Craterellus fallax*
*C. cornucopioides*
*C. foetidus*

Black Trumpet (*Craterellus fallax*)

## KEY IDENTIFYING CHARACTERISTICS

1. Two to five inches high, vase- or trumpet-shaped mushroom with thin, brittle flesh
2. Hollow stalk flaring open at the top, solid at the base
3. Upper-inner surface smooth to slightly wrinkled or minutely scaly; grayish brown to almost black
4. Undersurface brownish gray to gray, sometimes tinted pinkish orange; smooth to slightly veined or wrinkled
5. Found on the ground in woods

**DESCRIPTION:** A mushroom of any of these three species is distinctly vase or trumpet shaped, usually with an inrolled cap edge at first but with a very lobed or wavy, flaring cap edge at maturity. The upper-inner surface of the Black Trumpet (*Craterellus fallax*) is grayish brown to dark brown or almost black, with tiny brown scales. The flesh is thin and fairly brittle. The under-outer surface is gray or brownish gray (sometimes tinted orange) and is either smooth, or slightly veined or wrinkled. The stalk is actually an extension of the flaring "cap," not a separate, well-defined structure. The base is solid and very narrow, becoming hollow and wider above, flaring open to the edge of the cap. The mushroom is two to five inches high, two to four inches wide at the top, and has a fruity or fragrant odor.

The Horn of Plenty (*C. cornucopiodes*) is strikingly similar, but the upper-inner surface is not as dark and the flesh is more elastic. The easiest way to separate these two is by spore print color: the Black Trumpet has a pale yellow to apricot-colored spore print, and the Horn of Plenty has a white spore print.

The Fragrant Black Trumpet (*C. foetidus*) has thicker flesh near the cap center and more conspicuous dark brown scales on the upper-inner surface. It has an intensely fragrant odor. The under-outer surface has very shallow, blunt, forked veins, which are especially prominent near the edge of the cap.

KS

Horn of Plenty (*Craterellus cornucopioides*)

**FRUITING:** All three species can be found under deciduous trees. The Horn of Plenty and the Fragrant Black Trumpet also grow under conifers. The Black Trumpet and the Horn of Plenty are widely distributed in North America, but the Black Trumpet is more common in the east, especially in mixed woods with beech. The range of the Fragrant Black Trumpet is apparently more limited. It has been reported mostly in the northeastern United States. All three species fruit from midsummer through midfall and may be found scattered about or in groups or in clusters. The Fragrant Black Trumpet is usually found amid moss in oak and pine woods.

**SIMILAR SPECIES:** Two other similar but inedible *Craterellus* species occur in North America. *C. caeruleofuscus* and *C. cinereus* lack a fragrant or fruity odor, and their flesh has a slightly to distinctly disagreeable taste. The Common Fiber Vase (*Thelephora vialis*) appears somewhat similar, but it has tough, leathery flesh and lacks a pleasant odor.

**EDIBILITY:** These edible species, whose common names are often used interchangeably, are consistently rated highly by those who have tried them, though they're not as well known in North America as in Europe.

If they don't look too appetizing at first glance, they make up for this at first smell: they're strongly flavored, aromatic mushrooms. Because of their fragrant aroma, they are frequently dried and pulverized for use as a seasoning for everything from soup to steak, as are some of the closely related chanterelles. They're easy to dry— twenty-four hours in a food dehydrator is enough.

Some mycophagists find these species most enjoyable as a lightly sautéed side dish; certainly, little additional seasoning is necessary. Whether you choose to sauté them fresh or dry them, clean and prepare them by cutting off the solid part of the stalk base, slice them in half lengthwise, and gently wipe them clean with a moist paper towel or cloth.

Fragrant Black Trumpet (*Craterellus foetidus*)

These are among the most difficult edibles to find. The drab gray-ish color and small size coupled with their tendency to fruit after some leaves and other tree debris have started littering the ground in late summer make it a challenge to spot them. Once you find the first one, scour the ground in the immediate vicinity on your hands and knees, and you're apt to find at least a dozen more.

The Fragrant Black Trumpet is a special treat indeed. Its combined aroma and flavor are intensely satisfying, rivaled by no other mushroom the authors have sampled.

## LOBSTER MUSHROOM

*Hypomyces lactifluorum*

### KEY IDENTIFYING CHARACTERISTICS

1. Yellowish orange to orangish red mushroom completely covered with tiny, gritty, sandlike bumps
2. Longitudinal section reveals white-fleshed gilled mushroom inside and a very thin orangish layer on the outer surface of stalk, gills, and cap
3. Found on the ground in woods or under trees

**DESCRIPTION:** *Hypomyces lactifluorum* is not a mushroom, actually. It is an orangish moldlike sac fungus that parasitizes several white mushroom species of the genera *Lactarius* and *Russula*, causing them to grow in a rather disfigured manner. The overall shape of the para-sitized mushroom is somewhat like the bell end of a trumpet, except that the edge is usually quite wavy or lobed. The stalk portion is typi-cally very thick in relation to the width of the cap. The surface of the entire mushroom—cap (top and bottom) and stalk—has a texture somewhat like sandpaper. This grit is actually tiny, sandlike bumps that are partially embedded in the exterior flesh of the parasitized

Lobster Mushroom (*Hypomyces lactifluorum*)

mushroom. The entire mushroom is normally three to six inches high and four to eight inches wide, and the stalk is usually two to four inches thick. A longitudinal section reveals a white disfigured gilled mushroom, but the distorted gills may not be evident. No spore print can be obtained.

**FRUITING:** The Lobster Mushroom is found from midsummer through midfall throughout most of North America, sometimes solitary but usually scattered over an area on the ground under trees.

**SIMILAR SPECIES:** The only similar-looking mushrooms (those with unobscured true gills are, of course, easily ruled out) are orangish chanterelle species, each of which is edible and covered in this book. There are several other fairly common species of *Hypomyces* that parasitize, cover, and disfigure gilled mushrooms in a similar manner, but none are orange. This is called the Lobster Fungus in some field guides. We have chosen to use the name Lobster Mushroom for aesthetic reasons—it simply sounds more appetizing.

**EDIBILITY:** Although some mushroom field guides recommend caution to those who would sample mushrooms parasitized by this colorful and unusual species of fungus, suggesting that it could possibly be parasitizing a poisonous species, there is no evidence whatsoever to justify this concern. Some generalized field guides recommend that positive identification of the host mushroom should be obtained, yet this would be impossible for any but the most advanced mycologists. The Lobster Mushroom (so named for its color) is very popular among educated mycophagists, who are frequently able to gather it in abundance. Ironically, the mushrooms known to serve as host species are normally unpalatable. Rather odd, when you think about it: something that's edible only if it *does* look moldy!

# 7.

## Gilled Mushrooms

Some of the most difficult mushrooms to identify accurately are gilled mushrooms, or agarics. There are more than two thousand species of agarics in North America. Identifying most of them to family or genus on the basis of field characteristics, including spore print color, is not an insurmountable task for the well-studied amateur with a few good books. Identifying them to species is another matter. In many cases, the only way to distinguish one species from its closest relatives is through examination of microscopic and chemical characteristics.

Most of the deadliest species are gilled mushrooms, so be extra careful about the identification of the edible species. There are, however, a good number of fairly distinctive edible agarics that can be safely identified on the basis of field characteristics alone. In some cases, several species are difficult to tell apart, but each is edible; some of these groups share a common set of key identifying characteristics.

One important characteristic is spore print color, which is listed as a key identifying characteristic for most of the edible gilled mushrooms covered in this book. Under no circumstances should anyone forgo determining spore print color—or any other field characteristic—if it's listed as a key identifying characteristic. Too many over-anxious novices have made regrettable errors simply because they didn't have the patience to make a spore print. For the many species of gilled mushrooms that don't require spore print color as a key identifying characteristic, we have listed it at the end of the mushroom's full description.

When you become proficient at identifying gilled mushrooms, you might consider expanding your collecting to other agaric species that aren't included in this book. Most mushroom field guides tell which species are known to be safe for the table, and truly advanced mycophagists can eventually double the number of edible mushrooms they can identify. If you do eventually progress to that level, we hope one thought will stick in your mind: be ever cautious about identifications. Carelessness can make even the most experienced mushroom hunter sick . . . or worse.

Meadow Mushroom (*Agaricus campestris*)

# MEADOW MUSHROOM

*Agaricus campestris*

## KEY IDENTIFYING CHARACTERISTICS

1. Cap fleshy, dome shaped to flat, 1½–5 inches wide; top surface smooth, dry, white or off-white
2. Gills pink, pinkish brown, or dark brown; very closely spaced; free from stalk at maturity
3. Gills covered at first by white, membranous partial veil; mature specimens have membranous white ring around stalk
4. Stalk white, thick; no volva present
5. Found in grass on lawns or pastures, not near trees
6. Flesh white; color unchanged when cut or bruised; no unpleasant odor
7. Spore print dark chocolate brown

**DESCRIPTION:** The cap is at first dome shaped, nearly flat in larger specimens, and its surface is white, dry, and smooth, graying and cracking somewhat in maturity. The cap flesh is thick, soft, and white. The gills are bright pink at first, very crowded, often slightly attached to the stalk when young but always free in age. In small buttons, the gills are covered by a white membranous partial veil. As the mushroom expands, the veil ruptures to expose the gills, which darken until they're a rich chocolate brown. The ruptured veil leaves a white membranous ring around the stalk. The stalk is white, less than three inches long, and one-half to three-fourths inch thick. There is no volva around the stalk base. Mature specimens reach a height of up to four inches and a width of five inches. There is no unpleasant odor and no bruising effect associated with this species. The spore print is dark chocolate brown.

**FRUITING:** The Meadow Mushroom is sometimes found singly, but it is usually grouped or scattered, less frequently in small clusters, in grass on lawns or pastures, especially in moist spots. It can be found throughout North America, usually during summer and fall. The

## The Meadow Mushroom

This is the first kind of mushroom I ever enjoyed. When I was eight, my father invited me to "go mushrooming" in the local cow pastures. I was sure I didn't like mushrooms, but I was certainly willing to go for a walk with my dad, especially in a place where we might have to flee from an ornery old bull.

I don't recall whether we found any mushrooms that crisp, early autumn morning, but I do remember the first time I hesitantly tasted Mom's "Creamed Meadow Mushrooms on Toast." This, I knew at first bite, was serious good food, quite unlike those horrid cans of pieces and stems.

For several years afterward, when I got off the school bus each fall afternoon, I'd grab a wire-handled tomato basket and head straight for the back pastures of the nearest dairy farm to find a side dish for supper.

To this day, the first one of us that finds some Meadow Mushrooms dutifully notifies the other. And I still like to go out and soak my sneakers on the dew-drenched grass with Dad.

—DAVID FISCHER

mycelium is perennial, producing mushrooms in the same spot year after year.

**SIMILAR SPECIES:** Some deadly *Amanita* species look similar in the button stage; however, these Amanitas lack the Meadow Mushroom's characteristic pink to brown gills and dark chocolate brown spore print. Also, *Amanita* species always grow under or near trees. The Meadow Mushroom is sometimes found under trees, too, so if you choose to gather it near trees, examine each specimen very carefully to confirm the other key identifying characteristics. Be especially certain that each specimen has pink to brown gills and no volva.

There are a number of poisonous *Agaricus* species. Most grow under or near trees. Some are quite similar to the Meadow Mushroom, but they have an unpleasant odor frequently described as "creosotelike," and most of them bruise yellow, at least on the base of the stalk.

The Spring Agaricus (*A. bitorquis* or *A. rodmani*) is edible. Its cap is tannish, its gills are grayish pink at first, and it grows primarily on hard-packed ground in late spring and early summer. The Horse Mushroom (*A. arvensis*), which is edible (see next entry) is much larger than the Meadow Mushroom. It bruises yellow but has a pleasant odor. The Prince (*A. augustus*), also edible (see p. 40), has a yellowish brown scaly cap. Like the Horse Mushroom, it bruises yellow but has a pleasant aroma.

**EDIBILITY:** This is perhaps North America's best known, most popular edible wild mushroom. Probably every dairy farmer on the continent has either gathered it or been asked by others for permission to scour the cow pastures.

Although it is next-of-kin to the button mushroom found at the grocery store, the Meadow Mushroom is far richer in flavor. It is superior in any recipe that calls for its relatively bland, cultivated brother.

Some people eat the Meadow Mushroom raw, but we must advise against this practice in light of its preference for well-manured soil. Cooking thoroughly will destroy potentially harmful bacteria.

When this species is fruiting, scanning lawns and cow pastures from a car, with or without a pair of field glasses, can be a very effective foraging technique. Also, the Meadow Mushroom tends to be abundant, especially in moist cow pastures. Usually a large quantity can be located in the area where the first specimens were found. A return trip to the same place a week later will often yield a bonus crop.

# HORSE MUSHROOM

*Agaricus arvensis*

## KEY IDENTIFYING CHARACTERISTICS

1. Cap large (four to eight or more inches wide), round; surface dry; white to cream, bruising yellowish; smooth to slightly cracked
2. Gills pale gray to pink in young specimens, chocolate brown at maturity; free from stalk

Horse Mushroom (*Agaricus arvensis*)

3. White partial veil leaving white, membranous skirtlike ring on stalk; lower surface of partial veil or ring has white cottony patches
4. Stalk thick, white, bruising yellowish; no volva present
5. Found on lawns and pastures, not near trees (spruce excepted)
6. Odor pleasant, anise- or almondlike
7. Spore print dark chocolate brown

**DESCRIPTION:** The cap is round and large, two to eight inches in diameter. It is white to cream, bruising yellowish within three minutes. The cap surface is smooth but slightly cracked in large specimens. The gills are free from the stalk. They are pale gray to pink, finally aging to chocolate brown. The partial veil is white and membranous, with white cottony patches on its undersurface. In mature specimens, it leaves a skirtlike ring on the stalk and remnants on the edge of the cap. The stalk is three to six inches long, thick (½–1½ inches) and smooth surfaced, white to cream, bruising yellowish. There is no volva at the base of the stalk. This mushroom has a pleasant odor, similar to almonds or anise. The spore print is dark chocolate brown.

**FRUITING:** The Horse Mushroom appears singly to grouped or scattered, sometimes in fairy rings, on lawns, in pastures, or around spruce trees. It is quite common in urban areas, and it's found throughout North America, fruiting from midsummer through early fall. The mycelium is usually perennial, producing mushrooms year after year.

**SIMILAR SPECIES:** Some deadly Amanitas look similar in the button stage; however, they lack the Horse Mushroom's dark chocolate brown spore print and thick, sturdy, robust stalk. The white *Amanita* species also have a volva at the stalk base; *Agaricus* species do not.

The Yellow-foot Agaricus (*Agaricus xanthodermus*), a poisonous West Coast species (see page 153), usually has a darker and rougher cap surface, but some specimens are reportedly white and smooth enough to be confused with the Horse Mushroom. Both species bruise yellowish, but *A. xanthodermus*'s odor is strong and foul.

Several other poisonous *Agaricus* species occur under or near trees. But few of them have the white cap of the Horse Mushroom, and those that do have a disagreeable creosotelike odor.

**EDIBILITY:** Like other yellow-staining *Agaricus* species, the Horse Mushroom can accumulate large amounts of heavy metals, so avoid roadsides and industrial areas when collecting this species.

The Horse Mushroom's flavor makes it a very popular species. Its relatively huge size and coloration—it is often mistaken from a distance for a Giant Puffball—make it hard to overlook. Unfortunately, insect larvae find it as delicious as mycophagists do. Lucky is the mushroom hunter who finds several large specimens that haven't been invaded.

Its flavor is not extremely rich, but it's certainly not delicate. The taste is somewhat like the distinctive aroma: mild, pleasant, and nutty, reminiscent of almonds or anise. When cooking, be careful not to overwhelm it with other flavors.

Surprisingly, the Horse Mushroom is regarded suspiciously by many of the same rural folk who are thoroughly familiar with the Meadow Mushroom and the Giant Puffball. This is unfortunate for them but fortunate for those who have adopted it as a favorite edible.

## PRINCE

*Agaricus augustus*

**KEY IDENTIFYING CHARACTERISTICS**

1. Caps of buttons dome shaped but usually flat on top (like a marshmallow); caps of mature specimens nearly flat and at least five inches wide
2. Cap surface shows white flesh between fibrous, yellowish brown scales
3. Cap flesh white, staining yellow when cut or bruised
4. Mature specimens have white, membranous, skirtlike ring; no volva present
5. Odor fragrant, anise- or almondlike
6. Spore print dark chocolate brown

**DESCRIPTION:** The cap is large (four to ten inches wide, sometimes even larger), with white flesh showing between fibrous, yellowish brown scales. The cap is initially marshmallow to dome shaped, expanding until it is quite flat; the edge of the cap is often upturned in mature specimens. The flesh is thick and white, bruising yellowish. The gills are white in very young specimens, become pinkish, and finally turn brown; they are closely spaced and free from the stalk. In the button stage, the Prince's gills are covered by a white, membranous veil that bears cottony patches on its lower surface. The stalk is three to eight inches long and ¾–1½ inches thick; it is white and silky near the top and fibrous to somewhat scaly below, becoming brownish in age. The stalk usually extends well down into the ground. Mature specimens have a white, membranous, skirtlike ring on the

ST

Prince (*Agaricus augustus*)

stalk. This mushroom has a fragrant odor reminiscent of anise or almonds. There is no volva. The spore print is dark chocolate brown.

**FRUITING:** This robust mushroom is primarily a western North American species, though it has been reported from many other parts of the continent. It fruits on the ground—singly, in groups, scattered, sometimes even in small clusters—mostly in late summer and fall but sometimes even in springtime. Although the Prince is "naturally" a woodland species primarily associated with various conifers, it is also found in many other habitats (e.g., in grassy areas or disturbed soil, along paths or roads).

**SIMILAR SPECIES:** The Prince's overall form and dark chocolate brown spore print distinguish it as a species of the genus *Agaricus;* its specific description, large size, and pleasant aroma effectively rule out its close relatives. The odor is an important characteristic for all species of this large genus, in that the species that cause digestive upset consistently have a distinctly unpleasant odor of phenol (like creosote). Dangerous *Amanita* species have a volva and produce white spore prints; *Stropharia* species have dark purplish brown spore prints and attached gills.

**EDIBILITY:** This regal *Agaricus,* like other yellow-staining species of the genus, can accumulate a large amount of heavy metals, so don't collect it near roads or industrial areas.

The Prince is one of the favorites among devoted mycophagists in western North America, where it is most common. Like many of its relatives, the Prince is consistently rated as a choice edible: meaty, flavorful, and frequently abundant enough to fill a freezer. As a close relative of the *Agaricus* found on grocery store shelves, the Prince is suitable for use in any general recipe calling for mushrooms.

Some people eat this species raw, but we cannot recommend it. Especially when the Prince is found near agricultural or settled areas, there is no way to rule out the presence of bacteria that could cause gastrointestinal upset.

Like all mushrooms, the Prince should be eaten in moderation when trying it for the first time. Some people react to certain proteins present in various mushroom species, and the genus *Agaricus* is no exception.

# WINE-CAP STROPHARIA

*Stropharia rugosoannulata*

**KEY IDENTIFYING CHARACTERISTICS**

1. Cap two to ten inches wide, dry (slimy only when wet), smooth or cracked; dome shaped to flat; purplish red to reddish brown
2. Gills closely spaced, attached to the stalk but notched; white, becoming purplish brown
3. Stalk fairly thick, solid, with yellowish white to purplish brown ring with radial lines on the upper surface; no volva present
4. Found on the ground, especially in wood chips, sawdust, lawn mulch, gardens, or near compost heaps
5. Spore print dark purplish brown

**DESCRIPTION:** The cap is two to ten inches wide; initially dome shaped but then expanding until flat or even depressed at the center; and the color of red wine (purplish red to reddish brown), fading to pale yellowish brown at maturity. The cap surface is smooth, and the cap flesh is thick and white to yellowish white. At first, the gills are covered by a white, thick, wrinkled, membranous partial veil that is packed tightly against and between the gills. When the mushroom matures, the partial veil leaves a ring on the stalk that bears distinct radial lines on the upper surface and toothlike projections on the lower edge. In small, immature specimens whose gills are still covered by the partial veil, the gills are white; once the cap expands and ruptures the veil, the gills begin to turn purplish brown, eventually becoming nearly black. The stalk is white, often tinted yellowish below the ring and/or purplish brown above it. The stalk is three to five inches high, typically ½–1½ inches thick, and is slightly enlarged at the base. Thick white strands of mycelium (rhizomorphs) are usually attached to the stalk base. The spore print is dark purplish brown.

**FRUITING:** The Wine-cap Stropharia is found scattered or in groups, sometimes almost clustered, often in large numbers. It typically appears on or near mulch, compost, sawdust, or wood chips. It is found throughout most of North America, fruiting from late spring through early fall. Its mycelium will usually continue to produce mushrooms throughout the season until the substrate has been depleted.

**SIMILAR SPECIES:** Hard's Stropharia (*S. hardii*) is not known to be edible or poisonous. It is similar in stature, but the cap is yellowish brown, lacking the Wine-cap Stropharia's distinct purplish brown coloration. No other species can be considered as a look-alike if one considers all the key identifying characteristics listed above.

**EDIBILITY:** Although opinions differ concerning the quality of this mushroom's flavor, many mycophagists rate it as choice. However, avoid gathering it from garden mulch or other places where shrubs or other ornamental vegetation may have been treated with fertilizers, pesticides, or similarly dangerous chemicals.

In some places, the Wine-cap Stropharia has been cultivated commercially. If you have a compost heap or a pile of untreated garden mulch, you can try "planting" pieces of this species' cap there in the spring. By the summer's end, if you keep it well-watered, there's a good chance that you'll be able to gather a basketful. This species generally makes an excellent substitute for the grocery store mushroom. It can be gathered in sufficient quantity to last through winter.

Wine-cap Stropharia (*Stropharia rugosoannulata*)

## KEY IDENTIFYING CHARACTERISTICS

1. Open caps more than three inches wide, with white flesh showing between tan or pinkish to reddish brown fairly concentric scales
2. Cap flesh thick, white; not staining immediately brown when cut
3. Gills free from stalk, very closely spaced, white to dingy white or tinted reddish
4. Thick, white, membranous partial veil covering gills at first, then leaving a movable, bandlike ring on upper stalk
5. Stalk smooth, much thicker at middle or base; white at top, tan to reddish brown below, bruising yellow, orange, or reddish brown; *or* stalk slender, showing white between tiny brownish scales; base bulbous
6. Thickest part of stalk (or its base) at least one inch thick
7. No volva present
8. Spore print white, not greenish

## SHAGGY PARASOL, REDDENING LEPIOTA, AND PARASOL MUSHROOM

*Lepiota rachodes*
*L. americana*
*L. procera*

Shaggy Parasol (*Lepiota rachodes*)

**DESCRIPTION:** The Shaggy Parasol (*Lepiota rachodes*) is initially a button with a smooth well-rounded tan or light brown cap two to three inches wide; it has broad, white, closely spaced gills that are covered by a thick, white, membranous partial veil. The stalk is white at first, with an enlarged base. The Reddening Lepiota (*L. americana*) button is similar, but the button cap is slightly smaller (one to two inches wide) and more reddish brown. Its stalk is thickest at the middle. The Parasol Mushroom (*L. procera*) button is two to three inches wide at first, tan to brownish, egg shaped, and covered with woolly fibers or scales.

As these mushrooms mature, the cap surface breaks up into distinct, tannish to reddish brown, concentric scales showing white flesh between. The Shaggy Parasol's scales are coarse, and each scale is fairly smooth surfaced; the other two species' scales are cottony or woolly. The caps are eventually nearly flat, up to six inches (Reddening Lepiota), eight inches (Shaggy Parasol), or ten inches (Parasol Mushroom) wide, with a brownish or reddish brown disk or knob (umbo) at the top center of the cap. The veil ruptures, exposing the gills and leaving a thick, membranous, white, bandlike, movable ring on the upper stalk. (The ring may break and fall off, but it must be present to confirm identification.)

In all three species, the cap flesh is thick and white. In the Reddening Lepiota and the Shaggy Parasol, the cut flesh quickly stains yellow to pinkish orange, then slowly turns reddish brown. The Parasol Mushroom's flesh exhibits no immediate staining effect.

In all three species, the stalks remain white or off-white above the ring, but age or bruise tan to brown (Shaggy Parasol) or reddish brown (Reddening Lepiota) below the ring. When mature, the stalks are up to six inches high and one-fourth to one inch thick, except for the Parasol Mushroom: its stalk is no more than one-half inch thick (except, perhaps, at the very base), and may grow as high as a foot or more. It is slender, with a slightly bulbous base, and is covered with

Reddening Lepiota (*Lepiota americana*)

tiny brownish scales showing white between them. The surface of the stalk of the Shaggy Parasol and the Reddening Lepiota sometimes breaks into tough, curved scales that peel away from the middle of the stalk.

These three species produce white spore prints.

**FRUITING:** The Parasol Mushroom is found on the ground on lawns and in open woods. The Shaggy Parasol and the Reddening Lepiota are typically found on the ground under trees or near stumps, in wood chips or sawdust, in gardens, or on lawns with high wood content. The Shaggy Parasol is associated especially with conifer needles, particularly spruce. The authors have also discovered it growing indoors at the base of potted Norfolk Island pines.

All three species may be found from midsummer through midfall. The Shaggy Parasol usually doesn't appear before late summer; it and the Parasol Mushroom are often collected during winter in the southern United States. The Reddening Lepiota usually grows in groups or clusters; the Shaggy Parasol in close groups or fairy rings; and the Parasol Mushroom either singly, in loose groups, or well scattered.

The Shaggy Parasol is found throughout much of North America. The others are widely distributed, but the Reddening Lepiota is uncommon and the Parasol Mushroom unknown west of the Rocky Mountains.

**SIMILAR SPECIES:** Several of the key identifying characteristics above are intended to rule out two poisonous species in the *Lepiota* family—the Green-spored Lepiota and the Browning Parasol. The Green-spored Lepiota (*Chlorophyllum molybdites;* see p. 154) is difficult to distinguish at first look, especially from the Parasol Mushroom. But the gills of the Green-spored Lepiota quickly develop a greenish tint, and the spore print is pale green. This unhandy look-alike causes acute nausea and vomiting that last for at least a day or two, so make sure the spore print is white, not pale green.

Parasol Mushroom (*Lepiota procera*)

The Browning Parasol (*Lepiota brunnea*) is so similar to the Shaggy Parasol that, until quite recently, it was considered to be merely a variety of *L. rachodes*. It can, however, be distinguished by its distinct staining characteristic: the flesh quickly stains brown when cut or bruised, without first staining yellow to pinkish orange. The Browning Parasol has only been reported from the West Coast, primarily in California; it causes gastric upset, but not nearly as severe as that caused by the Green-spored Lepiota.

There are many smaller species of *Lepiota* that are poisonous, even deadly; however, they are rather dainty little mushrooms, not large and robust like the edibles. Don't gather the edible species unless the opened caps are each more than three inches wide, and do carefully confirm all key identifying characteristics.

These large *Lepiota* species are classified by some mycologists in a separate genus—*Macrolepiota,* which simply means "large *Lepiota*." Others classify one or another of the large *Lepiota* mushrooms as either *Leucoagaricus* or *Leucocoprinus* species.

**EDIBILITY:** These three *Lepiota* species are delicious edibles. The Parasol Mushroom and its shaggy brother are especially prized by those who know them. Strong-flavored, large, and sometimes abundant, they're a welcome find for mycophagists who are just starting to stock up on wild mushrooms for winter. They're not very moist to begin with, so drying thin slices of these is a fine way to save a large collection for later use. Canning, pickling, and freezing all work well, too. The Reddening Lepiota is not so highly prized as the other two species, but it is regularly collected for the table in areas where it's more common than its big brothers.

All three of these meaty, edible Lepiotas are capable of soaking up quite a bit of butter, oil, or margarine, so it's a good idea to cook them long and slow, using a moderate amount of butter or oil. You can add a splash of water if the mushrooms threaten to dry out as you sauté them.

Each of these mushrooms is particularly tasty baked or broiled, either stuffed first with just a dab of garlic butter or served with a dollop of seasoned sour cream. The Reddening Lepiota takes on a red wine color when cooked; you can be creative in deciding what it should accompany as a side dish. The Shaggy Parasol, on the other hand, becomes rather black when cooked; for this reason, it is especially appropriate for use in meat gravies.

---

## KEY IDENTIFYING CHARACTERISTICS

# SHAGGY MANE

*Coprinus comatus*

1. White egg- to bullet-shaped mushroom, three to ten inches high
2. Cap surface covered with white to reddish brown, delicate, flaky scales
3. Caps dissolve into thick, black liquid, starting at edge, as they mature
4. Stalk white, slender, hollow
5. Gills extremely crowded, free from stalk; initially white, tinting pink to gray before turning black and dissolving
6. Found on lawns, pastures, or soil

**DESCRIPTION:** The cap is egg- to bullet-shaped, dry, and white except at the top center of the cap, which is invariably tan to reddish brown. The cap surface, except at the top center, is covered with delicate white to reddish brown flaky scales. The gills are extremely crowded and free from the stalk; they are initially white, soon off-white or grayish, tinting pinkish starting at the edge of the cap, and finally becoming black and dissolving into a thick, black liquid. Initially, the gills are protected by a delicate, cottony, white veil that either remains as a movable ring around the lower part of the stalk or breaks and falls off. The stalk is white, hollow, smooth or with delicate white fibers, usually thicker at the base, three to ten or more inches high and one-half to three-fourths inch thick at the middle. The spore print is black.

**FRUITING:** This common mushroom is found singly or in groups, sometimes scattered about an area, on lawns, in pastures, or almost anywhere on the ground. It is found throughout most of North America, usually fruiting from late spring through early summer and again from late summer through early fall, but almost year-round in the southern states. It frequently appears in the same place twice each year for several consecutive years, especially in places where it is abundant.

**SIMILAR SPECIES:** The Shaggy Mane is a very common member of the Inky Cap (*Coprinus*) genus of mushrooms. Some *Coprinus* species are poisonous; however, none more than superficially resemble the Shaggy Mane. There are no dangerous look-alikes. Some other *Coprinus* species are also edible; one, the Mica Cap, is covered in this book (see next entry). Most of the *Coprinus* species share the strange

Shaggy Mane (*Coprinus comatus*)

method of spore dispersal called "deliquescence": the gills literally dissolve into a thick, black liquid; the spores are then carried by insects or water rather than by the wind.

**EDIBILITY:** Most dedicated mycophagists have eaten this common, abundant, and distinctive species. Most consider it excellent, though others use less enthusiastic terms. It is perhaps the most tender edible mushroom covered in this book, and it is especially suitable for sauces, soups, or gravies.

It is important to cook these mushrooms very soon after picking, or the gills will soon begin their process of autodigestion. This process will occur even in the refrigerator and, in fact, quite rapidly in the freezer. It can be delayed only by cooking or parboiling the mushrooms before storing them.

The stalks do not dissolve, though. They can be removed and stored in the refrigerator for several days. If you hold the mushroom cap in one hand, and gently but firmly twist the stalk with the other, they will easily separate from each other. Frequently, the gills will already have started turning pinkish or dark gray near the edge of the cap; if so, just cut off the lower portion of the cap.

Once the stalks have been removed, the caps are ideal for stuffing. They should be lightly sautéed first; otherwise, autodigestion may occur in the oven.

Shaggy Manes, which are called "Lawyer's Wigs" in England, can often be gathered by the bushel—if you hurry. On a hot, sunny day, Shaggy Manes can dissolve in as little as three to four hours, leaving nothing but a small disk atop the stalk, still dripping the black liquid that contains the mature spores.

**KEY IDENTIFYING CHARACTERISTICS**

# MICA CAP

*Coprinus micaceus*

1. Cap yellowish tan to yellowish brown, bell or dome shaped, less than two inches wide
2. Cap covered with tiny, crystalline granules; cap also has radial lines, especially prominent near edge
3. Gills whitish to gray, turning inky black and dissolving in mature specimens
4. Stalk white, smooth to minutely fibrous, no more than three inches high; no ring, partial veil, or volva present
5. Found in dense clusters on rotting wood or wood debris

**DESCRIPTION:** This common member of the Inky Cap genus (*Coprinus*) is small—typically two to three inches high and one to two inches wide. Initially, each mushroom is completely enclosed in a universal veil; however, this veil is very fragile and breaks up when the mushroom is extremely small, leaving only tiny, glistening, crystalline granules on the cap. These granules rub or rinse off easily, but they must be present in order to confirm identification. The surface of the

Mica Cap (*Coprinus micaceus*)

cap is radially furrowed or lined, especially near the edge. It is yellowish tan, invariably richer in color at the center of the cap; the color fades to gray in mature specimens. The cap is dome, bullet, or bell shaped. The gills are initially white, turning grayish and finally blackish as they dissolve into an inky goo, as happens in most species of this genus. Also, there are no partial gills: each gill extends from the edge of the cap to the stalk and is attached to it. The stalk is white and very slender (one to three inches long and one-eighth to one-fourth inch thick), and its surface is either smooth or minutely fibrous. Usually some capless stalks are evident in each cluster, still standing even though their caps and gills have dissolved and melted away. The spore print is inky black.

FRUITING: The Mica Cap grows exclusively on well-decayed wood, including completely or partially buried wood. It is very adaptive in terms of wood type but has a decided preference for deciduous wood. It always grows in clusters, sometimes with hundreds, even thousands, of specimens on a single log. Its range includes most of North America, and it fruits from midspring through midautumn.

SIMILAR SPECIES: The micalike granules on the cap surface combined with the dissolving gills typical of the genus *Coprinus* make this species unmistakable. However, because many little brown mushrooms, commonly referred to as "LBMs," are poisonous, even deadly, be sure to confirm all five of the key identifying characteristics listed above.

EDIBILITY: Although unusually small for a popular edible mushroom, this species is made worthwhile by the sheer number of specimens in a typical fruiting. Like its big brother, the Shaggy Mane, the Mica Cap has a wonderful flavor and a very tender texture. It must, of course, be gathered and cooked fresh, while the gills are still whitish or light grayish.

Because it is quite fragile, harvesting the Mica Cap is a bit time-consuming. But, if enough specimens are still in good condition, it is certainly worth the effort. Because it often fruits in midspring, even before the Yellow Morels are out, it is frequently the first edible wild mushroom that can be gathered fresh each year.

Because of its small size, the Mica Cap dries quickly enough to preserve it that way, provided you have access to a food dehydrator. Otherwise, the gills will start dissolving, and the mushrooms will be a useless mess. And, like all *Coprinus* species, the Mica Cap cannot be refrigerated because it will dissolve nonetheless. Enjoy it fresh.

# FAIRY RING MUSHROOM

*Marasmius oreades*

## KEY IDENTIFYING CHARACTERISTICS

1. Cap one to two inches wide, smooth, minutely suedelike; light tan with slightly darker central knob, or umbo
2. Gills white or yellowish white, well spaced, slightly attached to stalk or free
3. Stalk 1½–3 inches high, pale yellow to light tan, slender, minutely suedelike, very pliable; no ring, veil, or volva present
4. Found on lawns
5. Spore print white to light tan

DESCRIPTION: The cap is initially dome shaped, soon becoming distinctly bell shaped with a raised knob, or umbo, at the top center of the cap. The cap is one to two inches wide, off-white to light tan on top, and the upper surface is smooth but minutely suedelike. The gills are off-white to pale yellowish tan, fairly well spaced but somewhat less so in small specimens. The gills are barely attached to the stalk. The stalk is slender (less than one-fourth inch thick) and one to

Fairy Ring Mushroom (*Marasmius oreades*)

three inches high. It, too, is minutely suedelike, essentially the same color as the top of the cap, and very resilient: it can be bent or twisted substantially without breaking in two (this is a very important characteristic to ascertain). This mushroom typically is fragrant. The spore print is white to light tan.

**FRUITING:** This common mushroom is found on lawns throughout North America, fruiting from late spring through early summer. As the common name we use here implies, this species frequently forms fairy rings, essentially circle-shaped patterns of mushrooms, on lawns. Sometimes the entire circle may not be evident, though. Frequently they will fruit in an arc-shaped pattern or simply in a line or in a small group.

**SIMILAR SPECIES:** One species, the poisonous Sweating Mushroom (*Clitocybe dealbata*; see p. 158), named for a symptom it typically produces, is sometimes mistaken for the Fairy Ring Mushroom. The Sweating Mushroom, however, can be easily distinguished. The entire mushroom is white to off-white; also, its gills are much more closely spaced and broadly attached to the stalk, usually descending it somewhat. The stalk of this poisonous, so-called look-alike is somewhat tough, but it can be broken without much effort. In contrast, the stalk of the Fairy Ring Mushroom is very difficult to break. The main cause of confusion between these two mushrooms is careless picking. Lawn-inhabiting species of *Inocybe* will be ruled out by their brown spore prints. As with all edible mushrooms, each specimen should be examined to avoid unpleasant mistakes. *Marasmius oreades* is also called the "Scotch Bonnet" by some mushroom hunters.

**EDIBILITY:** This small mushroom, which is very common yet unnoticed by most people, is a popular edible in many parts of the world, including much of Europe. Like almost all small mushrooms that are popular edibles, it makes up for its size by its abundance.

A large lawn can yield enough Fairy Ring Mushrooms in one fruiting to make a huge casserole or a large pot of gravy, and the mycelium will usually fruit several times each summer.

The stalks are worthless in the kitchen—they are far too tough to eat. Discard them after you're sure you've identified the mushroom specimens properly. The caps, though, are very tasty and tender. They lend themselves very well to drying; in fact, they are often already well dried by the time they're picked. Like other species of the genus *Marasmius,* the Fairy Ring Mushroom revives (reabsorbs enough water to look fresh again) readily when soaked or sprayed with mist from a spray bottle of the sort used for houseplants.

# PURPLE-GILLED AND COMMON LACCARIAS

*Laccaria ochropurpurea*
*L. laccata*

Purple-gilled Laccaria (*Laccaria ochropurpurea*)

## KEY IDENTIFYING CHARACTERISTICS

1. Cap slightly depressed at center
2. Gills pink (Common Laccaria) or purple (Purple-gilled Laccaria), producing no latex when cut
3. Gills attached to stalk, sometimes descending it slightly (Common Laccaria only)
4. No partial veil, ring, or volva present
5. Found growing in moss or soil
6. Spore print white (Common Laccaria) or pale lilac (Purple-gilled Laccaria)

**DESCRIPTION:** The Purple-gilled Laccaria (*Laccaria ochropurpurea*) cap is 1½–6½ inches wide; it is initially purple to brownish purple, fading to grayish white at maturity. The cap is rounded in young specimens, nearly flat—usually with a slight central depression—in mature ones. The cap surface is smooth to slightly roughened. The

Common Laccaria (*Laccaria laccata*)

cap flesh is dull white, often water soaked, and has a slightly dis-agreeable taste. The gills are pale to dark purple, widely spaced, and have thick edges; they are attached to the stalk. The stalk is grayish white to brownish purple, usually the same color as the cap surface, and slightly roughened. It is two to six inches long and three-eighths to three-fourths inches thick, not noticeably enlarged toward but fre-quently curved near the base. The spore print is pale lilac.

The cap of the Common Laccaria (*L. laccata*) is quite rounded and pinkish orange to pinkish brown in young specimens. As it matures, it fades to grayish white and becomes nearly flat, typically with a slight depression at the center. Also, the cap edge is typically uplifted and wavy in mature specimens. The cap ranges in width from one-half to three inches. The cap surface may be smooth or slightly roughened. A longitudinal section reveals thin, water-soaked, pinkish orange to pinkish brown flesh; it has no distinctive taste. The gills are pinkish brown to dingy pink, widely spaced, and thick edged; they are attached to the stalk, often descending it slightly. The stalk is nearly the same color as the cap surface and measures one to four inches long and one-eighth to one-fourth inch thick; it isn't notice-ably narrower or thicker near the top or bottom, but it's usually twisted or curved. The surface of the stalk is typically roughened by vertical streaks. The spore print is white.

**FRUITING:** The Purple-gilled Laccaria is found singly or in groups on the ground in grassy areas or under deciduous trees (especially oak) during summer and fall throughout eastern North America.

The Common Laccaria is also found either singly or in groups on the ground in poor soils and in damp mossy or boggy areas. It fruits during summer and fall throughout most of North America.

**SIMILAR SPECIES:** Several other species of *Laccaria* are found in North America; most require microscopic examination and under-standing of the scientific literature for positive identification. However, those that match all the characteristics described above have been collected and eaten without any adverse reactions. No *Laccaria* species are suspected of being poisonous.

**EDIBILITY:** Both of these species are good edibles, though neither has attained widespread gourmet status. They make mediocre side dishes but deserve rave reviews for their wonderful contribution to soups, sauces, and gravies. Each is firm in texture, which also makes them perfectly suitable for stews.

The stalks of the Common Laccaria tend to be elongated and rather fibrous and tough when found growing in sphagnum moss. On the brighter side, specimens gathered in bogs are almost invariably free of insect larvae and require little cleaning. Its frequent habitat in bogs makes the Common Laccaria a reliable and welcome find during droughts or dry spells when few other edible wild mushrooms can be found.

# ROSY GOMPHIDIUS

*Gomphidius subroseus*

Rosy Gomphidius (*Gomphidius subroseus*)

## KEY IDENTIFYING CHARACTERISTICS

1. Cap slimy, one to three inches wide; rosy pink to dull red, dome shaped to sunken at the center
2. Gills white to grayish, partially descending stalk
3. Stalk slimy, white, tapering to a narrow, yellow base
4. Thin, slimy, partial veil or ring; no volva present
5. Flesh of cap and upper stalk white, but yellow at stalk base
6. Spore print brownish black to black

**DESCRIPTION:** The cap is one to three inches wide, slimy, rosy pink to dull red; it is dome shaped at first, becoming flat to sunken at the center in age. A small, pointed knob, or umbo, is sometimes present at the center of the cap surface. The gills of young specimens are covered by a slimy, colorless partial veil; at maturity, it remains on the stalk as a thin, slimy ring. The gills are white at first, becoming grayish in age; they partially descend the stalk and are typically soft and waxy. The stalk is white but covered with a colorless layer of slime; it is one to three inches long and one-fourth to three-fourths inch thick, tapering to a narrow, yellow base. The ring around the upper part of the mature stalk is thin and slimy, usually tinted blackish from the spores. A longitudinal section reveals white flesh except at the stalk base, which is lemon yellow. The flesh has a mild taste. The spore print is brownish black to black.

**FRUITING:** This mushroom is found scattered or in groups on the ground under conifers, especially Douglas fir, during summer and fall. It is most common in the Pacific Northwest, but it also occurs in California, the Rocky Mountains, and rarely in mountainous areas from Virginia to North Carolina.

**SIMILAR SPECIES:** There are several other *Gomphidius* species in North America; they are all edible. Each species differs from the Rosy Gomphidius by one or more of the key identifying characteristics listed above.

**EDIBILITY:** The Rosy Gomphidius is a fleshy, mild-flavored mushroom. Some mycophagists place it high on their list of favorites, while others consider it mediocre. You'll have to decide for yourself. For aesthetic reasons, the slime layer should be removed before cooking. It can be wiped off easily.

---

# WOOLLY CHROOGOMPHUS

*Chroogomphus tomentosus*

**KEY IDENTIFYING CHARACTERISTICS**

1. Cap surface matted, feltlike to woolly, one to three inches wide, dull orange to brownish orange, dome shaped to nearly flat
2. Gills thick, widely spaced, dull orange to grayish orange, partially descending stalk
3. Stalk dull orange to brownish orange, dry, feltlike to woolly, tapering to a narrow base
4. Partial veil or ring thin and fibrous, often indistinct; no volva present
5. Flesh yellowish orange to brownish orange
6. Spore print grayish black to black

**DESCRIPTION:** The cap is dull orange to brownish orange, one to four inches wide; the surface is dry, covered with a feltlike or woolly mat of fibers. The cap is dome shaped when young, becoming nearly flat at maturity. The gills of young specimens are covered by a fibrous, pale yellow to dull orange partial veil that only sometimes leaves a noticeable ring of fibers near the top of the mature stalk. The gills are dull orange to grayish orange at first, becoming grayish orange to gray in age; they are widely spaced and partially descend

Woolly Chroogomphus (*Chroogomphus tomentosus*)

the stalk. The stalk is 2–7½ inches long and three-eighths to three-fourths inch thick, tapering downward to a narrow base; its surface has the same color and texture as the cap. The flesh is yellowish orange except at the stalk base, which is brownish orange. The flesh has a mild taste. The spore print is grayish black to black.

**FRUITING:** The Woolly Chroogomphus grows scattered or in groups on the ground under conifers, especially hemlock and Douglas fir. It is found during summer and fall along the West Coast and in the Rocky Mountains.

**SIMILAR SPECIES:** *C. leptocystis,* a very similar, edible species found under conifers during autumn in the Pacific Northwest, has a grayer cap. Other *Chroogomphus* and *Gomphidius* species have slimy to sticky cap surfaces.

**EDIBILITY:** This mushroom is usually plentiful during moist periods in autumn. It is appreciated more for its abundance than for its taste, which is a rather subjective matter among those mushroom fanciers who have tried it.

# BROWNISH CHROOGOMPHUS

*Chroogomphus rutilus*

## KEY IDENTIFYING CHARACTERISTICS

1. Cap surface sticky, one to four inches wide, reddish brown to orangish brown or greenish brown; cap dome shaped, often with a pointed knob, or umbo
2. Gills brownish yellow or greenish brown to grayish brown; widely spaced, partially descending stalk
3. Stalk tapering to a narrow base; dull brownish yellow to dull orange, often with reddish tints
4. Partial veil or ring thin and fibrous, often indistinct; no volva present

Brownish Chroogomphus (*Chroogomphus rutilus*)

5. Flesh pale brownish yellow to pale orange
6. Spore print grayish black to black

**DESCRIPTION:** The cap has a sticky, reddish brown to orangish brown or greenish brown surface; it is one to four inches wide, dome shaped, usually with a small, pointed knob, or umbo, at the center. The gills of young specimens are covered by a fibrous, pale orangish brown partial veil that may or may not leave a visible ring near the top of the mature stalk. The gills are brownish yellow to greenish brown at first, becoming grayish brown in age; they are fairly widely spaced and partially descend the stalk. The stalk is two to seven inches long and three-eighths to three-fourths inches thick, tapering downward to a narrow base; it is dull brownish yellow to dull orange, often with reddish tints in age. The flesh of the cap and stalk is pale brownish yellow to pale orange but darker toward the stalk base. The flesh has a mild taste. The spore print is grayish black to black.

**FRUITING:** This species is found scattered or in groups on the ground under conifers, especially pine trees. It is found from late summer through fall and into early winter in areas with milder climates. Its range includes much of North America.

**SIMILAR SPECIES:** The Wine-colored Chroogomphus (*C. vinicolor*), which is edible, is nearly identical, but it is smaller and grayish brown with wine-red or reddish orange stains. *Gomphidius* species have white cap flesh. Like other *Chroogomphus* species, *C. rutilus* was previously classified in the genus *Gomphidius*.

**EDIBILITY:** The Brownish Chroogomphus is often abundant during cool, rainy periods, particularly in the Pacific Northwest. Like many of its equally mild-flavored relatives, it has a close circle of devotees. Those who truly enjoy it appreciate the lack of competition from other mushroom hunters, though this species is perhaps the most popular edible in the *Gomphidius* family.

# GRAYLING

*Cantharellula umbonata*

Grayling (*Cantharellula umbonata*)

## KEY IDENTIFYING CHARACTERISTICS

1. Small, gray cap with a small, pointed, central knob, or umbo
2. Gills forked, descending stalk; white to cream colored, slowly bruising yellow to reddish
3. Stalk slender, sturdy, off-white
4. Found only in moss on the ground, not on moss-covered wood
5. Gills do not produce latex when cut
6. Spore print white

**DESCRIPTION:** The cap is ½–1½ inches, rarely two inches, in diameter. The cap surface is smooth and gray, typically with a small but distinct central knob, or umbo. The gills are repeatedly forked; they are white with a creamy or grayish tint. The gills bruise yellow to red, usually within ten minutes or so; they descend the stalk noticeably, and they produce no latex when cut. The stalk is off-white and slender but sturdy. The spore print is white.

**FRUITING:** The Grayling is found only in moss, usually in fairly sunny areas. It typically appears scattered about in a bed of moss, fruiting during cool periods from late summer through late fall. It tends to reappear in the same spot year after year; its known range is limited to northeastern North America.

**SIMILAR SPECIES:** The key identifying characteristics presented for the petite Grayling are very reliable. The only other species likely to be mistaken for this little mushroom are very small *Lactarius* species. They must be ruled out by cutting across the gills of a fresh specimen to determine whether latex is produced.

This species was formerly classified as *Cantharellus umbonatus*, the Knobbed Chanterelle.

**EDIBILITY:** The diminutive but distinctive Grayling tastes as delicious as the true chanterelles do, making it one of the smallest mushrooms worth gathering for the table. Once you've located the first few specimens, keep looking around in the same bed of moss and in others nearby; you're likely to find plenty more for your basket. Be especially careful to examine every specimen you pick, though, to make sure no other little mushrooms are inadvertently collected.

The Grayling is on the very short list of gilled mushrooms that can be dried without a significant loss in quality. The stalks may be slightly chewy after the mushrooms have been reconstituted, but the caps will certainly be just as tender and tasty as they are when fresh. Sauté them lightly, with just a dab of butter. Their size limits their versatility, but their rich, wonderful flavor makes them exquisite as a simple side dish. The flavor is strong enough that a fair quantity can even be used as a pizza topping. Omelets and other recipes that need only a small amount of mushrooms are appropriate for smaller collections.

## BLEWIT

*Clitocybe nuda*

Blewit (*Clitocybe nuda*)

### KEY IDENTIFYING CHARACTERISTICS

1. Cap dome shaped to flat, smooth, lilac with gray or tan tints, two to six inches wide
2. Gills pale violet to pinkish brown, notched at stalk
3. Stalk pale violet to brownish lilac; no ring, veil, or volva present
4. Spore print pale pinkish tan

**DESCRIPTION:** The cap is rounded to almost flat, two to six inches wide; it's purplish, but usually with some grayish or tannish areas. The cap surface is smooth and dry to moist. The gills are light purple, often tinted pinkish brown; they are closely spaced and attached to, but notched near, the stalk. The stalk is also purplish, with a white, silky sheen most noticeable in young specimens. It usually has an enlarged base and is rather stout—one-half to one inch thick and only one to three inches high. The spore print is pale pinkish tan.

**FRUITING:** Blewits are sometimes found singly but usually in groups, scattered or in small clusters, on or near leaves, pine duff, compost piles, old wood chips or sawdust, and on lawns under pine trees. They can be gathered throughout much of North America from late summer through late fall.

**SIMILAR SPECIES:** Few species of mushrooms—none of which are closely related—share the overall purplish coloration of the Blewit's cap surface, gills, and stalk. The distinctive spore print color will rule out other purplish mushrooms, including the poisonous Lilac Fiber Head (*Inocybe lilacina*) and *Cortinarius* species, which have brown and rusty-brown spores, respectively. The Blewit is also classified as *Lepista nuda*.

**EDIBILITY:** The Blewit is highly regarded among dedicated mycophagists, not only for its wonderfully rich flavor, but also for its frequent abundance. Its texture is very close to other fleshy, gilled mushrooms; it is accordingly versatile in the kitchen—a good all-purpose mushroom.

When it is found fresh and collected in quantity, the Blewit provides an excellent opportunity to stock up on wild mushrooms for the cold days of winter. Blewits can be frozen fresh with satisfactory results, but they retain their flavor better and take up less freezer space if they're partially cooked before freezing. Drying thin slices also works well, but freezing is the superior option.

# ORANGE-LATEX, ORANGE BOG, AND FROSTED ORANGE-LATEX MILKIES

*Lactarius deliciosus*
*L. thyinos*
*L. salmoneus*

**KEY IDENTIFYING CHARACTERISTICS**

1. Cap orange, somewhat concentrically zoned; *or* cap white and slightly velvety when young but orange and smooth when mature
2. Gills orange, immediately exuding an orange latex when cut
3. Stalk orange; no ring, partial veil, or volva present
4. Latex mild tasting (taste a tiny bit and then spit it out)

**DESCRIPTION:** The Orange-latex Milky (*Lactarius deliciosus*) has an orange cap, 2–5½ inches wide, with three to six rusty orange concentric zones. It is dome shaped when young, expanding until nearly flat, typically with a slightly sunken center. Fresh caps are moist and sticky. Green stains often develop in age, especially near the cap edge. The gills are orange, somewhat crowded, and attached to the stalk; they fade to orangish yellow in age and stain green when bruised. When cut, the gills immediately exude an orange latex that tastes mild. The stalk is orange, one to three inches long and three-eighths to one inch thick; its surface is smooth, sometimes with tiny, shallow pits. The stalk also usually develops green stains in age or when

DA          Orange-latex Milky (*Lactarius deliciosus*)

Orange Bog Milky (*Lactarius thyinos*)

bruised. The flesh of both cap and stalk is pale yellow, staining green; it is somewhat fragrant and tastes mild.

The Orange Bog Milky (*L. thyinos*) is very similar to the Orange-latex Milky; however, the cap has alternating concentric zones of orange and pale yellow, and it is usually somewhat slimy. Also, the stalk of this species is sticky and often distinctly pitted. The orange latex slowly stains the gills and other parts of the mushroom dull red, not green. As with the Orange-latex Milky, the flesh is somewhat fragrant and tastes mild.

The Frosted Orange-latex Milky (*L. salmoneus*) is also quite similar to the Orange-latex Milky. Its characteristic differences include a smaller, carrot-orange cap that is typically covered by a white, slightly velvety coating, especially in young specimens. As the mushroom matures, the white coating is worn away, exposing the orange cap surface. The gills, latex, and stalk of this species are also orange. The flesh of both cap and stalk is orange; again, it is somewhat fragrant and mild-tasting.

The spore prints of these species range from off-white to pale yellow.

**FRUITING:** These lactarii are found singly, grouped, or scattered on the ground in woods during summer and fall. The Orange-latex Milky is found in much of North America under conifers, especially pine. The Orange Bog Milky occurs in northeastern North America west to Michigan; it prefers bogs or wet woodlands, typically in moss. The Frosted Orange-latex Milky is found under pines in the southeastern United States from Florida to North Carolina and Texas.

Frosted Orange-latex Milky (*Lactarius salmoneus*)

**SIMILAR SPECIES:** Some fleshy *Lactarius* species found in North America are poisonous or cause adverse reactions. The key identifying characteristics rule them out.

**EDIBILITY:** Although the Orange-latex Milky is especially popular in Europe and the Soviet Union, these species are less highly rated by North American mycophagists. The texture is often somewhat granular, and the flavor is usually not outstanding. However, the flavor of these mushrooms and such strong-flavored freshwater fish as trout balance each other quite well when they are sautéed together. Pickling or use in stews brings out these common species' best flavors, and they are often abundant enough to make collecting them worthwhile.

Bleeding Milk-cap (*Lactarius rubrilacteus*)

# BLEEDING MILK-CAP
*Lactarius rubrilacteus*

## KEY IDENTIFYING CHARACTERISTICS

1. Cap two to five inches wide, orange to orangish brown or reddish brown, with concentric zones and sometimes with green tints
2. Stalk pale orange to pale orangish brown, hollow, distinctly narrower at base; no partial veil, ring, or volva present
3. Gills dull orange to pale reddish brown
4. Gills immediately exuding dull red to orangish red latex when cut; latex mild-tasting (taste a tiny bit and then spit it out)

**DESCRIPTION:** The cap is round topped with an inrolled edge at first, becoming broadly vase shaped. The cap is smooth and sticky, two to five inches wide; it is orange to orangish brown or reddish brown overall, with several concentric zones typically alternating in color between a pale yellowish orange and a dark orangish brown or reddish brown. Buttons may be green overall; mature specimens may have greenish stains or streaks on the cap surface. The cap flesh is thick, creamy white, and mild-tasting; it may slowly stain greenish after being exposed to air. The gills are dull orange to pale reddish brown, sometimes with greenish stains when bruised or older; they are closely spaced and attached to the stalk, sometimes descending it a bit. When cut, the gills immediately produce a scanty (especially in dry weather), mild-tasting latex that is dull red to orangish red. The stalk is pale orange to pale orangish brown; it is usually smooth, but it may have tiny, shallow pits. The stalk is 1–2½ inches long and ⅜–1⅛ inches thick at the middle, tapering to a narrower base; it is hollow, especially at maturity. The spore print is pale yellow.

**FRUITING:** This mushroom occurs from the Pacific Northwest south to California; it has also been found in New Mexico. It is found scattered or in groups on the ground under conifer trees; it fruits during summer and autumn.

SIMILAR SPECIES: The edibility of *L. barrowsii*, which is known only from New Mexico, has not been established; its cap lacks zones and is paler (whitish to pinkish tan), and its latex is darker, a port wine red. It is only considered a look-alike because its gills do stain green when bruised or in age.

The Bleeding Milk-cap was previously classified as *L. sanguifluus*.

EDIBILITY: The Bleeding Milk-cap is highly rated. It is a firm, tasty mushroom that makes a fine substitute in recipes that call for the better-known Orange-latex Milky.

## INDIGO, SILVER-BLUE, AND VARIEGATED MILKIES

*Lactarius indigo*
*L. paradoxus*
*L. subpurpureus*

### KEY IDENTIFYING CHARACTERISTICS

1. Cap concentrically zoned; dark blue, grayish blue, silvery blue, or wine red overall, with or without greenish stains
2. Gills dark blue, grayish blue, or reddish brown; slowly staining greenish in age or when bruised; slowly exuding a scant dark blue, wine red, or wine brown latex when cut
3. Stalk dark blue, grayish blue to grayish green, or wine red with dark reddish brown pits; with or without greenish stains; no ring, partial veil, or volva present

DESCRIPTION: The Indigo Milky (*Lactarius indigo*) has a concentrically zoned dark blue to grayish blue or silvery blue cap that typically develops greenish stains in age or when bruised. The cap is two to six inches wide; it is dome shaped with an inrolled edge when young, then becomes nearly flat and typically has a slightly sunken center at maturity. Fresh caps are moist and sticky. The gills are dark blue to grayish blue at first, eventually fading to greenish yellow, and slowly staining green when bruised or in age; they are fairly crowded, and are attached to the stalk. When cut, the gills exude a scant dark blue latex that slowly changes to dark green. The stalk is dark blue to grayish blue, 3/4–3 1/2 inches long and 3/8–1 inch thick; its surface is smooth and typically dry. The flesh of both cap and stalk is whitish, quickly staining blue when cut and slowly turning greenish; the flesh and latex taste mild to slightly bitter or somewhat peppery.

The Silver-blue Milky (*L. paradoxus*) has a concentrically zoned, grayish blue to silver blue cap that often has pinkish brown tones near the edge, and pale green stains in age or when bruised; it is 1–3 1/4 inches wide. Immature caps often lack concentric zones, and have a silvery sheen overall. The cap is dome shaped with an inrolled edge when young, expanding until it is nearly flat, typically with a somewhat sunken center. Fresh caps are moist and sticky. The gills are reddish brown, somewhat crowded, and attached to the stalk; they become grayish green in age, and stain green when bruised. When cut, the gills exude a scant reddish brown latex that slowly changes to green. The stalk is pinkish gray with green stains in age or when bruised; it is 1–1 3/4 inches long and 3/8–3/4 inch thick. The surface of the stalk is smooth and typically dry. The flesh of both cap and

Indigo Milky (*Lactarius indigo*)

Silver-blue Milky (*Lactarius paradoxus*)

Variegated Milky (*Lactarius subpurpureus*)

stalk is pale green and slowly darkens after exposure to air; it tastes mild to slightly bitter or somewhat peppery.

The Variegated Milky (*L. subpurpureus*) has a somewhat concentrically zoned dark wine red to pale pink cap that develops green stains in age; it is one to four inches wide, dome shaped with an inrolled edge when young, becoming nearly flat with a typically sunken center at maturity. Fresh caps are moist and sticky. The gills are wine red, becoming green-spotted in age and staining greenish when bruised; they are closely spaced and are attached to the stalk. When cut, the gills exude a scant, wine red latex that tastes mild to faintly peppery. The stalk is wine red, 1–3½ inches long and ¼–⅝ inch thick; its surface is smooth but has small, shallow, dark reddish brown pits. The flesh of both cap and stalk is whitish to pale pink, staining red and then greenish; it tastes mild to slightly peppery.

The spore prints of these species range from pale cream to yellow.

**FRUITING:** These lactarii are found singly, grouped, or scattered on the ground in woods during summer and fall; the Silver-blue Milky is also collected as late as February in its southern range. The Indigo Milky is found in eastern North America, west to Michigan and south to Texas; it prefers oak and pine woods. The Silver-blue Milky occurs from southeastern Canada to Florida and west to Texas. It grows under oak, pine, and palmetto palm trees, especially on wooded lawns. The Variegated Milky grows in mixed woods, especially hemlock and pine, from southern Canada to the Gulf Coast region.

**SIMILAR SPECIES:** Some fleshy "Milky" (*Lactarius*) mushrooms found in North America are poisonous or cause adverse reactions; the key identifying characteristics provided here easily rule them out.

**EDIBILITY:** The flavor and texture of these three species are quite similar to those of most of the other *Lactarius* species covered in this book. They are not generally regarded as choice, although they certainly have their following. Like most Milkies, they are suitable for a wide variety of recipes such as casseroles, and in some years these mushrooms can be collected in great quantity, filling the baskets of those who like to get their mushrooms fresh from the woods.

# VOLUMINOUS-LATEX, HYGROPHORUS, AND CORRUGATED-CAP MILKIES

*Lactarius volemus*
*L. hygrophoroides*
*L. corrugis*

### KEY IDENTIFYING CHARACTERISTICS

1. Cap and stalk dry, reddish brown to orangish brown, smooth to wrinkled, lacking concentric zones of alternating colors
2. Gills whitish to pale yellow, immediately exuding white to cream latex when cut
3. Latex tastes mild or slightly sour, not bitter or peppery (taste a tiny bit and then spit it out); latex doesn't become yellow after exposure to air
4. Cap and stalk flesh white; mild-tasting, not bitter or peppery; odor pleasant or fishlike
5. Stalk has no partial veil, ring, or volva

Voluminous-latex Milky (*Lactarius volemus*)

Hygrophorus Milky (*Lactarius hygrophoroides*)

**DESCRIPTION:** The Voluminous-latex Milky (*Lactarius volemus*) cap is dry, orangish brown, and two to five inches wide; its surface is smooth to slightly wrinkled and lacks concentric zones of alternating colors. It is typically flat; in mature specimens, there is a slight depression at the center of the cap. The gills are closely spaced and attached to the stalk; they are pale cream, slowly staining brown when bruised. When cut, the gills produce abundant white latex that has a mild taste and slowly turns a cream color (*not* yellow) and stains the gills brown. The stalk is two to four inches long and three-eighths to three-fourths inch thick, narrowing slightly at the base; it is orangish brown. The flesh of the cap and stalk is white, mild-tasting, and has a mild to fishlike odor, especially noticeable in mature specimens.

The Hygrophorus Milky (*L. hygrophoroides*) has an orangish brown cap and well-spaced white to cream-colored gills that descend

Corrugated-cap Milky (*Lactarius corrugis*)

the stalk noticeably and exude a mild-tasting white latex that neither changes color nor stains the gills.

The Corrugated-cap Milky (*L. corrugis*) has a reddish brown, distinctly wrinkled cap and closely spaced, pale yellow to yellowish brown gills that exude plentiful white latex that stains the gills brown. The flesh of the cap and stalk is white, mild-tasting, and has a mild to distinctly fishlike odor.

The spore prints of these species range from white to cream or pale yellow.

**FRUITING:** These mushrooms are found singly, scattered, or in groups on the ground in woods. They occur throughout eastern North America and west to Minnesota and Texas. All three species fruit from early summer through early autumn.

**SIMILAR SPECIES:** None of the many other North American *Lactarius* species have the unique combination of key identifying characteristics listed above.

**EDIBILITY:** All three of these species are widely rated as choice edible wild mushrooms by those mycophagists who've tried them. They are firm, meaty mushrooms that can be prepared and enjoyed in a wide variety of recipes. Casseroles and thick sauces are especially suitable. They frequently fruit in large numbers; so this, along with their fairly large size, makes them a prize find for the mushroomer.

Rooted Oudemansiella (*Oudemansiella radicata*)

# ROOTED OUDEMANSIELLA

*Oudemansiella radicata*

**KEY IDENTIFYING CHARACTERISTICS**

1. Cap tannish brown to gray, two to four inches wide, covered with a translucent, wrinkled, rubbery cuticle
2. Gills white, well spaced, attached to stalk
3. Stalk long, slender, white at top, whitish tan to grayish brown at base; long, rootlike appendage below ground; no ring, veil, or volva present
4. Found on the ground in deciduous woods or on lawns
5. Spore print white

**DESCRIPTION:** This is a tall, slender, and graceful gilled mushroom. The cap is slightly rounded to almost flat, one to four inches wide, and quite thin fleshed. It is covered with a rubbery, translucent cuticle that is fairly wrinkled—especially near the center of the cap—and there is usually a central knob, or umbo. The cuticle is very slippery when moist. The gills are white, fairly well spaced, and fairly resilient (bending considerably without breaking); they are attached to the stalk. The stalk is slender, no more than one-half inch thick except at the very base (where it is thickest), and white near the top but usually streaked with grayish tan to brown hues toward the base. The stalk is three to ten inches tall, except in very immature specimens. Holding the base of the stalk gently but firmly and pulling up slowly will reveal the "root"; it is three to six inches long, tapering to a point. (This underground appendage is sometimes difficult to pull up, especially on lawns.) The spore print is white.

**FRUITING:** This distinctive species is very common in deciduous woods and on lawns throughout eastern North America and into the Midwest during summer and fall.

**SIMILAR SPECIES:** The edible *O. longipes* is nearly as tall and slender stalked, but it has a smaller, brown, velvety cap. No other mushroom species really come close to matching the key identifying characteristics listed above, especially if one considers the distinctive cap cuticle and the rootlike stalk appendage. The Rooted Oudemansiella is classified as *Xerula furfuracea* by some mycologists; it was previously called *Collybia radicata*.

**EDIBILITY:** This mushroom has a wonderful flavor, though some people complain that the rubbery cuticle makes it undesirable. Since the cuticle is almost impossible to remove, it is wise to cook the Rooted Oudemansiella until the top surface of the cap is well browned and dry. Grilling works very well. The stalk tends to be a bit chewy, but it can be removed quite easily. Mushroom hunters who are familiar with this species often collect the caps only and leave the stalks standing in place.

The long stalk has its advantage: insects never seem to get to the cap until at least a couple of days after the mushroom fruits. If you gather a good quantity, these handsome mushroom caps are thin fleshed enough that they dry quickly. Unfortunately, the cuticles are just as rubbery after the dried mushrooms have been reconstituted. Again, the best bet is to cook them until the top surface of each cap is dry.

# GYPSY

*Rozites caperata*

**KEY IDENTIFYING CHARACTERISTICS**

1. Cap orangish yellow to orangish brown, with a faint white coating, especially at the center; two to six inches wide, egg shaped to nearly flat
2. Gills of young specimens covered by yellowish white, membranous partial veil
3. Gills pale yellowish white to dull brown; closely spaced, attached to stalk
4. Stalk pale yellow to yellowish brown, moderately thick
5. Stalk of mature specimens has distinct, membranous, yellowish ring
6. Found on the ground in woods
7. Spore print rusty brown

**DESCRIPTION:** The cap is orangish yellow to orangish brown, with a distinct white coating, especially near the center. The cap is two to six inches wide, egg shaped at first but nearly flat at maturity. The cap flesh is thick and white. The gills of very young specimens are covered by a yellowish white, membranous partial veil. The gills are initially pale yellowish white, becoming yellow and finally dull brown. The stalk is pale yellow to yellowish brown, two to five inches long and three-eighths to three-fourths inch thick; it is narrower toward the top. All but the smallest specimens whose gills are still covered by the partial veil have a distinct, yellowish, membranous ring near the top of the stalk. The spore print is rusty brown.

**FRUITING:** The Gypsy is usually found scattered, often in groups and rarely singly, on the ground in woods. It is primarily a fall mushroom but often fruits during cooler periods from middle to late sum-

Gypsy (*Rozites caperata*)

mer. Its range includes many parts of northern North America, but it most frequently occurs in the Northeast and the Pacific Northwest; it also occurs at higher elevations in the southern United States.

**SIMILAR SPECIES:** Few mushrooms of this size produce rusty brown spore prints *and* have membranous partial veils or rings. Diligent confirmation of all the key identifying characteristics listed above will rule out all other species.

**EDIBILITY:** The Gypsy is an excellent edible mushroom, often collected in large quantities in the northern corners of the United States. It is equally common and popular in many parts of Europe, where it is sometimes sold commercially. This tender-fleshed mushroom should be preserved, prepared, and cooked like most other fleshy gilled mushrooms.

# WHITE MATSUTAKE

*Tricholoma magnivelare*

**KEY IDENTIFYING CHARACTERISTICS**

1. Caps of buttons white, two to five inches wide, with cottony, inrolled edges
2. Expanded caps large and robust (at least four inches wide) with yellowish brown to reddish brown fibers and scales
3. Flesh thick and firm, with spicy, fragrant odor; white, not changing color when cut
4. Gills very closely spaced; attached to but notched near stalk; white, staining pinkish brown when bruised
5. Gills of buttons covered by thick, white, cottony-membranous partial veil
6. Stalk white with yellowish brown to pinkish brown scaly patches beneath a thick, membranous ring
7. Ring white on top, yellowish brown to pinkish brown below
8. Spore print white

White Matsutake (*Tricholoma magnivelare*)

**DESCRIPTION:** The cap is white at first, fairly smooth surfaced, and rounded, with a cottony, inrolled edge; it develops yellowish brown to reddish brown fibers and scales and is nearly flat in age. The cap is 2–7½ inches wide. The cap flesh is thick, firm, and white and does not change color when cut or bruised. The gills are white, staining pinkish brown when bruised; they are very closely spaced, attached to the stalk, and notched near it. The gills of young specimens are covered by a thick, white, membranous partial veil. The stalk is white in young button specimens. As the mushroom matures, the partial veil ruptures, leaving on the stalk a thick, white, membranous ring that is white on the upper surface and yellowish brown to pinkish brown on the lower surface. In mature specimens, the stalk is white above the ring, but below the ring, the stalk is covered by scaly, yellowish brown to pinkish brown patches. The mature stalk is two to six inches long and ¾–1½ inches thick, narrowing toward the base. This species has a distinctly spicy, fragrant odor. There is no volva or universal veil. The spore print is white.

**FRUITING:** This large mushroom is found singly or in groups, on the ground in wet or sandy soil under conifers, especially hemlock and fir. It occurs throughout much of northern North America—from Maine west to the Rocky Mountains and the Pacific Northwest—fruiting from late summer through fall, even into late winter in places with relatively mild climates (such as the Puget Sound area).

**SIMILAR SPECIES:** The Fragrant Tricholoma (*T. caligatum*), which is edible (see next entry), shares the White Matsutake's distinct, spicy aroma, but it has a smaller, reddish brown cap and a white partial veil or ring with reddish brown patches below. The Imperial Cat (*Catathelasma imperialis*), also edible (see p. 74), has a larger, dingy grayish brown cap and a thick stalk with a flaring, double-layered ring and lacks the other species' distinctive aromas. The White Matsutake is sometimes classified as *Armillaria ponderosa*.

EDIBILITY: This fleshy, robust mushroom is usually rated as an excellent edible, though a few people find it too rich and aromatic for their tastes. It is especially popular among Japanese Americans, who know it from their ancestors' home across the Pacific Ocean.

One large cap will liven up a big soy sauce stir-fry, but this fragrant mushroom works well in any recipe that calls for the typical commercially available mushroom or any other fleshy variety. If you're looking for a mushroom whose character will not be lost amid strong cheeses and such, the White Matsutake is an excellent candidate.

## FRAGRANT TRICHOLOMA

*Tricholoma caligatum*

### KEY IDENTIFYING CHARACTERISTICS

1. Cap two to five inches wide; rounded to nearly flat; whitish or tan between reddish brown to brown scales and hairlike fibers
2. Gills white, staining brownish in age; closely spaced, attached to stalk
3. Stalk white to pale tan above a flaring, membranous, white to brownish ring
4. Stalk covered with reddish brown to brown scales and fibers below ring; no volva present
5. Fragrance distinctly spicy
6. Spore print white

DESCRIPTION: The cap is two to five inches wide, dome shaped to nearly flat; it has whitish to brownish flesh showing between dry, flattened, reddish brown to brown scales and fibers. The cap flesh is thick and white. The gills are closely spaced and attached to the stalk; they are white, often staining brownish in age. The gills of young specimens are covered by a whitish, membranous partial veil that later remains on the stalk as a white to brownish ring. At first, the ring is flared open at the top. The stalk is two to four inches tall and ¾ –1¼ inches thick, sometimes thickest at the middle; it is white to pale tan above the ring but covered with reddish brown to brown scales and fibers below the ring. This mushroom has a distinctly fragrant, spicy aroma. The spore print is white.

FRUITING: The Fragrant Tricholoma is found singly or scattered and occasionally in groups on the ground in woods and typically fruits in late summer or fall. It is especially associated with oak and pine trees on the East Coast and with various conifers on the West Coast. Its range includes many parts of North America, excluding the Midwest and the Rocky Mountains, but it is only common in eastern North America.

SIMILAR SPECIES: Some varieties of this species apparently lack the spicy aroma (some reportedly smell unpleasant); such specimens are nonetheless pleasant after cooking. The edible Fetid Tricholoma (*T.* [or *Armillaria*] *zelleri*) has orangish brown scales and fibers, and an

SM

Fragrant Tricholoma (*Tricholoma caligatum*)

unpleasant odor and taste; like the unpleasant-smelling varieties of the Fragrant Tricholoma, it is enjoyable once cooked. The White Matsutake (*T. magnivelare*), also edible (see preceding entry), shares the spicy aroma; it is larger, and is not as distinctly scaly and hairy as the Fragrant Tricholoma. The Fragrant Tricholoma is sometimes classified as *Armillaria caligata* and called the Fragrant Armillaria.

**EDIBILITY:** This is rated as a choice edible mushroom. Its taste and aroma are remarkably similar to those of the White Matsutake; we, therefore, refer you to that species' "Edibility" section for culinary suggestions.

## IMPERIAL CAT

*Catathelasma imperialis*

### KEY IDENTIFYING CHARACTERISTICS

1. Cap six to sixteen inches wide, dome shaped to nearly flat; dingy gray to dingy brown
2. Gills broad, closely spaced, descending stalk; yellowish to gray, sometimes tinted greenish
3. Stalk thick, tapered downward to a pointed base; two-layered ring on stalk; no volva present
4. Spore print white

DA

Imperial Cat (*Catathelasma imperialis*)

**DESCRIPTION:** This is a huge gilled mushroom, sometimes attaining a cap width of sixteen inches but more typically five to fourteen inches. The cap is dome shaped at first, becoming nearly flat at maturity; the cap surface is sticky to dry, smooth, dingy gray to dingy brown, sometimes with greenish tints. The gills are covered at first by a two-layered, membranous veil; the outer layer encloses the entire stalk of the button. The gills are broad, closely spaced, and descend the stalk; they are yellowish to gray, sometimes tinted greenish. The stalk is 5–7½ inches long and two to three inches thick; it tapers to a distinctly pointed base. The mature stalk bears a two-layered ring. The spore print is white.

**FRUITING:** This giant mushroom's North American range is restricted to the Rocky Mountains and the Pacific Northwest. It is found singly or scattered on the ground in conifer forests, fruiting from late summer through fall.

**SIMILAR SPECIES:** Few other gilled mushrooms approach the proportions of this species; none can be considered look-alikes. The Swollen-stalked Cat (*C. ventricosa*) is very similar, edible, and also has a two-layered ring, but the cap is only three to six inches wide. The Imperial Cat's two-layered ring rules out large *Armillaria* and *Tricholoma* species.

**EDIBILITY:** The Imperial Cat's popularity among mushroom hunters in the Rocky Mountains and the Pacific Northwest is largely due to its gigantic size: one mature specimen goes a long way. This is fortunate because one specimen is frequently all that can be found! This mushroom's flavor is pleasant, and its texture is very firm in comparison to most other species. It can be substituted in any recipe that calls for fleshy mushrooms.

# PLATTERFUL MUSHROOM

*Tricholomopsis platyphylla*

Platterful Mushroom (*Tricholomopsis platyphylla*)

## KEY IDENTIFYING CHARACTERISTICS

1. Cap dark grayish brown to pale gray, streaked with dark fibers
2. Gills white, attached to stalk, moderately spaced, very broad
3. Stalk white; thick, white cords attached to base; no partial veil, ring, or volva present
4. Found on or about well-decayed wood
5. Spore print white

**DESCRIPTION:** The cap is dark grayish brown when young, becoming pale gray in age; it is usually darkest at the center and is streaked with dark fibers. It is quite rounded at first, expanding until nearly flat; it is two to seven inches wide, with a smooth, moist surface. The cap flesh is thin, white, and firm, with a mild to bitter taste. The gills are white, attached to the stalk, moderately spaced, and very broad. The stalk is white and fibrous, three to six inches tall, and three-eighths to one inch thick; it is not noticeably thicker at the top, or at the base, but there are thick, white cords attached to the stalk base. This mushroom has no veil, ring, or volva. The spore print is white.

**FRUITING:** The Platterful is one of the earliest gilled mushrooms of considerable size to appear in the spring; it typically first appears during morel season—in May or even earlier—and continues to appear until midfall. It is found singly or in groups, always on or near well-decayed deciduous wood. It is very common and abundant in its range, which includes eastern North America west to Iowa. It has also been found along the Pacific Coast.

**SIMILAR SPECIES:** The Fawn Mushroom (*Pluteus cervinus*), which is edible (see next entry), and other *Pluteus* species are generally smaller, are found in the same kind of habitat, and look similar from the top; however, they can be distinguished by their free gills and salmon pink spore prints.

**EDIBILITY:** A small percentage of mycophagists develop mild gastric upset after eating the Platterful Mushroom, but most people who eat this species enjoy it without any adverse reaction. Eat only a small portion the first time you try it. Mature specimens sometimes have an unpleasant or bitter taste, even after cooking; adding a teaspoon of lemon juice while cooking them will eliminate the bitterness.

The Platterful Mushroom is often collected by morel hunters—especially unsuccessful ones. There is some disagreement about the quality of its taste and texture: some rate it highly, while others classify it as mediocre. It is fairly large, fleshy, and often abundant, so it is much appreciated by a great many mycophagists. It is ideal for use in soups, sauces, gravies, and casseroles. For those who enjoy it, it makes an attractive side dish—brush the cap with butter or margarine, and charcoal grill it with the gills facing up.

# FAWN MUSHROOM

*Pluteus cervinus*

Fawn Mushroom (*Pluteus cervinus*)

## KEY IDENTIFYING CHARACTERISTICS

1. Cap grayish brown to dark brown
2. Gills white to pinkish, free from stalk
3. No veil, ring, or volva present
4. No greenish or bluish stains on base of stalk
5. Found on well-decayed wood
6. Spore print salmon pink

**DESCRIPTION:** The cap is grayish brown to dark brown, smooth, and moist; it is two to five inches wide, rounded at first but nearly flat in mature specimens. The cap flesh is thick, soft, and white. The gills are initially white, becoming pinkish as the mushroom matures; they are free from the stalk and closely spaced to fairly crowded. The stalk is white, sometimes coated with tiny, grayish brown "hairs"; it is two to four inches long and one-fourth to three-eighths inch wide, usually somewhat enlarged at the base. The spore print is salmon pink.

**FRUITING:** The Fawn Mushroom is found singly or in groups on well-decayed wood from spring through fall; it is also frequent during winter in the southwestern United States. Its range includes most of North America.

**SIMILAR SPECIES:** The key identifying characteristics listed above eliminate all species but other members of the genus *Pluteus;* they are distinguished from other gilled, cap-and-stalk mushrooms primarily by their salmon pink spore prints, free gills, habit on decaying wood, and the lack of any veil, ring, or volva. *P. salicinus* reportedly contains psilocybin, a psychoactive toxin; the base of its stalk has greenish to bluish stains, so it is ruled out by the key identifying characteristics. No other Pluteus species is suspected of being poisonous.

One of the more common species in this genus is the edible Sawdust Mushroom (*P. petasatus*). It has a dingy white cap with tiny brown scales near the center and white gills that are free and pinkish at maturity. It occurs on sawdust and decayed wood. The Platterful Mushroom (*Tricholomopsis platyphylla*), which is edible (see preceding entry), looks quite similar but is usually larger and has attached gills and a white spore print. *Entoloma* species, some poisonous and others suspected of being poisonous, which are sometimes found on decaying wood, have pink spore prints but are much smaller and have attached gills.

The Fawn Mushroom is classified by some mycologists as *P. atricapillus.*

**EDIBILITY:** This is a fine, common edible mushroom, suitable for use in general recipes that call for mushrooms—especially sauces, soups, gravies, casseroles, and the like. Because of the short list of characteristics that distinguish it from dangerous mushrooms, it is especially well-suited for the novice mycophagist.

Its flavor is different from, though neither superior nor inferior to, that of the common cultivated button mushroom. We cannot claim that it makes an outstanding side dish all by itself, but it is tender, fleshy, and wholly worthwhile. Because it is so very common, it provides an alternative to "collecting" mushrooms at the supermarket.

Unfortunately, it is also quickly riddled by insect larvae, especially during hot weather; therefore, it is best gathered and cooked when quite young. Early (and late) in the season, larger specimens may be found with caps that are pristine and uninvaded. These have the richest flavor, and some experienced mushroom hunters place such prime specimens fairly high on their list of favorite mushrooms.

Abortive Entoloma (*Entoloma abortivum*)

# ABORTIVE ENTOLOMA

*Entoloma abortivum*

## KEY IDENTIFYING CHARACTERISTICS

1. Whitish, firm to spongy, round or oval or irregularly shaped, lumpy fungal mass; flesh whitish, with pink to pinkish red marbling
2. Found on the ground in woods
3. Less than three inches high

**DESCRIPTION:** The key identifying characteristics listed above describe the strange, aborted form of a mushroom of the genus *Entoloma*. Sometimes the aborted form is found by itself, and sometimes it is found directly adjacent or even clustered with the normal form of this species. The normal mushroom also sometimes occurs alone. The aborted form is typically one to two inches high and two to four inches wide.

The normal, unaborted mushroom has a grayish to grayish brown cap that is first rounded but is nearly flat at maturity; it is two to four inches wide, and its surface is smooth to minutely hairy. The gills are pale gray, maturing to salmon pink; they are closely spaced and attached to the stalk, usually descending it somewhat. The stalk is grayish white, one to four inches long, and one-fourth to three-fourths inch thick; in some specimens, it is enlarged near the base.

The spore print is salmon pink.

**FRUITING:** This odd species is found scattered or in groups during autumn on the ground in woods. It's fairly common in the eastern United States, but it's also found as far west as Kansas and Arizona.

**SIMILAR SPECIES:** The aborted form has no look-alikes if one observes the size and whitish interior flesh with pinkish to pinkish red marbling. However, the nonaborted form can easily be mistaken for poisonous species of the genus *Entoloma*, some of which are known to cause severe and prolonged nausea, vomiting, and diarrhea. Some mushroom field guides call this the Aborted Entoloma.

**EDIBILITY:** This strange but common freak of nature is regarded by many experienced mushroom collectors as a choice edible. Both the aborted and nonaborted forms are tableworthy. It's essential, though, to avoid what you think may be the normal form of this mushroom unless it is found clustered with or immediately adjacent to the aborted form for reasons explained above. The mushroom hunter should appreciate the way the aborted form of this species distinguishes it as safe in an otherwise dangerous and confusing genus.

Cook the Abortive Entoloma any way you choose—sauté it or deep-fry it after breading it or dipping it in batter. If you have enough, use it in whatever recipe appeals to your palate. The flavor is mild, so don't overwhelm it: delicate white wine sauces provide an excellent treatment for this frequently abundant mushroom. Because of the spongy nature of the aborted form, be careful not to use much butter, margarine, or cooking oil because the flesh can soak up a lot of fat during cooking. Avoid specimens that are mushy (note the difference between this adjective and "spongy").

# BRICK CAP AND SMOKY-GILLED NAEMATOLOMA

*Naematoloma sublateritium*
*N. capnoides*

## KEY IDENTIFYING CHARACTERISTICS

1. Cap two to four inches wide; orange to red at center, yellow to orange or red at edge, but not yellow or greenish yellow overall; surface smooth, moist
2. Gills closely spaced, attached to stalk; whitish or pale yellow to grayish, finally purplish brown in age
3. Gills of young specimens covered by cobwebby (fibrous) partial veil
4. Gills of young specimens not yellowish green or greenish yellow
5. Stalk whitish or pale yellow to brownish, not bright yellow; slight ring of fibers on upper stalk
6. Found clustered on wood
7. Cap flesh mild-tasting, not bitter (taste a tiny bit and then spit it out)
8. Spore print purplish brown

**DESCRIPTION:** The cap of the Brick Cap (*Naematoloma sublateritium*) is quite round with an inrolled edge in young specimens, expanding until virtually flat. It is one to four inches wide, brick red at the center and usually pale orange at the edge; the surface is smooth and moist. The gills of young specimens are covered by a whitish, cobwebby veil, though it may appear fairly membranous in young specimens. The gills are very pale yellow in young specimens but soon become purplish gray to dark grayish purple; they are closely spaced and attached to the stalk, though they are easily separated from it. The stalk is whitish at the top to very pale yellow at the middle, typically reddish orange near the base, and slowly stains darker where bruised. It is two to four inches long and one-fourth to five-eighths inch thick. Mature specimens have a ringlike zone of yellowish brown fibers near the top. The cap flesh is mild-tasting.

Brick Cap (*Naematoloma sublateritium*)

The cap of the Smoky-gilled Naematoloma (*N. capnoides*) is at first quite round with an incurved edge, but it expands until broadly dome shaped. The cap is orangish yellow at the edge and orange with a slight brownish tint at the center; it is one to three inches wide, with a smooth, moist surface. The gills of young specimens are covered by a dense, whitish, cobwebby partial veil. The gills are initially grayish white but soon become distinctly grayish, then grayish brown, and finally dark purplish brown in age. The gills are closely spaced and attached to but easily separated from the stalk. The stalk is grayish white to pale grayish brown, typically darker near the base; mature specimens display a slight ringlike zone of fibers near the top of the stalk. The stalk is two to three inches long and one-eighth to three-eighths inch thick. The cap flesh is mild-tasting, not bitter.

Both species produce purplish brown spore prints.

**FRUITING:** Both of these *Naematoloma* species are found in clusters on wood during autumn. The Brick Cap is found on deciduous logs and stumps throughout most of eastern North America, and it is frequently gathered in very late fall, after most other species have ceased fruiting. The Smoky-gilled Naematoloma is restricted to coniferous wood, with a preference for spruce and Douglas fir; it is widely distributed in North America. It can often be gathered in large quantity in pure stands of fir or spruce trees.

**SIMILAR SPECIES:** Several of the key identifying characteristics listed above are expressly designed to rule out the poisonous Sulphur Tuft (*N. fasciculare;* see p. 159). It occasionally has been mistaken for the Smoky-gilled Naematoloma, but the toxic species has a greenish yellow to bright orangish yellow cap and, usually, bitter-tasting flesh. The gills of young Sulphur Tufts are greenish yellow to sulphur yellow, darkening to purplish brown in age. Because it can be mistaken for the Smoky-gilled Naematoloma, it is especially important to examine specimens in various stages of development. This is rarely

Smoky-gilled Naematoloma (*Naematoloma capnoides*)

a problem, inasmuch as most fresh clusters include specimens in all stages.

The Dispersed Naematoloma (*N. dispersum*), whose edibility is unknown, has a brownish yellow cap less than two inches wide; a long, thin stalk; and mild-tasting flesh. It grows on conifer needles and decaying wood and fruits scattered or in groups in the Pacific Northwest and the Rocky Mountains.

*Naematoloma* species are sometimes classified in the genus *Hypholoma*.

**EDIBILITY:** Both species are fine edibles, especially when young.

# VELVET FOOT

*Flammulina velutipes*

### KEY IDENTIFYING CHARACTERISTICS

1. Cap one to two inches wide; golden yellow to reddish yellow or reddish brown, palest at cap edge; slimy to sticky
2. Gills white to pale yellow, closely spaced, attached to stalk
3. Stalk yellow at top, brown to brownish black and velvety at base; no partial veil, ring, or volva present
4. Found in clusters on logs, stumps, or dead trees
5. Spore print white

**DESCRIPTION:** The cap is reddish yellow to reddish brown, noticeably darker at the center, sometimes yellow at the cap edge; it is one to two inches wide, round with an inrolled cap edge in young specimens, nearly flat in mature ones. The cap surface is slimy or sticky. The gills are white to pale yellow, closely spaced, and attached to the stalk. There is no partial veil. The stalk is quite slender, one-eighth to one-fourth inch thick and one to three inches long, narrowing toward the base. The stalk is yellow to brownish near the top and

Velvet Foot (*Flammulina velutipes*)

brown to brownish black at the base; it is covered with tiny, velvety "hairs" near the base, sometimes nearly to the top of the stalk. There is no ring or volva present. The spore print is white.

**FRUITING:** This dainty mushroom grows in clusters on deciduous logs, stumps, and decaying trees, particularly willow, aspen, elm, and poplar. It is found throughout much of North America, typically fruiting from fall through spring during cold weather but also when the temperature is above yet near the freezing point.

**SIMILAR SPECIES:** The key identifying characteristics listed above rule out everything but the Velvet Foot. The Deadly Galerina (see p. 160) has a ring, a rusty brown spore print, a typically nonclustered growth habit, and several other distinctly different features. The Velvet Foot is sometimes called the Winter Mushroom because it prefers near-freezing temperatures. It was formerly in the genus *Collybia*.

**EDIBILITY:** Despite its small size, this is a very popular edible mushroom—not just among experienced mushroom hunters but among urban gourmets as well: it is widely cultivated. Commercially, it is sold fresh in oriental food stores and sometimes in supermarket produce sections as Japanese Enotake. You won't recognize the wild Velvet Foot just because you've seen Enotake at the market, though: the cultivated mushrooms' caps don't develop normally.

Ironically, the cap is the best part of this species; the stalks are quite tough. But we don't claim this mushroom to be one of Mother Nature's greatest gifts. Rather, it seems to have earned its popularity because it comes out when no other mushrooms do.

In fairness, it *is* a tasty and tender mushroom, it sometimes fruits in enough quantity to permit a good-sized harvest, and it is rarely ruined by insect larvae. But it would probably be ignored by all but the most enthusiastic mushroom hunters if it fruited when there were alternatives.

# HONEY MUSHROOM

*Armillaria mellea* complex

Honey Mushroom (*Armillaria mellea* complex)

## KEY IDENTIFYING CHARACTERISTICS

1. Cap surface and stalk yellowish brown to pinkish brown
2. Erect, dark "hairs" (not scales) on center of cap surface
3. White, cottony to membranous partial veil covering gills of small specimens
4. Whitish, cottony to membranous ring on stalk of larger specimens
5. Found in clusters on wood or at base of trees or stumps
6. Spore print white

**DESCRIPTION:** The cap is quite round in young specimens, flat at maturity, one to six inches wide; the color of the cap surface varies from yellowish brown to pinkish brown, with dark, erect, hairlike fibers on the center of the cap surface (sometimes covering much of the cap). Otherwise, the cap surface is sticky to slippery. The gills are moderately to well spaced, attached to the stalk and descending it only slightly; they are white in young specimens, staining yellowish, orangish, or reddish, especially at maturity. The gills of young specimens are covered by a white, cottony to membranous veil. The stalk is slightly fibrous, whitish to yellowish brown or pinkish brown, more or less the same color as the cap surface; it is two to six inches long and ⅜–1½ inches thick, sometimes being even thicker at the base. Mature specimens bear a cottony or membranous ring near the top of the stalk. Thick white to blackish "shoestrings" (rhizomorphs) are attached to the base of the stalk. There is no volva around the stalk base. The spore print is white.

**FRUITING:** The Honey Mushroom is typically an autumn species, but it sometimes appears as early as midsummer to late summer during cool weather; it is found throughout North America. Typically, it grows in clusters, but single specimens are found occasionally. It is most frequently found at the base of tree trunks and around stumps,

Honey Mushroom (*Armillaria mellea* complex)

but it also appears on dead or dying wood (especially buried wood or tree roots) or on the ground in open areas.

**SIMILAR SPECIES:** The Deadly Galerina (*Galerina autumnalis*), which is fatally poisonous (see p. 160), is smaller, lacks erect hairs on the cap surface, and produces a brown spore print. The Big Laughing Gym (*Gymnopilus spectabilis*), which is poisonous (hallucinogenic), is orange and has an orangish brown spore print. The Jack O'Lantern mushrooms (*Omphalotus illudens* and *O. olivascens*), also poisonous (see p. 148), produce whitish spore prints but are orangish and lack erect hairs on the cap surface. *Pholiota* species—some are edible, but others are poisonous—have brownish spore prints.

The Ringless Honey Mushroom (*Armillaria tabescens*) is quite similar but has no ring or partial veil; it does have a dry and smooth to slightly hairy or scaly cap surface. It is edible, but causes gastrointestinal upset in some people. Its range is limited to eastern North America, and it is sometimes classified as an *Armillariella*.

The Honey Mushroom is quite variable in color, wood preference, and other characteristics. These differences exist because the Honey Mushroom is actually a large complex of very similar species. They are best distinguished by other less obvious and microscopic characteristics.

The various species are classified by some mycologists in the genus *Armillariella*.

**EDIBILITY:** Some of the species in the Honey Mushroom complex cause gastrointestinal upset in some people, especially if the mushrooms are not cooked thoroughly. Because the numerous species are difficult to distinguish, it is wise to sample only a small amount of each collection to determine your individual reaction before making a meal of these delicious fungi. Fortunately, an exception can be made for specimens gathered from the same immediate area as previously tested collections. In other words, if you find a log, stump, or tree with the Honey Mushroom growing on or around it and if you subsequently try it and have no adverse reaction, you can gather more from the same spot next year and enjoy them without worry. There is some evidence that specimens that have been frozen when fresh (picked or unpicked) or that fruited after first frost are more likely to cause gastrointestinal upset.

Except for the relatively few untoward reactions, the Honey Mushroom is extremely popular among experienced mushroom hunters—in Europe and other parts of the world as well as in North America. It is a scrumptious, versatile species, well suited for almost anything one can do with an edible mushroom. The flavor is fairly rich and distinctive, though it's not sweet, as one might expect from its common name. "Honey" actually refers to the various colors of the caps, which fairly closely parallel the range of colors of honey.

Because these mushrooms should be cooked thoroughly, a slow, low-heat sauté is preferable to a two-minute scorching in butter. Many mushrooms are at their best when they've been browned slightly, but this technique doesn't do justice to the flavor or texture of the Honey Mushroom.

The Honey Mushroom is often very abundant. Its mycelium spreads via shoestringlike runners called "rhizomorphs," which can extend, tree hopping, several hundred feet. For this reason, there are almost always more Honeys to be had wherever the first specimen or cluster is found. An acre of woods can supply enough Honeys to fill the largest basket in just a few hours. This is just one of the many reasons why the Honey Mushroom is many mycophagists' favorite sweetheart.

## TREE VOLVARIELLA

*Volvariella bombycina*

**KEY IDENTIFYING CHARACTERISTICS**

1. Cap three to ten inches wide; surface dry, silky, white to yellowish white
2. Gills free from stalk, white to pink; no ring or partial veil
3. Stalk dry, white, arising from a volva
4. Found on wood
5. Spore print pink or pinkish brown, not white

**DESCRIPTION:** The cap is three to ten inches wide, oval at first to nearly flat when mature. The cap surface is dry, silky (with fine "hairs"), and white to yellowish white. The flesh is thin and white. The gills are free from the stalk, broad, and quite crowded together; they are white in young specimens, pink at maturity. There is no partial veil. The stalk is smooth and white, three to eight inches long and three-eighths to three-fourths inch thick, with a somewhat thicker base. There is no ring on the stalk, which arises from a deep, thick, membranous, cuplike volva that is usually within a wound or hole in a tree, stump, or log. The spore print is pink to pinkish brown.

Tree Volvariella (*Volvariella bombycina*)

**FRUITING:** This mushroom is usually found growing from wounds of living trees. It also occurs on logs, stumps, and dead trees, where it also prefers wounds. It is an eastern North American species, found singly or in groups during summer and fall. The range extends into southern swamps and bayous.

**SIMILAR SPECIES:** No other mushrooms conform to all the key identifying characteristics listed above.

**EDIBILITY:** This large mushroom is both handsome and tasty. There's just one problem: it's frequently found growing from a tree wound so far off the ground that it's all but impossible to reach it! This is a large, firm, fleshy mushroom, with a modest but pleasant flavor. It is fairly common in its range but, unfortunately, not very abundant. Not to worry, though—one good-sized specimen will make a fine side dish for two.

# OYSTER MUSHROOM

*Pleurotus ostreatus* complex

**KEY IDENTIFYING CHARACTERISTICS**

1. Cap white to pale brown or gray; fan or oyster shell shaped; surface smooth
2. Gills white to yellowish cream, descending stalk; gill edges not serrate
3. Stalk short, lateral, white; distinctly downy or hairy
4. Found on trees, logs, or stumps; usually clustered
5. Spore print white or pale grayish lilac

**DESCRIPTION:** The cap surface is white to pale brown or gray; it is smooth and dry to moist. The cap is quite fleshy, fan or oyster shell shaped, two to six inches or more in width. The gills are white to pale yellowish white, with nonserrate edges (this can be seen more easily with a hand lens, or magnifying glass); the gills descend a short,

Oyster Mushroom (*Pleurotus ostreatus* complex)

white, lateral stalk that is hairy or downy. (Often the stalk is not evident.) This mushroom sometimes has a pleasant, fragrant aroma like anise or licorice. The spore print is either white or very pale lilac gray.

**FRUITING:** Oyster Mushrooms usually grow in clusters on wood, favoring maple, aspen, beech, poplar, and willow. They fruit throughout North America during cool, wet periods, especially during spring and fall, but year-round under favorable weather conditions. The mycelium lives for one to three years or more in the same wood, frequently producing multiple fruitings even in the same year.

**SIMILAR SPECIES:** There are no toxic look-alikes. The inedible Orange Mock Oyster (*Phyllotopsis nidulans*) has an orange, hairy cap surface, yellow to orange gills, a pinkish spore print, and an unpleasant odor. Inedible, lateral-stalked species of the genera *Lentinus* and *Lentinellus* have serrate (toothed) gill edges.

There are several edible, closely-related *Pleurotus* species: *P. cornucopioides'* gills descend to the very base of the stalk and produce a pale gray to lilac spore print. *P. sapidus* also has pale grayish lilac spores; it may, in fact, be the same species as *P. cornucopioides.* (This entire group is the subject of continuing study.) Angel's Wings (*Pleurocybella porrigens*) (see next entry) and Leaf-like Oyster (*Hohenbuehelia petaloides*), both edible, are very thin fleshed; the latter usually has a light brown cap surface.

The only similar-looking species that warrant concern are members of the genus *Crepidotus.* None is known to be poisonous or suspected of being, though none is considered edible. They can be easily ruled out by their smaller size, thin flesh, and brownish spore prints.

**EDIBILITY:** The Oyster Mushroom is second only to the grocery store button mushroom as the most widely cultivated mushroom in North America. It can be purchased fresh and at a reasonable price in an increasing number of grocery store produce departments. Increased

Oyster Mushroom (*Pleurotus ostreatus* complex)

cultivation—mostly on grain-laden straw—has taken this choice mushroom from the domain of gourmet specialty shops, where it long commanded exorbitant prices. Look for it in the supermarket: once you've seen it, you'll likely recognize it immediately when you find it growing wild.

This is an easy species for home cultivation. It will readily colonize an aspen, poplar, or willow log. Simply drill a few small holes into the wood, poke in some small pieces of an Oyster Mushroom, and keep the log well watered. When practical, you can even bring home a log that already has Oysters growing from it. Cut the mushrooms off close to the wood, keep the log moist, and it will likely fruit again.

Unfortunately, the Oyster is highly susceptible to infestation by insect larvae; the mushrooms must, therefore, be harvested quickly after they fruit. On the brighter side, it tends to fruit in large clusters—up to twenty pounds or more from a single log!—so when you find it in good condition, you might be able to fill your freezer (but cook it partially before freezing it).

Although it's not extraordinarily rich in flavor, the Oyster Mushroom is tender and tasty enough to make an outstanding side dish. It is also quite versatile, lending itself to any recipe that calls for fleshy mushrooms. The Oyster is also one of the few wild mushrooms that is safe as a raw edible.

**KEY IDENTIFYING CHARACTERISTICS**
1. Thin fleshed, fan to shell shaped, stalkless gilled mushroom, one to four inches wide
2. Cap surface white, smooth to minutely velvety; cap edge not radially lined
3. Gills crowded, white; gill edges not serrate
4. Found on logs or stumps
5. Spore print white

# ANGEL'S WINGS

*Pleurocybella porrigens*

Angel's Wings (*Pleurocybella porrigens*)

**DESCRIPTION:** The cap surface is white and smooth to minutely velvety. The cap is one to four inches wide, thin fleshed, with crowded white gills descending to a stubby lateral base; it is fan to shell shaped with a smooth edge. The spore print is white.

**FRUITING:** Angel's Wings is found scattered or in overlapping clusters, rarely singly, on conifer logs and stumps, especially hemlock. It usually fruits from late summer through midautumn. Its range includes most of northern North America, extending as far south as North Carolina and northern California.

**SIMILAR SPECIES:** Numerous white *Crepidotus* species look similar but produce brown spore prints. The Orange Mock Oyster (*Phyllotopsis nidulans*) and the Stalkless Paxillus (*Paxillus panuoides*) are orangish or yellowish overall and produce pinkish or yellowish spore prints, respectively. *Lentinellus* species have serrate gill edges. *Panellus* and *Panus* species are not white overall. (The above species and genera are mostly inedible, but none are known to be poisonous.)

The Leaf-like Oyster (*Hohenbuehelia petaloides*), which is edible, has a pale brown cap and whitish to pale gray gills. Mushrooms categorized in the Oyster Mushroom complex (*Pleurotus* species), which are also edible (see preceding entry), have thicker flesh and (usually) a distinct lateral stalk.

Angel's Wings was formerly classified in the genus *Pleurotus,* where some mycologists still place it.

**EDIBILITY:** This is a fine little white mushroom, very similar in taste and appearance to its cousin, the Oyster Mushroom. It is not nearly as fleshy as the Oyster, but Angel's Wings is frequently abundant enough to fill the mushroom hunter's basket, especially when it fruits in overlapping clusters on large fallen hemlock trunks.

This common autumn species is, in fact, so close to the Oyster Mushroom that we recommend treating them in the kitchen as one and the same, with only two significant differences to keep in mind. First, on the negative side, Angel's Wings' thin flesh can easily become saturated by the frying medium. Second, on the positive side, the flesh of Angel's Wings is much more tender than that of the Oyster Mushroom, and the house chef needn't be concerned about tough, fibrous stalks, which can be a problem with the latter.

Late Fall Oyster Mushroom (*Panellus serotinus*)

# LATE FALL OYSTER MUSHROOM

*Panellus serotinus*

## KEY IDENTIFYING CHARACTERISTICS

1. Cap greenish yellow, sometimes purplish tinted; fan to shell shaped; smooth
2. Gills yellow, not orange; gill edges not serrate
3. Stalk stubby, lateral, downy or hairy; gills attached to stalk
4. Found on wood, often in clusters, from middle to late fall

**DESCRIPTION:** This is a fan- or oyster shell–shaped, shelflike mushroom. The cap surface is smooth to minutely velvety; the color is highly variable, typically a mixture of gray, green, and yellow, usually with purple or brown tints, especially near the edge. Each cap is one to six inches wide. The gills are yellow, not orange, and they do not have serrate edges (this can be seen more easily with a hand lens, or magnifying glass). The gills are attached to and slightly descend a yellow, stubby, lateral stalk that is downy or hairy. A longitudinal section reveals a thin gelatinous layer beneath the cap cuticle. The spore print is yellowish.

**FRUITING:** As implied by its common name, the Late Fall Oyster Mushroom's season is limited to autumn, mostly after the first frost. It grows on a wide variety of deciduous and coniferous logs and stumps, usually fruiting in overlapping clusters. It is very common throughout most of North America.

**SIMILAR SPECIES:** This is a distinctive mushroom, if one simply observes all the key identifying characteristics presented above. (Use the color photograph also as a guide.) There are a variety of other gilled mushrooms that grow on wood and appear shelflike, but none can really be called look-alikes. For example, the nasty-smelling Orange Mock Oyster (*Phyllotopsis nidulans*), which is inedible, is, as one would presume, orange. Very few species of mushrooms have any greenish coloration on the cap surface; none even approach the overall appearance of the Late Fall Oyster Mushroom. This mushroom is often called the Greenback, and was previously classified in the same genus as the so-called true Oyster Mushroom (*Pleurotus*).

**EDIBILITY:** This may be one of the most underrated of the distinctive, edible, gilled mushrooms. It can usually be gathered in quantity after most other fungi have ceased fruiting.

The stalk is too tough to eat, but a good collection of the more tender caps is a worthwhile harvest. Some people find it slightly bitter. This may be related to the tree species on which it's found, but extended slow cooking seems to eliminate that problem. Regardless, slow but thorough cooking tends to bring out the Late Fall Oyster's best flavor and keep it tender. It can be used in most any recipe. It is moist, fleshy, and flavorful enough for soups, sauces, gravies, and casseroles, or it can be simply sautéed after simmering.

Those of us who look to this green-backed beauty for end-of-the-season salvation may be only the most dedicated of wild mushroom eaters, but we will not betray our last refuge. Some mushroom hunters even insist that it is superior to its more popular distant cousin, the Oyster Mushroom (see p. 87). It certainly has its advantages: it's there when we're going through mushroom withdrawal, and its late season debut usually spares it from the ravages of insect larvae. Its occurrence on a wide variety of wood types makes it abundant. And if it's less than outstanding, it's by no means mediocre.

# 8

# *Boletes*

Mushrooms of this large family, technically called the Boletaceae, look like the gilled cap-and-stalk mushrooms. Setting the boletes apart, however, is a layer of vertically arranged tubes in the cap that have openings or "pores" at the bottom. Most polypores (see p.121) grow on wood, while boletes are normally found on the ground. Boletes can be distinguished from the few polypores that grow on the ground by two typical characteristics. First, the boletes are fleshy; most polypores are tough (leathery to woody). Second, the boletes' tube layers can be easily separated from the cap flesh with a blunt knife; the polypores' tube layers are almost impossible to remove.

Members of the Bolete family are very diverse. Some are large and statuesque; others are small and inconspicuous. Cap, stalk, and pore surface colors practically span the rainbow. Distinguishing among many of the species is generally difficult, even for professional mycologists. The number of species known in North America (and other parts of the world) is the subject of continual study; however, the entire group is a remarkably safe one for the mycophagist, provided two simple principles are followed.

First, many of the species whose pore surfaces are orange to red are poisonous. Second, parts of many species will bruise blue, usually quickly but sometimes more slowly, and many of these species, too, are poisonous. All boletes known to be poisonous or suspected of being feature one or both of these characteristics. Some of the others taste bitter or are otherwise unpalatable, and some that exhibit one or even both of these two warning signs are perfectly safe. Reassuring, though, in such a confusing group of mushrooms with so many delicious species is that recognizing these two characteristics can effectively eliminate the risk of poisoning. Some longtime mushroom hunters even insist that *all* boletes, except the bitter-tasting ones, are edible, provided they're well cooked. We discourage such experimentation.

The three bolete genera with the greatest number of species are *Boletus, Leccinum,* and *Suillus.* In general, the caps of *Boletus* species are smooth and dry to moist, and *Suillus* caps are scaly or slimy to tacky. Also, most suilli have a partial veil. *Leccinum* species are distinguished from the other genera by the scabers—tiny, stiff, granular points—on the stalk surface. On mature specimens, the scabers are always darker than the color of the cap.

Beyond these quick-and-easy field characteristics, accurately identifying many species requires studying each specimen thoroughly with the aid of the ever-changing technical literature, chemical reagents, and a microscope. Spore print color, shape and arrangement of the tubes, color, bruising reaction (if any), habitat, and a variety of other features are used to distinguish between the several hundred species in this large mushroom family.

Boletes are, as a rule, mycorrhizal with trees. Many are associated with specific tree species, especially various conifers; others are more versatile. Most boletes are summer mushrooms, fruiting before most of the large gilled mushrooms do. A few species are found as early as midspring, but bolete season, especially for the species with orange or red pore surfaces, is really under way by midsummer. As summer progresses, cool rains will bring out a greater variety of boletes, including many of the most popular edibles. Fruiting continues right into autumn when the *Suillus* species are most abundant. In most species, the mycelium is perennial, producing mushrooms year after year.

Boletes, in general, lend themselves well to preservation by drying. If the cap cuticle is slimy, it should be removed. This is also true of the tubes if they've become soft and mushy.

I had barely begun trying to identify mushrooms with a single field guide when a short stroll in the woods produced three specimens of a handsome, smooth-capped bolete. I knew from the field guide that the family was fairly safe (and these specimens featured neither of the two warning signs) and that some species were highly prized by gourmets.

I was sure I had found the King Bolete (*Boletus edulis*). An anxious review of its field guide description—I was *far* too smart to make a foolish mistake!—confirmed my identification, except that my specimens lacked a white reticulation. (A spore print, of course, seemed wholly unnecessary.) This single inconsistency didn't sour my appetite, though. I knew that there were many similar species, all wonderfully edible.

At home, I cut one mushroom into pieces, threw some butter into my pan, and tossed the pieces in to sauté them. What a delightful aroma! Surely, this must be the King Bolete, I decided. If it tastes only half as good as it smells, it will be wonderful! My wife agreed, eyeing the pan hungrily.

When the mushroom was cooked, I removed the pan from the heat and gently pushed the tines of a fork into the tender flesh of a piece of the cap. I was not just anticipating, I was drooling. With great expectations, my nose tickled pink by the aroma and my heart rejoicing at my prize find, I put the small piece in my mouth and began chewing.

I wonder what my wife thought as my smile quickly gave way to a bitter, hurt expression. I dashed to the kitchen garbage pail and spat the offender out.

"Yech!" I said. "This is worse than baking chocolate!"

A more detailed review of my field guide pinpointed my error. I had found the common Bitter Bolete (*Tylopilus felleus*). Since then, I have heard this same sad story (with variations) from many mushroom hunters. My nickname for this species? Fool's Bolete. *But I won't be fooled again.*

—DAVID FISCHER

King Bolete (*Boletus edulis*)

# KING, CHALKY-WHITE, AND WHITE KING BOLETES

*Boletus edulis*
*B. albisulphureus*
*B. barrowsii*

## KEY IDENTIFYING CHARACTERISTICS

1. Cap dome shaped to flat; mature specimens four or more inches wide; white, pale gray, or dull tan to reddish brown; surface smooth, not slimy
2. Cap flesh white, mild-tasting (taste a tiny bit and then spit it out)
3. Pore surface white to yellow, not pink, orange, or red; not bruising blue
4. Stalk thick, white to pale yellowish brown, with distinct, white to pale yellow, netlike ridges over the upper portion or all of the stalk

**DESCRIPTION:** The King Bolete (*Boletus edulis*) cap is pale yellowish brown to reddish brown with a moist surface. It is three to ten inches wide and dome shaped when young but nearly flat when mature. The stalk is thick and firm and often club shaped; it is white to pale yellowish brown, three to ten inches long and 1–3½ inches thick, with distinct, white, netlike ridges over (at least) the upper third. The flesh of the cap and stalk is white and mild-tasting. The cap undersurface has a white to yellow pore surface that doesn't stain blue when bruised.

The Chalky-white Bolete (*B. albisulphureus*) is similar overall but has a soft, dry, milky white cap and stalk. The cap is much smaller, only two to five inches wide; the stalk is two to five inches long and ¾–1½ inches thick, with distinct, yellow, netlike ridges near the top. The pore surface is yellow and doesn't bruise blue.

The White King Bolete (*B. barrowsii*) has a dry, white to pale gray or dull tan cap and stalk. Like the King Bolete, its cap is large—three to ten inches wide. The stalk is typically club shaped, especially in young specimens, and measures three to eight inches long and ¾–2¼ inches thick. The stalk also has distinct, white to pale yellow, netlike ridges on the upper part. The pore surface is white to pale

Chalky-white Bolete (*Boletus albisulphureus*)

KS

White King Bolete (*Boletus barrowsii*)

yellow in young specimens and greenish yellow in mature ones. It doesn't bruise blue.

The spore prints of these species are greenish brown.

**FRUITING:** These boletes are found on the ground singly or in groups, during summer and fall. The King Bolete is found throughout much of North America in woods, often in great quantity. The Chalky-white Bolete is primarily a species of southeastern U.S. oak and pine woods and commonly collected as far west as Mississippi. It has also been reported from northeastern areas including Maine and New Jersey. The White King Bolete grows under both deciduous and coniferous trees in the southwestern United States and in parts of California, where it is often collected during winter.

SIMILAR SPECIES: The boletes are a large and diverse group of mushrooms, but only these three safe and delicious edibles conform to the key identifying characteristics listed above. The most important characteristics for those gathering boletes for the table are typified by these species: (*a*) pore surfaces that aren't orange or red and don't stain blue when bruised or cut and (*b*) mild-tasting flesh.

The Bitter Bolete (*Tylopilus felleus*), which is inedible (see p. 163), is often confused with the King Bolete; however, it has dark brown netlike ridges and bitter-tasting flesh.

EDIBILITY: All three of these species are choice edibles. They are large, firm, and meaty, and they tend to fruit in large quantity wherever they're found. Unfortunately, they are as much a prize find for insect larvae as they are for the mycophagist. The best way to harvest them, once you understand their key identifying characteristics, is to check the stalk for larvae. Cut it off at the base, then look to see if larvae have invaded. If they have, cut farther up and look again. As a last resort, break the stalk free from the cap, and check to see whether the larvae have reached the cap. If they haven't, you're in luck!

Like morels and a few other kinds of mushrooms, boletes lend themselves well to drying. For more information on this, see part 4, "Wild Mushrooms in the Kitchen."

# ADMIRABLE BOLETE

*Boletus mirabilis*

## KEY IDENTIFYING CHARACTERISTICS

1. Cap two to eight inches wide; dark maroon, maroon-brown, or reddish brown; surface granular or roughened
2. Pore surface yellow to greenish yellow, slowly staining darker yellow where bruised
3. Stalk maroon-brown; enlarged at base, with coarse, netlike ridges on upper stalk
4. Found on or beside rotting stumps or logs

DESCRIPTION: The cap is two to eight inches wide; it is dome shaped at first, often remaining dome shaped but sometimes becoming nearly flat or even depressed at the center in age. The cap surface is dark maroon to maroon-brown at first, becoming reddish brown to dull chocolate brown in age. The cap surface is granular and/or roughened, slippery in young specimens but velvety and dry in mature ones. The undersurface of the cap bears a spongelike layer of tubes with a yellow to greenish yellow pore surface that slowly stains darker yellow where bruised. The pores are round or angular, and quite large. The cap flesh is thick, firm, and mild-tasting; it is pale lemon yellow, tinged red near the cuticle, and does not change color when bruised or cut. The stalk is thick, firm, and solid; it is four to eight inches long and one-half to two inches thick with an enlarged base. The stalk is maroon-brown to dark reddish brown with yellowish streaks and has a coarse pattern of netlike ridges near the top. The spore print is greenish brown.

Admirable Bolete (*Boletus mirabilis*)

**FRUITING:** The Admirable Bolete is usually found singly, but occasionally in groups, on rotting stumps and logs of conifers, especially Western hemlock, Douglas fir, and Western red cedar. It fruits from fall through early winter, primarily in the Pacific Northwest.

**SIMILAR SPECIES:** *B. projectellus* (edible) has a dry, slightly velvety, reddish brown cap cuticle that projects beyond the cap flesh and tube layer. Its stalk is reddish brown and has coarse, netlike ridges over nearly the entire length. It is found on the ground under pines along the East Coast from Nova Scotia south to North Carolina, and it has also been reported from Michigan.

**EDIBILITY:** The Admirable Bolete truly deserves its name: not only is it very handsome, but it is also a popular, choice edible. The thick, firm flesh, when sautéed in butter, has a distinctly lemony flavor. It serves well in a wide variety of recipes, but is excellent simply sautéed in butter and served as a side dish with fish or meats.

## TWO-COLORED BOLETE

*Boletus bicolor*

**KEY IDENTIFYING CHARACTERISTICS**

1. Cap dry; two or more inches wide; dark rose red to pale pinkish red, sometimes dull yellow at edge
2. Pore surface yellow, slowly staining blue where bruised
3. Cap flesh pale yellow, slowly staining blue when cut
4. Stalk yellow at top; stalk flesh yellow throughout
5. Lower two-thirds of stalk surface dark rose red

**DESCRIPTION:** The cap is initially dome shaped, becoming nearly flat in maturity; it is two to seven inches wide. The cap surface is dry and unpolished, dark rosy red at first and then fading to pale pinkish red with a dull yellow edge at maturity. Older caps may be somewhat cracked, and the color often fades to dull yellow with rosy tints. The

Two-colored Bolete (*Boletus bicolor*)

pale yellow flesh of both cap and stalk is mild-tasting and slowly stains blue when cut. The pore surface is yellow, sometimes with reddish stains in age; it slowly stains blue where bruised (only after several minutes). The pores are tiny and usually appear more polygonal than round when viewed with a hand lens. The stalk is two to four inches long and ½−1¼ inches thick, nearly equal in thickness overall or slightly thicker toward the base. The stalk has a dry surface; it is yellow at the top but covered with a thin layer of dark rosy red over the lower two-thirds. There is no partial veil, ring, or volva. The spore print is greenish brown.

**FRUITING:** The Two-colored Bolete is found scattered or in groups on the ground under oak (especially where mixed with pine) and aspen trees. It fruits during summer and fall in a range that extends from Nova Scotia south to Florida and as far west as Minnesota.

**SIMILAR SPECIES:** The Brick-cap Bolete (*B. sensibilis*) is poisonous (see page 162); it is similar to the Two-colored Bolete, but its flesh and pore surface stain blue *instantly* when bruised or cut. *B. bicolor* var. *borealis* (edibility unknown) has an orange-red pore surface with olive tints.

**EDIBILITY:** This bolete is as delicious as it is handsome—just as good, according to many mycophagists, as the King Bolete. It is common and often abundant in oak and pine woods on many parts of the East Coast.

# CHESTNUT, BLUING, AND PALE-CHESTNUT BOLETES

*Gyroporus castaneus*
*G. cyanescens*
*G. subalbellus*

Chesnut Bolete (*Gyroporus castaneus*)

## KEY IDENTIFYING CHARACTERISTICS

1. Cap one to four inches wide, surface dry
2. Pore surface white to yellow, may bruise blue; pores tiny, depressed around stalk
3. Stalk hollow, at least near the base, in mature specimens
4. Spore print pale yellow or yellow

**DESCRIPTION:** The Chestnut Bolete (*Gyroporus castaneus*) cap has a dry, chestnut brown to orangish brown or yellowish brown surface. It is one to four inches wide and round topped in young specimens but nearly flat in mature ones. The cap undersurface has a white to pale yellow pore surface and tiny round to slightly angular pores that are depressed around the stalk and don't stain blue when bruised. The stalk is pale yellowish brown to brownish orange, smooth surfaced, and typically dry; it is either equal in thickness from top to bottom or slightly enlarged at the base—1–3½ inches long and ¼–½ inch thick at the middle. Also, the stalk is hollow in mature specimens, especially near the base. The flesh of both cap and stalk is white and mild-tasting.

The Bluing Bolete (*G. cyanescens*) is similar in most respects; however, it has a straw-colored, slightly velvety cap and stalk, and all parts of the mushroom immediately stain blue when cut or bruised.

The Pale-chestnut Bolete (*G. subalbellus*) has dull white to yellowish cap and stalk surfaces, with tints of apricot or pink, and yellowish brown stains in age. The pore surface is white to yellow and stains reddish brown where bruised. In other respects, it fits the description of the Chestnut Bolete.

These species produce yellow spore prints.

**FRUITING:** These three members of the genus *Gyroporus* are found singly or in groups on the ground in woods during summer and fall. The Chestnut Bolete is commonly found in eastern North America

Bluing Bolete (*Gyroporus cyanescens*)

Pale-chesnut Bolete (*Gyroporus subalbellus*)

(rarely on the West Coast) in deciduous woods (oak trees are frequently noted). The Bluing Bolete is also an eastern species but occurs in both coniferous and deciduous forests. The Pale-chestnut Bolete is found in the eastern United States, west to Texas; it prefers sandy soil in oak and pine woods.

**SIMILAR SPECIES:** The edible Red Gyroporus (*G. purpurinis*) is so similar to the three species described above that it fits their key identifying characteristics. Its cap is dry, velvety, and purplish red, and its stalk is dark red and hollow. Like the other *Gyroporus* species, its pore surface is white to yellow, with tiny round pores that are depressed around the stalk. The Red Gyroporus is an eastern U.S. species; it is associated with deciduous trees, especially various species of oak. No other species meet all the key identifying characteristics listed above.

**EDIBILITY:** All three of the illustrated boletes, as well as the Red Gyroporus (described as a similar species), are fine edibles. The rule of thumb that warns against eating boletes that stain blue when bruised is shattered by the Bluing Bolete. There are, in fact, a number of perfectly safe, edible boletes that *do* bruise blue. Unfortunately, most of the others are more difficult to distinguish from their poisonous look-alikes and thus remain—as well they should—prizes reserved for only the most experienced mushroom hunters.

# RED-CAPPED SCABER STALK

*Leccinum aurantiacum*

Red-capped Scaber Stalk (*Leccinum aurantiacum*)

**KEY IDENTIFYING CHARACTERISTICS**

1. Cap two to eight inches wide; surface bright to dull orangish red, dry or slightly sticky
2. Pore surface white, staining greenish brown when bruised
3. Cap flesh thick; white, slowly staining wine red, then grayish, and finally purplish black when cut
4. Stalk thick, firm, solid; white with scabers
5. Scabers dingy white on stalks of young specimens, orangish brown to brown or black on mature ones

**DESCRIPTION:** The cap is bright to dull orangish red; it is dry but slightly sticky in wet weather. It is rounded in young specimens, nearly flat in mature ones, and two to eight inches wide. The pore surface is white, staining greenish brown when bruised; the pores are minute and nearly round. The stalk is thick, firm, and solid; it is white with tiny, stiff, granular projections, or scabers. The stalk is about the same thickness from top to bottom or somewhat thicker at the base. It measures three to eight inches long and three-fourths to two inches thick. The stalk scabers of young specimens are dingy white, darkening to orangish brown as the mushroom grows, and become brown to black in age. The spore print is yellowish brown.

**FRUITING:** This mushroom is found on the ground singly or in groups throughout much of North America. It fruits in both deciduous and coniferous woods during summer and autumn.

**SIMILAR SPECIES:** In North America, there are several other *Leccinum* species, or Scaber Stalks, with orangish red caps. They are generally difficult to distinguish from *L. aurantiacum*, but each differs from this species by at least one of the features listed above as a key identifying characteristic. As far as is known, all are edible. There have been no reports of any adverse reactions despite frequent consumption by avid mushroom hunters.

**EDIBILITY:** The Red-capped Scaber Stalk is rated by some mycophagists almost as highly as the King Bolete (*Boletus edulis*), which is edible (see p. 95), while others say it is only mediocre. This is a good example of the subjective nature of the sense of taste, at least as applied to mycophagy. At any rate, the Red-capped Scaber Stalk is often abundant, especially under aspen and pine, following heavy rains in summer and fall. It often fills the large baskets of delighted mushroom hunters.

Slippery Jack (*Suillus luteus*)

# SLIPPERY JACK AND ALLIES

*Suillus luteus*
*S. grevillei*
*S. caerulescens*
*S. americanus*

**KEY IDENTIFYING CHARACTERISTICS**

1. Cap two to six inches wide; surface smooth; sticky or slimy
2. Cap surface bright yellow to golden yellow, yellowish brown to orangish brown, or reddish brown to bright red
3. Cap flesh white to yellow, not staining blue when cut or bruised
4. Pore surface white or yellow to yellowish brown, not staining blue when bruised; may be covered by partial veil
5. Spore print greenish brown to yellowish brown

DA

Larch Suillus (*Suillus grevillei*)

WS

Blue-staining Suillus (*Suillus caerulescens*)

**DESCRIPTION:** The Slippery Jack (*Suillus luteus*) has a slimy to sticky reddish brown to yellowish brown cap; it is two to five inches wide, dome shaped at first but nearly flat in age. Young specimens have a white, membranous partial veil. As the cap expands, the veil ruptures, exposing a white to yellow pore surface that soon becomes mottled with brownish spots but doesn't stain blue when bruised. The cap flesh is white to pale yellow, not staining blue. The stalk is white to pale yellow, with pinkish to brownish dots; it is 1−3½ inches long and three-eighths to one inch thick. The mature stalk is adorned by a membranous ring with a white upper surface and a purple undersurface. The stalk is thick, firm, solid, and fairly equal in thickness from top to bottom. The spore print is greenish brown to yellowish brown.

The Larch Suillus (*S. grevillei*) cap is two to six inches wide, with a

Chicken-fat Suillus (*Suillus americanus*)

slimy, bright red to brownish red or bright yellow surface. The cap flesh is pale yellow, staining pinkish red when bruised. Young specimens have a pale yellow partial veil. The pore surface is pale yellow to olive yellow, slowly staining rusty brown when bruised. The stalk is dry, pale yellow with reddish or brownish spots and streaks; mature specimens have a white, cottony ring. The spore print is greenish brown.

The Blue-staining Suillus (*S. caerulescens*) cap is two to six inches wide. The cap surface is sticky to slimy, dull reddish brown to yellowish brown near the center, and dingy yellow near the edge. The cap flesh is pale yellow, staining pinkish. Young specimens have a white to pale yellow partial veil that will rupture to leave a whitish, cottony ring on the mature stalk. The pore surface is medium to dark yellow. The stalk is 1–3½ inches long and ¾–1¼ inches thick; it is dry and yellow to dingy yellow with reddish to brownish spots and streaks. The flesh of the stalk base stains blue to green when cut. The spore print is brown to yellowish brown.

The Chicken-fat Suillus (*S. americanus*) cap is sticky to slimy and bright yellow with cinnamon brown to reddish streaks and spots. The cap flesh is yellowish, staining pinkish brown when exposed. At first, the pore surface is covered by a yellowish partial veil that leaves no ring on the stalk—rather, it sticks to the edge of the mature cap. The pore surface is yellow, staining brownish when bruised or in age; the pores are large and angular (not round). The stalk is bright to dull yellow, with brown spots and streaks and no ring; it is relatively narrow—1–3½ inches long and only one-eighth to three-eighths inch thick. The spore print is yellowish brown.

**FRUITING:** These *Suillus* species are found singly or in groups on the ground under specific kinds of trees. The Slippery Jack occurs in eastern North America under red pine, Scotch pine, and spruce; it fruits from fall through early winter. The Larch Suillus, as its name implies, is found under larch (tamarack) trees and is common in northern North America from late summer until early winter. The Blue-staining Suillus is found only under Douglas fir in the Pacific Northwest and California, fruiting from fall through early spring. The Chicken-fat Suillus grows only under eastern white pine from Nova Scotia south to the Carolinas and west to Michigan; it fruits during summer and fall, sometimes in fairy rings.

**SIMILAR SPECIES:** Each of these four species has a look-alike, each of which is edible. The Slippery Jill (*S. subluteus*) is similar to her brother, the Slippery Jack, but has a thicker partial veil that leaves a baggy ring that lacks purplish coloration. *S. proximus* is similar to the Larch Suillus, but it lacks the bright red cap color, and the flesh of its stalk base stains green when exposed. *S. ponderosus* is similar to the Blue-staining Suillus but has a sticky to slimy reddish brown to dingy yellow cap and a sticky yellow to orange veil. *S. sibiricus* is similar to the Chicken-fat Suillus but has a thicker stalk (one-fourth to five-eighths inch) and sometimes has a yellow ring; also, the cap is typically darker yellow to yellowish brown with darker, reddish brown streaks. No mushrooms other than edible *Suillus* species conform to the key identifying characteristics listed above.

**EDIBILITY:** All these *Suillus* species are good, frequently abundant edibles. The slime layer on the caps should be removed; otherwise, gastric upset may occur in some individuals. It is also wise to remove the tube layers because these often become slimy, especially when cooked. This is unnecessary if the mushrooms are to be dried.

Despite these slightly bothersome preparations, the slimy-capped *Suillus* species are very popular among mushroom hunters. The flesh of both cap and stalk is tender and flavorful and works especially well in sauces and gravies. As with all boletes, drying is a popular way to preserve suilli. Pickling is also a tasty option for these common and abundant mushrooms.

# 9

# Tooth Mushrooms

Two genera are included in this chapter: *Hydnum,* which are ground-inhabiting cap-and-stalk mushrooms, and *Hericium,* which are white to yellowish, iciclelike mushrooms found on logs, stumps, and dead or dying trees. The species covered here—and only a handful of species of each genus occur in North America—are among the most easily identifiable edible mushrooms. In both genera, the mushrooms produce spores on downward-pointed "teeth," or spines. Few other mushrooms produce spores on similar-looking structures, and most of them are shelflike. They are also, in the dual opinions of the authors, among the most delicious.

The *Hydnum* (also called *Dentinum*) species look like gilled mushrooms or boletes, but they are quickly and easily distinguished by the spines, rather than gills or pores, on the underside of each cap. The *Hericium* species are odd but beautiful; they are whitish masses of iciclelike spines that appear on trees, stumps, and logs.

These are particularly safe mushrooms for the novice because no dangerous fungi look anything like them. They are also highly regarded among experienced mycophagists, for they have excellent texture and taste.

# SWEET TOOTH

*Hydnum repandum*

Sweet Tooth (*Hydnum repandum*)

## KEY IDENTIFYING CHARACTERISTICS

1. Pale to rich orange cap and stalk
2. Pointed spines beneath cap
3. Found on the ground in woods or bogs

**DESCRIPTION:** The cap is orange and two to six inches in diameter; the surface is smooth or slightly roughened, sometimes cracked; often it is slightly sunken in the center. The cap edge is inrolled in young specimens and wavy or lobed in mature ones. The under-surface of the cap is covered with short, pointed spines that usually extend somewhat onto the stalk. The spines are yellowish to orange, always lighter in color than the surface of the cap. The stalk is yellow-ish orange, fairly thick, smooth, and often slightly off-center. The spore print is white.

**FRUITING:** The Sweet Tooth is found singly or scattered on the ground in a variety of forest types. It fruits from midsummer through midautumn and is found throughout North America. It will usually reappear in the same area year after year.

**SIMILAR SPECIES:** There are many cap-and-stalk mushrooms with spines beneath the cap; none are known to be poisonous. Several are fine edibles: *H. umbilicatum* is smaller, with a darker orange cap sur-face and an almost invariably sunken center; it grows in wet conifer-ous forests and bogs. The Scaly Tooth (*Sarcodon imbricatum*) has a brown, distinctly scaly cap and brown spines and stalk; it fruits in late spring and early summer on the ground in woods. Another species, *Sarcodon scabrosum,* is similar but has a black stalk base and a de-cidedly bitter taste.

    *H. albidum* (edibility unknown) is chalky white at first and then creamy with very pale orangish yellow tints; it has a peppery taste. The Sweet Tooth also has variants that are lighter in color, especially whitish or pale yellow; they are just as edible as the orange varieties.

Other cap-and-stalk mushrooms with teeth or spines on the under-surface of the cap bear little resemblance to the edible species recommended here. The Sweet Tooth is sometimes called the Hedgehog or Spreading Hedgehog mushroom. Both it and *H. umbilicatum* are sometimes classified in the genus *Dentinum*.

**EDIBILITY:** The distinctive Sweet Tooth and its little brother, *H. umbilicatum,* are both delicious edibles. Synonyms aside, a Sweet Tooth by any other name would still taste as sweet. Specimens of the larger species look, from a short distance, much like the Golden Chanterelle, because of similar size, color, and shape. This shouldn't lead to any disappointment, though: both the Sweet Tooth and *H. umbilicatum* have a pleasant, mild flavor, making each a prize find for the mushroom hunter. They are firm, fleshy mushrooms and can be prepared in a variety of ways. The chef should be careful not to disguise the delicate flavor, though. Unless you have a large collection, they are best served as a simple, sautéed side dish.

Some mycophagists rate the Scaly Tooth as high as they do the Sweet Tooth, while others find it far less appealing. Apparently, its flavor varies considerably from place to place.

If there are insects hiding in the spines, they can easily be removed with the edge of a knife.

JC

Comb Tooth (*Hericium coralloides*)

# COMB TOOTH AND BEAR'S HEAD TOOTH

*Hericium coralloides*
*H. americanum*

**KEY IDENTIFYING CHARACTERISTICS**

1. White mass, resembling coral in shape, with iciclelike (downward-pointing) spines
2. Found on logs, stumps, or trees

**DESCRIPTION:** A mushroom of either species is essentially a mass of white to cream-colored, iciclelike spines. Each is composed of a series of branches. The Bear's Head Tooth (*Hericium americanum*) is

Bear's Head Tooth (*Hericium americanum*)

usually more compact than the Comb Tooth (*H. coralloides*). Whereas the former species' branches are packed fairly closely together, the latter species' branches are generally more spread out. The most practical way to distinguish between the two species is by examining the arrangement of the spines or teeth. Spines are fairly evenly distributed along the length of each branch of the Comb Tooth (hence, its common name); the spines of the Bear's Head Tooth are found mostly in bundles, especially at the tip of each branch. Both species are typically three to ten inches high, four inches to a foot wide, and project three to six inches from the wood on which they grow. Some specimens are pale pinkish or yellowish; yellow specimens are usually not very fresh. Both species produce white spore prints.

**FRUITING:** These species are found either alone or with several mushrooms on the same log from midsummer through midfall. The Comb Tooth is found throughout much of North America. The Bear's Head Tooth is confined primarily to eastern North America; it is occasionally found growing on living trees. The two species' tree preferences include beech, maple, oak, and birch.

**SIMILAR SPECIES:** The Bearded Tooth (*H. erinaceus*) lacks branches; the entire mushroom appears much more rounded, and the spines hang from a central wad of tissue. It occurs almost exclusively on wounds of living trees, especially oak. *H. abietis* is most similar in form to the Bear's Head Tooth; it grows on conifer logs, stumps, and dead branches in western North America. Both of these other species are equally edible. No other fungi even remotely resemble mushrooms of this genus.

Recent comparisons of North American and European specimens have cleared up some previous taxonomic errors but caused much confusion about the scientific names of the North American *Hericium* species: Our Comb Tooth used to be called *H. ramosum*, and the Bear's Head Tooth used to have what is now the Comb Tooth's name.

EJ

Bearded Tooth (*Hericium erinaceus*)

**EDIBILITY:** All *Hericium* species are delicious edibles when fresh. Because they are usually fairly large, they are wonderful finds for the mushroom hunter—and the photographer.

Pick them by cutting as close to the wood as possible. Sometimes, the mushroom will be found quite high on a standing tree trunk or tall stump; a long, sturdy stick can be used to dislodge it. Once you have the *Hericium* in hand, shake it vigorously. This eliminates most of the insects that may be hiding in the spines or among the branches.

When you get the mushroom home, slice it like bread. This is slightly difficult with the Comb Tooth and *H. abietis* because of the numerous branches; simply break the branches free from each other. In the case of the Bear's Head Tooth and the Bearded Tooth, though, the central mass of tissue helps hold the slices together better. After slicing, it is fairly easy to evict any remaining insects by simply blowing them away.

When fresh, young, and white, the *Hericium* mushrooms are a wonderful treat for the palate. The Bearded Tooth may develop a sour taste unless it is very fresh; the others retain their quality longer.

These strange but beautiful mushrooms can be prepared in a variety of ways, but most devotees of the genus prefer simply to sauté the slices or pieces and eat them rather than compromise their distinctive, mildly sweet flavor with other foods. The numerous branches of the Comb Tooth and *H. abietis* lend themselves well to drying and develop a striking golden color; however, they are more tender—and tastier—when cooked fresh. If you do dry them, reconstitute them with cream.

Slices of the Bear's Head Tooth and the Bearded Tooth can also be baked or broiled with excellent results; another scrumptious alternative is to dip the slices in batter and deep fry them.

Baked or broiled morsels of any *very* fresh *Hericium* mushroom makes a most unusual hors d'oeuvre: dipped in melted butter, the mushroom has a taste and texture reminiscent of broiled lobster tail.

# 10.

## Coral-shaped, Club-shaped, and Cauliflower-shaped Mushrooms

The mushrooms in this section represent fungi from two families: the coral mushrooms and the polypores. Of the four species of coral mushrooms, only the first looks like marine coral. The second looks like a club, but it is nonetheless classified as a member of the coral family of fungal fruit. The remaining two, which are look-alikes, look quite like the polypores in this chapter. The three polypores have shapes like bushes rather than the typical shelflike form of most polypores.

These disparate mushrooms are all quite easy to identify, but their culinary value is clearly a matter of personal opinion.

# CROWN-TIPPED CORAL

*Clavicorona pyxidata*

Crown-tipped Coral (*Clavicorona pyxidata*)

## KEY IDENTIFYING CHARACTERISTICS

1. Many-branched, pale yellow, corallike mushroom with a tiny, crown-shaped tip on each branch
2. Found on wood

**DESCRIPTION:** This mushroom is pale yellow, sometimes almost off-white; it is composed of a series of very slender, repeatedly branching stalks with a tiny, crown-shaped structure at the tip of each branch. Some specimens are as much as six inches high, but four inches is more typical. Each branch is one-sixteenth to one-eighth inch thick. The spore print is white.

**FRUITING:** This species grows on dead deciduous logs either as a single cluster or in groups. It is especially common on moss-covered logs; preferred wood types are aspen, poplar, willow, and cottonwood. It is common in most parts of North America and fruits from late spring through early fall. The same log often produces two or more fruitings in the same year.

**SIMILAR SPECIES:** There are many other species of multibranched, corallike fungi; some are poisonous and some are edible. Most of the poisonous species grow on the ground. Of the other species that grow on wood, none have the Crown-tipped Coral's distinctive crown-shaped branch tips. The only close relative of this species, *C. avellanea* (edibility not established), is grayish brown; it grows on coniferous wood in the Pacific Northwest. The Crown-tipped Coral was previously classified in the genus *Clavaria*.

**EDIBILITY:** This common and distinctive fungus has been reported to cause mild diarrhea in some people; therefore, exercise moderation, especially when trying it for the first time. It is delicious.

Each specimen should be cut from the log near the base of the stalk, cleaned of any wood or moss particles, wrapped carefully in waxed paper to prevent drying, and later fried in a very small amount of butter. Use a covered frying pan because this mushroom has an entertaining, if peculiar, tendency to jump right out of the pan as it fries!

The Crown-tipped Coral makes a fun pizza topping; its unique flavor and texture complement the traditional Italian-style pizza ingredients. Baking it or frying it thoroughly makes it delightfully crispy, though it sometimes becomes a bit chewy if not gathered and cooked when fresh and moist. It can be preserved by drying, but, like most mushrooms, it's more chewy that way. Better to enjoy when fresh.

# FLAT-TOPPED CORAL MUSHROOM

*Clavariadelphus truncatus*

Flat-topped Coral Mushroom (*Clavariadelphus truncatus*)

## KEY IDENTIFYING CHARACTERISTICS

1. Club-shaped, flat-topped mushroom, two to six inches high
2. No gills, pores, or spines
3. Found on the ground in conifer woods
4. Not white or pale pinkish white overall

DESCRIPTION: This distinctive mushroom is shaped like a flat-topped club, two to six inches tall, with a base much narrower (one-fourth to one-half inch wide) than the top (one to three inches wide). Both the flattened top and the outer sides are distinctly wrinkled, but less so near the base of the club. The surfaces of the mushroom are yellowish orange to pinkish brown, usually more yellowish on top and more pinkish on the sides. The flesh is white and usually spongy but sometimes fairly firm; it tastes sweet in fresh specimens. The base of the mushroom is usually covered with white hairlike fibers. Older specimens frequently split at the top, sometimes revealing a hollow interior (the split may or may not run down into the stalk). The spore print, which can be obtained by laying the mushroom on its side on white paper, is pale yellowish brown.

**FRUITING:** The Flat-topped Coral Mushroom is found on the ground—either singly, scattered, or in groups—in conifer woods. Its season runs from summer through autumn, and it is found throughout most of North America.

**SIMILAR SPECIES:** The Pestle-shaped Coral (*C. pistillaris*), which is edible, is nearly identical but has a rounded (not flattened) top and bitter-tasting flesh; it occurs on the ground in deciduous woods. Although it is technically edible, we know of no mycophagists who have been pleased with this look-alike.

*C. ligula* (edibility unknown) is quite similar in shape but is much smaller; also, it doesn't taper noticeably toward the base, is not flat-topped, and is usually decidedly pinkish or orangish. It, too, has bitter-tasting flesh.

It is unlikely that anyone could mistake a specimen of another species as a Flat-topped Coral, provided one notes the overall shape and size, flat top, and downward-tapering stalk; however, the Pestle-shaped Coral is sometimes nibbled at the top by slugs—in which case a taste of the flesh will rule it out.

**EDIBILITY:** This is a fine edible wild mushroom—often firm, always tasteful, and certainly unusual. Those unfamiliar with North America's diverse fungal flora wouldn't likely realize that this is a mushroom at all. Sauté it or bread and deep-fry it for an unusual side dish.

---

# EASTERN AND ROOTING CAULIFLOWER MUSHROOMS

*Sparassis spathulata*
*S. radicata*

Eastern Cauliflower Mushroom (*Sparassis spathulata*)

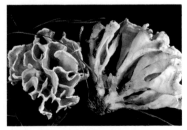

A more mature specimen showing leaflike lobes and flattened branches.

## KEY IDENTIFYING CHARACTERISTICS

1. Round, cauliflower- or lettucelike cluster of mushroom tissue, at least six inches high and six inches wide
2. Found on decaying wood or on the ground in woods

**DESCRIPTION:** The Eastern Cauliflower Mushroom (*Sparassis spathulata*) is a fairly round, compact cluster of fungal tissue, shaped

Rooting Cauliflower Mushroom (*Sparassis radicata*)

very much like a head of lettuce or cauliflower. It is composed of cream to pale yellow, flattened, leaflike branches that are grossly wrinkled, curled, and folded. Each "leaf" is usually lightest in color at the edge. The flesh is white, thin, and fibrous. The mushroom is six inches to one foot wide and six to ten inches high. The branches arise from a slight, cordlike, rooting base. The mushroom has a fairly mild, pleasant odor.

The Rooting Cauliflower Mushroom (*S. radicata*) is very similar, but it is generally less compact and has a tough, deeply rooting, dark brown to black stalk, three to five inches long and one to two inches thick. Each "leaf" is usually darkest in color at the edge. The mushroom is usually bigger than its East Coast sibling, sometimes growing as large as three feet wide and twenty inches high.

The spore print of either species is white.

**FRUITING:** The Eastern Cauliflower Mushroom is found on the ground (rarely on well-decayed wood) in oak and pine woods, especially in sandy soil at the base of trees or on their roots; it fruits from midsummer through mid-fall. The Rooting Cauliflower Mushroom is found in coniferous forests west of the Rocky Mountains, from British Columbia south to northern California. It is especially frequent in the Pacific Northwest and has also been reported at high elevations in Arizona. It is usually found at the base or on the roots of conifer trees but occasionally on well-decayed logs or stumps; it fruits during autumn.

**SIMILAR SPECIES:** No other mushrooms closely resemble these strange species. Three edible members of the polypore family—the Hen of the Woods (*Grifola frondosa;* see next entry), the Umbrella Polypore (*Polyporus umbellatus;* see p. 119), and the Black-staining Polypore (*Meripilus giganteus;* see p. 120) are vaguely similar because of their size and compound structure, but each can easily be distinguished from the *Sparassis* mushrooms by comparing their photographs and descriptions.

The scientific names of these species have been confused a great deal. The Eastern Cauliflower Mushroom is sometimes classified as *S. herbstii,* and the Rooting Cauliflower Mushroom is also known as *S. crispa.* The Eastern Cauliflower Mushroom has often been mistakenly called *S. crispa.* These mushrooms are among the relatively few species whose common names are more universally agreed upon than their scientific names, though at least one field guide calls the Eastern Cauliflower Mushroom by the name Ruffles.

**EDIBILITY:** Disagreement over the nomenclature of these species doesn't spill over into the matter of edibility—they are both consistently rated choice. Although the flesh is somewhat fibrous, especially in the Rooting Cauliflower Mushroom, long, slow cooking tenderizes it quite effectively. Stews, soups, gravies, casseroles, and a variety of other kinds of dishes are well suited for these flavorful mushrooms.

Drying is absolutely undesirable for either species, because it makes them leathery tough; pickling, canning, or partial cooking and freezing are the popular ways to preserve them for later use. But because the Rooting Cauliflower Mushroom sometimes takes on gigantic proportions—up to forty pounds or more, according to some Pacific Northwest mycophagists—the amount of work involved with these techniques for such large mushrooms is considerable. They are more frequently shared with other mushroom enthusiasts and eaten when fresh.

The Rooting Cauliflower Mushroom will usually reappear in the same spot for several years in a row if the "leaves" are carefully cut off with a sharp knife and the inedible root left in the ground.

---

# HEN OF THE WOODS

*Grifola frondosa*

**KEY IDENTIFYING CHARACTERISTICS**

1. Pale gray to grayish brown, bushlike cluster of fan-shaped caps at least six inches wide and four inches high
2. Found on the ground in woods, usually at the base of a tree or stump

**DESCRIPTION:** This mushroom is a large cluster of overlapping, pale gray to grayish brown more or less fan-shaped caps, each three-quarters to three inches wide and one-eighth to one-fourth inch thick near the edge. The undersurface of each cap is white to yellowish white; it bears tiny, shallow pores that descend a white lateral "branch." These branches are fused together in bundles, all arising from a white, short-but-thick, basal stalk. The flesh is white, thick, and somewhat fibrous; it has a mushroomy or mealy odor and a slightly sweet taste. Each mushroom is typically six inches to two feet wide and four to fourteen inches high. The spore print is white.

Hen of the Woods (*Grifola frondosa*)

Bill Chapman with a beautiful
Hen of the Woods (*Grifola frondosa*)

**FRUITING:** This mushroom is found mostly in eastern North America, but it has also been reported from Louisiana, the Pacific Northwest, and the midwestern states. It fruits singly or in groups during summer and fall. It is found on the ground at or near the base of a deciduous tree or stump, especially oak; it is sometimes found in association with conifers.

**SIMILAR SPECIES:** Several edible mushrooms are vaguely similar in size and the overall compound structure. These include the Cauliflower mushrooms (*Sparassis* species; see preceding entry), the Umbrella Polypore (*Polyporus umbellatus;* see next entry) and the Black-staining Polypore (*Meripilus giganteus;* see p. 120). Idahoans may find the yellowish *Polyporus illudens* near conifer trees; we have no information on its edibility and therefore cannot recommend it. The Hen of the Woods, which was formerly classified as *Polyporus frondosus,* has no dangerous look-alikes.

**EDIBILITY:** The Hen of the Woods is widely regarded as an excellent edible mushroom in Europe as well as in North America. Its flesh is fairly fibrous, especially in mature specimens, but long, slow cooking makes it thoroughly palatable.

This is a mildly sweet mushroom that lends itself well to a variety of dishes. It and the Cauliflower mushrooms serve well as substitutes for each other in dishes that call for one or another of these large mushrooms. Fresh, tender, young specimens are even worthy of presentation as a side dish with meat, fish, or poultry. Preferred methods for preserving the Hen of the Woods are pickling and canning; freezing—even raw—will suffice, if you have enough space in your freezer.

If you find a Hen of the Woods, remember where you discovered it. This species tends to reappear in the same place for at least several years.

GL

Umbrella Polypore (*Polyporus umbellatus*)

# UMBRELLA POLYPORE

*Polyporus umbellatus*

## KEY IDENTIFYING CHARACTERISTICS

1. White to tan, bushlike cluster of round caps ⅜–1½ inches wide; cluster is at least three inches wide
2. Undersurface of caps whitish to pale yellow, bearing tiny, shallow pores that descend a white, slender, centrally attached "branch"
3. Found at the base of a tree or stump or on buried wood or roots

**DESCRIPTION:** The Umbrella Polypore is a fairly large cluster of overlapping, white to tan, circular caps, each ⅜–1½ inches wide. The undersurface of each cap is white to pale yellow; it bears tiny, shallow pores that descend a white, centrally attached "branch." These branches are fused together in bundles, all arising from a white basal stalk. The stalk, in turn, arises from a very firm, black, underground "root" that is white inside. Each mushroom cluster is three to twenty inches wide and four to ten inches high. The spore print is white.

**FRUITING:** This species is found primarily in northeastern North America, south to Tennessee and west to Ohio; it has also been reported from Iowa, Idaho, and Washington. It fruits on the ground at the base of deciduous trees and stumps or on buried wood or tree roots during spring and fall.

**SIMILAR SPECIES:** The only similar mushrooms are equally edible species—the Cauliflower mushrooms and the Hen of the Woods are vaguely similar. None of the look-alikes, however, have circular caps centrally attached to branches. This is an extraordinarily safe mushroom for the novice because it has no dangerous look-alikes.

**EDIBILITY:** The Umbrella Polypore is consistently rated as a choice edible. It is generally less common than its cousin, the Hen of the Woods; but unlike the Hen, it is almost invariably tender and doesn't require long, slow cooking.

# BLACK-STAINING POLYPORE

*Meripilus giganteus*

Black-staining Polypore (*Meripilus giganteus*)

Alan Bessette holding a good-sized Black-staining Polypore (*Meripilus giganteus*)

## KEY IDENTIFYING CHARACTERISTICS

1. Cluster of large, thick, fleshy, shelflike caps two to eight inches wide
2. Undersurface of each cap bears very tiny white pores that stain blackish when bruised or in age
3. Found at the base of trees or stumps

**DESCRIPTION:** This mushroom is a cluster of thick, fleshy, grayish white to grayish yellow or yellowish brown, shelflike caps, two to eight inches wide and usually one-fourth to one-half inches thick. The undersurface of each cap bears minute pores that are whitish to pale gray and that easily bruise blackish within several minutes. The flesh is white and a bit fibrous. Each cluster is six inches to two feet wide and sometimes even wider. The spore print is white.

**FRUITING:** This polypore is found on or about deciduous trees and stumps, most frequently beech and oak. It fruits in summer and fall, and its range includes much of the eastern United States, west to Missouri and Louisiana.

**SIMILAR SPECIES:** There are only a few similar fleshy polypores; none exhibit the overall form and black-bruising reaction of this species. The Black-staining Polypore was previously classified in the genus *Polyporus;* a recent taxonomic study suggests it be *M. sumstinei.*

**EDIBILITY:** Although not frequently collected, it is a worthwhile edible. In *The Audubon Society Field Guide to North American Mushrooms,* Gary H. Lincoff compares the taste and texture to beef liver. Like most tableworthy polypores, it requires long, slow cooking. It can be frozen fresh.

Again, like most other edible members of the polypore family, this mushroom tends to be quite large. Sometimes its size borders on the ridiculous—up to fifty pounds or more in a single cluster.

# Shelflike Mushrooms, Puffballs, Morels, and Jelly Fungi

## Shelflike Mushrooms

All three of the edible species covered in this section on shelflike mushrooms are fleshy members of the Polypore family, though they are classified within three separate genera. While most polypores are hard and woody, these three are fleshy and soft. There are no known poisonous species among the polypores.

Polypores are distinguished from other fungi primarily by two field characteristics: they usually grow on wood, and they have pores (not gills or teeth) on their undersurface. This is a particularly safe, though rather limited, group of edible mushrooms for beginners.

## Puffballs

Almost everyone has noticed puffballs. The characteristic puffs of smoke produced when a mature puffball is touched or stepped on always delight children. This "smoke" is actually a cloud of spores. Puffballs differ from most other mushrooms in that they produce their spores as an interior mass called the "gleba," rather than on exterior surfaces such as gills or pores.

Most puffballs are also delicious edibles. The Giant Puffball is one of the world's best-known and most widely distributed edible wild mushrooms. Its huge size—some specimens exceed two feet in diameter—makes it easily identifiable. Several similar species of large puffballs are equally prized as food, and one good-sized specimen is sufficient to serve as a side dish for a very large and hungry family. There are also several smaller edible puffballs. Everyone who has ever taken a summer or fall walk in the woods has noticed them, but few realize that most woodland varieties are every bit as delicious as the larger ones. What the smaller species lack in size, they make up for by their usual abundance. A common species of "puffball" (actually, this is a false puffball), the Pigskin Poison Puffball (see p. 164), is toxic, and it can be easily identified by its leathery, warted exterior skin, as can its untrustworthy brothers.

Most edible puffballs grow on the ground. The most common exception is the Pear-shaped Puffball, which grows in clusters on stumps and logs. The edible species have two principal field characteristics in common: a relatively thin and resilient skin on the outside and an initially pure white interior. As a puffball matures, the solid white interior develops a greenish, yellowish, brownish, or purplish coloration and soon turns into a powdery mass of spores. Without exception, puffballs should only be eaten when the interior is pure white. Once the gleba starts to change color, each species has the potential of causing gastrointestinal upset.

The various edible puffball species taste quite the same. Attempting to describe the flavor would be pointless because it is truly unique. The texture is just as delightful and somewhat like French toast. Devotees of the large species are always thrilled to find a specimen in good condition. That's the biggest problem with puffballs. They start to mature quickly, and once they are, they're no longer fit for the table. For this reason, a puffball is a true gourmet mushroom—if it's not *perfectly* fresh, forget it.

Some people have allergic reactions to some species of puffballs, particularly the Giant. These allergies develop, at least in some cases, after years of eating them. In the absence of any evidence to the contrary, and considering the similarities in taste and texture between the numerous species, it would be wise for persons suffering such reactions to avoid the entire group lest they have a serious reaction to a species new to them that may produce the same reaction. Allergic reactions tend to worsen each time a susceptible individual is exposed to the allergen.

## Morels

There is only one genus—*Morchella*—of true morels. These are all safe, delicious edibles, highly prized by mushroom lovers and gourmets alike. In some areas, they're hard to find; in other areas, they're as common as weeds. Consider yourself lucky if you live in their midst.

All three species that are recognized by most North American mycologists are covered in this single section. Several varieties that may be (but *haven't* been conclusively proven to be) separate species are known to be safe; they're covered by the key identifying characteristics and description here also.

Beware of false morels offered by neighbors. Three genera of so-called false or early morels—*Verpa*, *Gyromitra*, and *Helvella*—are all either proven to have or suspected of having toxic species. Stay with the real thing, and you'll avoid unpleasant possibilities, including cancer that may not develop for decades after you've enjoyed such "treats."

## Jelly Fungi

The jelly mushrooms are, perhaps, the mushrooms least likely to be called such by those who are unfamiliar with the Fungi Kingdom's remarkable diversity. The flesh of these jellylike fruiting bodies is always distinctly gelatinous, a characteristic that will readily distinguish them from all other groups of mushrooms. Most jelly fungi produce irregular, bloblike mushrooms; the two species described here are among the few with a more distinctive form. No jelly mushrooms are suspected of being poisonous, but their only redeeming culinary value is the sheer novelty of their form. They demand the gourmet cook's creative magic to give them taste and to present them in a manner that will please the eye, for they have no flavor of their own.

Dryad's Saddle (*Polyporus squamosus*)

# DRYAD'S SADDLE

*Polyporus squamosus*

## KEY IDENTIFYING CHARACTERISTICS

1. Fleshy, lateral-stalked, fan- or saddle-shaped, shelflike mushroom, four or more inches wide, with flattened, tan to brown scales on top
2. Undersurface covered with minute, polygonal, white to yellow pores
3. Interior flesh moist; white with or without brownish marbling
4. Found clustered on logs, stumps, or trees

**DESCRIPTION:** This mushroom is at first almost cylindrical, usually in clusters of several "fingers" (or stalks) that are white to tan except for the ends, which are yellowish brown and depressed. In this immature form, tiny, honeycomblike pores can be seen on the lower side of each finger. As it grows, the end of each finger flares out to become the edge of the cap. The upper surface continually develops brownish, flattened, fibrous scales, showing yellowish tan flesh between. Soon the cap becomes fan or saddle shaped; the pores, which extend onto the stalk, become deeper and wider. The stalk thickens and toughens, darkening until the base is black and quite hard. Fully grown caps range from four inches to one foot or more in width and project nearly that far from the wood on which they're growing. The pores are yellowish white to yellow in mature specimens. The flesh is white, usually marbled with brownish streaks near the upper cap surface, and has a distinct aroma similar to cucumber or watermelon rind. The spore print is white.

**FRUITING:** Dryad's Saddle is usually found in overlapping clusters (but sometimes singly) on deciduous stumps and logs and on dying trees. Within its range—mostly northeastern North America, but as far south as North Carolina and into the Midwest—it is extremely common in spring but less so during summer cold spells and in the fall. This distinctive species is especially abundant on elm, beech, birch, oak, maple, and willow. Each stump will produce mushrooms for at least several years, often more than once in each season.

**SIMILAR SPECIES:** This is the most common of a very few large, fleshy, shelflike polypores; there are no dangerous look-alikes. A few other *Polyporus* species are vaguely similar to Dryad's Saddle, but no other fleshy species of this size closely match its appearance. The scientific name simply means "scaly polypore."

**EDIBILITY:** If the morel is the "lobster" of springtime mushrooms, then Dryad's Saddle is that season's meat and potatoes. Within its range, this conspicuous fungus is easy to find—it fruits on deciduous stumps, often in great quantity, especially during spring. And while Dryad's Saddle—some call it the Rider's Saddle or Pheasant's-back Polypore—isn't as prized as the morel, its unique flavor is good. Dryad's Saddle's big spring season is a sure sign of morel season, and it can provide a hefty consolation prize for the unsuccessful morel hunter.

The only problem with this species is its toughness. Young, fresh specimens are quite tender—enough so to slice and dry them for later use—but whole, mature ones are often too tough to be considered palatable.

Most mushroom hunters familiar with this species harvest it by simply slicing off only the most tender edges of the caps, leaving the rest behind. Determining how much of the cap edge to harvest is easy enough: if a moderately sharp knife slices through it readily, you won't be disappointed. But cut the rest of the mushroom off the stump anyway. The mycelium will be more likely to fruit again in the same year. Cook the pieces slowly, but don't overcook them. Otherwise, even the most tender pieces will become chewy, with a taste and texture similar to burned pork chops (actually, this may appeal to some barbecue fanatics with good teeth). Dryad's Saddle can be eaten raw, too, but only in modest quantity. Tender slices have a slightly crunchy texture, and the flavor is somewhat like watermelon (but without any sweetness). These can add a nice touch to salads.

Consider yourself lucky if you find some of the strange-looking, immature fingers of Dryad's Saddle. At this stage, the entire mushroom is quite tender and generally richer in flavor. If you get to the Saddles later than that, there is another option. Cut the whole mushroom off the wood. When you cook it, simmer it for awhile, discard the mushroom, and strain the liquid. This will make a fine base for soup, gravy, or sauce.

# SULPHUR SHELF

*Laetiporus sulphureus*

## KEY IDENTIFYING CHARACTERISTICS

1. Shelflike, stalkless mushroom found in overlapping clusters on trees, stumps, or logs
2. Upper surface smooth to suedelike, bright orange
3. Undersurface bright yellow with tiny pores

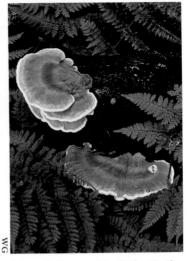

Sulphur Shelf (*Laetiporus sulphureus*)

Young fresh caps of the Sulfur Shelf. Note bright sulfur-yellow cap edge. Caps become dull orange as they age.

**DESCRIPTION:** The mushroom is fan to kidney shaped, stalkless, and shelflike; it is bright yellowish orange to orange on the upper surface and bright yellow on the undersurface. Each shelf is two to ten inches wide, projecting one to six inches from the wood it's growing on, and one-half to three inches thick. The top surface is smooth at first, becoming minutely suedelike; the undersurface is composed of tiny pores. The edge of each cap is noticeably wrinkled or folded. A longitudinal section reveals pale yellow to pale orange flesh, literally dripping with moisture when fresh. In age, the bright orange and yellow colors fade until the mushroom is white and the flesh becomes dry and chalky, at which stage the mushroom is inedible. The spore print is white.

**FRUITING:** This strikingly beautiful mushroom is usually found in overlapping clusters, sometimes totaling fifty pounds or more. It is most commonly found on deciduous trees, stumps, and logs, but also sometimes on conifers. It is found throughout much of North America. It fruits mostly from midsummer through midfall, but it is sometimes found as early as midspring or as late as early winter. It will frequently fruit a second time during the same season on the same tree, stump, or log, especially if the first fruiting was harvested. It also tends to grow on the same tree, stump, or log for several years in succession.

**SIMILAR SPECIES:** No other polypore looks like the Sulphur Shelf. There is a paler variety (*L. sulphureus* var. *semialbinus*), which is edible and typically pale orange on top and white on bottom.

**EDIBILITY:** The Sulphur Shelf reportedly causes gastric upset, at least in some people, particularly when it is picked from Eucalyptus or hemlock trees, or from some other conifers. Such specimens are best avoided. A recent report also suggests that alcoholic beverages should be avoided if one consumes specimens found growing from

During a late summer trip to the Tug Hill Plateau east of Lake Ontario, I spotted an immense cluster of Sulphur Shelves as my truck bounced down an old logging road. I stopped, got out of the truck, and walked over to the tree. The cluster extended at least ten feet up the north side of a huge black cherry tree, but the lowest part of the cluster was eight feet above the ground. Without a ladder, I had one chance: a large fallen branch was leaning against the tree.

(*continued*)

(*continued*)

Using a long, sturdy pole as a brace, I carefully inched my way up the log. I was grateful—the mushrooms were so fresh that they dripped at the slightest touch! Bracing myself with the pole in my left hand, I pulled my pocket knife out with my right, opened it, and stuck it into the trunk. I reached into my back pocket for a folded paper lunch bag, shook it open, and carefully set it down on the log. I pulled the knife from the wood, cut off a nice, wet slice of mushroom, and managed to hold onto it with my knife hand. I aimed carefully, then dropped it into the bag.

I continued until the bag threatened to burst, then reluctantly worked my way back down the log. On the way home, I kept second-guessing myself about a dozen other ways I might have been able to harvest more. I had five or six pounds, but I left another fifty pounds on the tree. It never fails: the less prepared I am, the more mushrooms I find.
—DAVID FISCHER

honey locust trees; those who ignore this warning may experience nausea and vomiting. The Sulphur Shelf has also been known to cause allergic reactions, including swollen lips, in a few individuals. Most fans of this colorful edible insist that it must be collected and cooked while it is very fresh, actually dripping juice when it is cut. Some mycophagists, though, prefer it after it has aged a bit and isn't so wet.

The alternate common name, the Chicken Mushroom, is a culinary comparison: its flavor and texture are, indeed, remarkably similar to those of chicken breast fillets. Perhaps this is an unflattering comparison. Most people who enjoy the Sulphur Shelf would argue that it is superior to its fowl namesake. Nonetheless, it is often substituted in traditional chicken dishes, producing recipes from Mock Chicken Cacciatore (p. 224) to Faux Coq au Vin.

From a calorie-counting perspective, this is an ideal species. Like most mushrooms, it has negligble caloric value and could thus help justify the cheeses and other fattening ingredients that are used in so many wonderful chicken recipes.

When you find a fresh cluster of Sulphur Shelf mushrooms, use a sharp knife to cut each shelf off as close as possible to the tree, stump, or log. When it's juicy, the Sulphur Shelf usually requires little or no cleaning, and insects are rarely a problem.

Unlike most mushrooms, the Sulphur Shelf can be frozen uncooked with little or no damage to its flavor or texture. This is fortunate indeed, considering that one large tree will sometimes yield fifty pounds or more of this excellent edible. Some mushroom hunters eat the whole thing, but the moist edge of each shelf is decidedly the most tender part.

# BEEFSTEAK POLYPORE

*Fistulina hepatica*

## KEY IDENTIFYING CHARACTERISTICS

1. Red-topped, shelflike mushroom found growing on wood
2. Flesh moist to juicy; undersurface bears tubes that are not attached to each other

**DESCRIPTION:** This is a shelflike mushroom shaped somewhat like an oyster shell, three to ten inches wide and ¾–2½ inches thick. It is orangish red or pinkish red to deep red on top. Its pinkish red flesh is juicy and rather gelatinous when fresh. The undersurface bears very small tubes that are free from each other; the pore surface appears yellowish brown to reddish brown. When a stalk is present, it is lateral, short, and thick and colored like the upper surface of the cap. The spore print is pinkish salmon to pale orangish brown.

**FRUITING:** The Beefsteak Polypore is found only on oak or chestnut wood, either at the base of a tree or on a stump or log. It is found in eastern North America, most frequently in the southeast, and it is uncommon in the northeastern United States and Canada. It fruits in summer and fall.

JB

Beefsteak Polypore (*Fistulina hepatica*)

**SIMILAR SPECIES:** No other mushroom comes close to this distinctive species.

**EDIBILITY:** This unmistakable species is a subject of much disagreement among ardent mycophagists at mushroom club meetings. Some rate its al dente texture and tart, acidic flavor the highest; others decry it as a sour-tasting waste of time in the field as well as in the kitchen. Without doubt, there is a significant difference in the qualities of fresh, juicy specimens and older, drier ones, but these variances don't likely account for the wide-ranging opinions of experienced mushroom eaters. Rather, it is the eclectic nature of taste.

This is one of only a few species that we can recommend as a safe edible *uncooked*. Those who do enjoy it like to cut it up raw and toss it into salads. The Beefsteak Polypore should be cooked over low heat in order to preserve its tender texture. It can also be frozen fresh.

## KEY IDENTIFYING CHARACTERISTICS

1. Large (four inches to two feet wide), white to light brown, round mushroom; surface smooth to coarsely warted
2. Interior solid, undifferentiated, white (no gills or stalk)
3. Found on the ground, not on wood; not clustered

**DESCRIPTION:** These species all share a single key trait: the interior is a solid white mass (gleba) of feltlike tissue. There is no true stalk, but some species have a sterile basal structure, the flesh of which is spongy. The Giant Puffball (*Langermannia gigantea*) is particularly huge—up to two feet or more in width. It is covered by a smooth, feltlike skin, and it is sometimes creased, almost like buttocks, on the outside. The Purple-spored and Skull-shaped Puffballs (*Calvatia cyathiformis* and *C. craniformis*) are very similar, but never quite so

# GIANT PUFFBALL AND ALLIES

*Langermannia gigantea*
*Calvatia sculpta*
*C. booniana*
*C. cyathiformis*
*C. craniformis*

Giant Puffball (*Langermannia gigantea*)

EJ

Purple-spored Puffball (*Calvatia cyathiformis*)

huge. The Purple-spored Puffball usually has a pinkish tan exterior; the Skull-shaped Puffball has a whitish skin and large wrinkles near the base. The Western Giant Puffball (*C. booniana*) grows as large as the Giant Puffball, but the outer surface is covered with tan, polygonal "warts." The Pyramid Puffball (*C. sculpta*) is very distinctive: it is covered with pointed, pyramid-shaped warts. In each case, the interior eventually begins turning into a mass of powdery spores, ranging in color from brownish yellow to rich purple.

At maturity, the outer skin of these species cracks or splits open, or even breaks free from the base, allowing the wind to disperse the spores from the cuplike base, which remains in place. In others, the entire puffball breaks free from the ground and is blown about by the wind.

EJ  Skull-shaped Puffball (*Calvatia craniformis*)

KS  Western Giant Puffball (*Calvatia booniana*)

**FRUITING:** These species appear in a variety of habitats and have various ranges as well. As a group, one or another can be found almost anywhere on the continent except along the Gulf Coast and in the Deep South. The Giant Puffball is found throughout most of North America east of the Mississippi River and in California. The Skull-shaped Puffball is quite widespread; the Western Giant Puffball is restricted mostly to arid areas, such as the southwestern United States, and as far north as Idaho. The Purple-spored Puffball is rarely found in Canada or west of the Rocky Mountains. The Pyramid Puffball is found mostly in western North America, especially in the Pacific Northwest.

The Giant and Purple-spored Puffballs are primarily lawn mushrooms, though the Giant is also frequently encountered in open, wooded areas. The Skull-shaped Puffball prefers open woods, and

WS        Pyramid Puffball (*Calvatia sculpta*)

During September in upstate New York, I put a lot of miles on my car. I drive—sometimes aimlessly, sometimes along a carefully planned route—slowly but, I suppose, rather dangerously, as my eyes scan every meadow, pasture, and open grassy area along the way. No other mushroom is so perfectly suited for this type of four-wheel foraging: the large white puffballs are very easy to spot from the road.

I do wish, though, for laws prohibiting people from carelessly leaving volleyballs lying around in their yards and from painting large rocks white. This foolish, irresponsible behavior causes a great deal of unnecessary wear and tear on my car's brakes and wastes a lot of my time.

My wife, Leisa, is among the many people I know who prefer puffballs over every other kind of mushroom they've ever tried. My in-laws have a patch of bad grass, not thirty feet from their barbecue area, that produces at least a few large puffballs each year. I maintain that this is my wife's dowry. She is only grateful that her parents don't compete for these delightful mushrooms.

These are the only mushrooms whose lawn-owners regularly deny me permission when I knock at the door and ask if it is OK to pick some. I therefore have recently embarked upon a new, more scientific approach with folks when I spy large puffballs on their lawns: I tell them that I am conducting important mycological research.

—DAVID FISCHER

the Western Giant Puffball is usually found in brushy areas. The Pyramid Puffball is found under conifers at higher elevations. The Skull-shaped, Purple-spored, and Giant puffballs fruit mostly from late summer through midautumn; the other two species are encountered as early as late spring.

In each case, only one to three specimens will usually be found in a given area, but the Giant, Western Giant, and Purple-spored puffballs sometimes form fairy rings of up to a dozen mushrooms or more. The large puffballs tend to fruit year after year in the same spot.

**SIMILAR SPECIES:** The Sculptured Puffball (*Calbovista subsculpta*) is edible and is nearly identical to the Pyramid Puffball but has less conspicuous, somewhat flattened warts. It is commonly collected at higher elevations in the Rocky Mountains, northern California, and the Pacific Northwest. Several other less common species of *Calvatia* and their allies closely resemble one or another of the species described in this section, but none are suspected of being poisonous; however, among the smaller false puffballs, there is one notable, poisonous species: the Pigskin Poison Puffball (*Scleroderma citrinum*; see p. 164). Its interior is only white for a very short time, quickly turning purplish black with white marbling. Even when young, it can be easily distinguished from the edible puffballs: it has a very tough, rindlike skin, which is covered with minute warts that won't rub off, and a very firm interior.

**EDIBILITY:** The Giant Puffball, sometimes classified as *Calvatia gigantea*, is probably the world's best known edible wild mushroom; its sizable relatives are less commonly known but equally delicious. Two cautions apply to all edible puffballs. They should be cooked soon after picking, while the interior is still pure white. Also, some people experience indigestion after eating puffballs, particularly the Giant. For this reason, it is wise for each individual to eat only a small portion the first time.

KS                    Sculptured Puffball (*Calbovista subsculpta*)

Puffballs, especially the Giant, are immensely popular among ruralists in many regions. Occasionally, they even show up at farmers' markets. Most urban gourmets, however, are not familiar with puffballs. This is mostly because puffballs, unlike most recognized gourmet-quality mushrooms, cannot be dried or otherwise preserved in a way that effectively retains their delightful texture and flavor. The only practical way to preserve them is by freezing raw or partially cooked slices, but this is strictly a short-term option. The slices must be carefully separated by layering waxed paper between them, and extreme care must be taken to prevent freezer burn. It is equally critical to prevent moisture in the freezer from forming ice on the frozen slices. Either of these problems will turn a wonderful culinary delight into a wholly mediocre mushroom. Frozen slices should be cooked immediately after they are removed from the freezer. If they thaw first, they will be a disappointment.

Those who know the Giant Puffball and its large relatives almost invariably rate them very high. If some individuals would employ trickery for a basketful of morels or chanterelles, others would lie, cheat, or steal to get their hands on a large, firm, fresh Giant Puffball. The delicate taste and texture are truly unique and wonderful.

Only two cooking techniques are recommended: The simple slice-and-sauté approach, and the batter-dip-first technique. In either case, go easy with the spices because the delicate flavor is easily overwhelmed. Also, puffballs should be cooked slowly over low heat; otherwise, they will dry out, produce a lot of smoke, and become somewhat bitter.

There are two primary competitors in the race for fresh, large puffballs: centipedes and tiny, wormlike larvae. The former often create fairly large tunnels at the base of the mushroom, but they can be ousted as easily as slugs. The latter, though, are frequent victors. They begin their invasion at the bottom and then work their way up. Consequently, they sometimes only ruin half of the puffball. Puffball devotees often find it necessary to carefully dissect each specimen and remove the infested areas. "It is," they smile and say, "worth the effort."

# GEM-STUDDED AND PEAR-SHAPED PUFFBALLS

*Lycoperdon perlatum*
*L. pyriforme*

**KEY IDENTIFYING CHARACTERISTICS**

1. White to tan mushroom without well-defined stalk or cap; no gills or pores present
2. Longitudinal section reveals white flesh throughout
3. Close inspection reveals no stalk or gills inside
4. Exterior surface covered with tiny, granular spines that rub off easily; *or* found clustered or grouped on wood
5. Outer skin not tough or leathery (easily cut with fingernail)

**DESCRIPTION:** The Gem-studded Puffball (*Lycoperdon perlatum*) is a white to pale tan, ball- to pear-shaped mushroom without a well-defined stalk or cap; its surface is coated with tiny, granular spines, most of which are easily rubbed off. It is 1–2½ inches wide and 1½–3½ inches high. Longitudinal section reveals pure white, undifferentiated flesh throughout. In age, the interior becomes greenish brown and powdery, and a "pore" opens on the top surface of the mushroom.

The Pear-shaped Puffball (*L. pyriforme*) is very similar, but it has a smoother surface and typically lacks the Gem-studded Puffball's exterior spines. It is usually slightly smaller than the Gem-studded Puffball, but in some areas, specimens are frequently gathered in autumn that are quite large—as much as five inches high. A longitudinal section will reveal a section of sterile flesh at the base, which is more spongy (less dense) than the upper flesh.

**FRUITING:** Both species fruit from middle or late summer through middle or late fall and are found throughout most of North America. The Gem-studded Puffball is found singly to grouped or scattered, rarely in clusters of two or three, on the ground. It usually occurs in woods but also appears in a variety of other habitats. The Pear-shaped Puffball almost always grows in groups or clusters of at least three specimens and is always found on wood or wood debris.

**SIMILAR SPECIES:** There are a number of closely related species of small puffballs that are difficult to distinguish from these two common ones. There have been only rare reports of adverse reactions to any of these, despite frequent consumption by avid mushroom enthusiasts. It is important to rule out white *Amanita* buttons, but this is easily accomplished if one adheres to all the key identifying characteristics listed above. Some species of false puffballs—such as the Pigskin Poison Puffball (*Scleroderma citrinum*), which is poisonous (see p. 164)—have white interior flesh when young; however, they can be ruled out by their leathery tough, rindlike skin.

The Gem-studded Puffball was previously classified as *L. gemmatum*; it is also referred to as the Devil's Snuffbox.

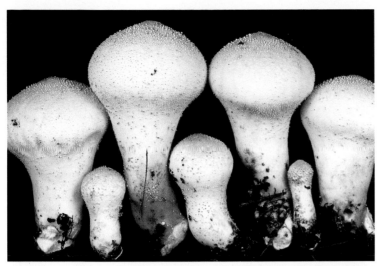

Gem-studded Puffball (*Lycoperdon perlatum*)

Pear-shaped Puffball (*Lycoperdon pyriforme*)

**EDIBILITY:** These common puffballs are every bit as delicious as their larger, more frequently collected cousins. The smallness of these two species and their equally delicious look-alikes requires that a sizable quantity be gathered for most culinary uses, but when they're fruiting in abundance, it's worth the time and effort to gather a basketful. As with all puffballs, these species should be eaten only when the interior is pure white.

These little puffballs' delicate flavor is best brought out by sautéing them slowly until slightly browned. Specimens should be cleaned, then sliced lengthwise. Although most puffballs taste quite the same, large specimens of the Pear-shaped and Gem-studded puffballs frequently have good-sized sterile (non–spore producing) bases; if cooked separately, these bases taste remarkably like morels.

# YELLOW, BLACK, AND HALF-FREE MORELS

*Morchella esculenta*
*M. elata*
*M. semilibera*

Yellow Morel (*Morchella esculenta*)

## KEY IDENTIFYING CHARACTERISTICS

1. Cap appears spongelike or honeycombed (distinct ridges surrounding pits)
2. Longitudinal section reveals single hollow chamber from base of stalk to top of cap
3. Longitudinal section of cap reveals no multichambered interior
4. Cap not draping from stalk as in *Verpa bohemica* (see photo on p. 166)

**DESCRIPTION:** The cap appears distinctly spongelike or honeycombed; its entire surface is composed of pits surrounded by ridges. The base of the cap is attached directly to the top of the stalk, except in the Half-free Morel (*Morchella semilibera*), whose cap's lower half drapes, like a skirt, below its point of attachment to the upper stalk. The ridges of morel caps range in color from white to almost black, but are most often yellowish brown to gray. Usually the inside of the pits are colored differently from the ridges. The pits of the Yellow (*M. esculenta*) and Half-free morels are usually dark, and the pits of the Black Morel (*M. elata*) are usually light. The stalk is textured with minute, granular ribs or bumps and ranges in color from white to yellow.

Slicing a morel open lengthwise reveals that the entire mushroom is hollow, with a single chamber extending from top to bottom. The inner surface of the morel is also textured with minute, granular bumps or ribs. The flesh of the stalk is quite thin, rarely more than one-fourth inch thick, except at the base of the stalk, which is sometimes thicker and multilayered, especially in large specimens.

The entire mushroom varies in height from three inches to one foot or more and in width from two to four or more inches. The proportional height of the cap, in relation to the stalk, is also quite variable. The Half-free Morel's cap usually makes up less than a fourth of the mushroom's overall height, while the other species' caps are usu-

This collection of Yellow Morels shows a wide range of colors, shapes, and sizes.

ally as tall as the stalks. In the case of the Black Morel, the stalk may make up only a small fraction of the mushroom's overall height.

The shape of the cap also varies tremendously. It may be cone shaped and rather pointed at the top, egg shaped, or nearly ball shaped. The stalk, cap, or both are frequently bent (this bending is caused by such obstacles as sticks that the growing mushroom meets).

As this description indicates, morels vary tremendously in size, shape, and color; however, they never vary from the four key identifying characteristics listed above. They are easily identified to the genus *Morchella*. The spore print, which is usually so slight that it's rather difficult to obtain, is white, cream, or pale yellow.

**FRUITING:** Morels are most often found in groups or scattered—but sometimes singly—in a variety of habitats. The Yellow and Black morels are found throughout much of North America, but the Half-free Morel is mostly limited to the eastern half of the continent and the Pacific Northwest. Morels fruit for a period of only four to six weeks in the springtime.

TB

David Fischer with Yellow Morels

Spring, of course, comes to different places at different times. In the Carolinas, the season's first morels appear as early as mid-March. In northern Canada and in mountainous areas at high elevations, they usually don't start fruiting until June. In most places, though, late April through late May is the core of morel season. In areas where morels are found in the greatest abundance—sections of Ohio, Indiana, the Michigan Peninsula, New England, Ontario and Quebec provinces, Northern California, and the Pacific Northwest are fortunate in this respect—foraging for morels is usually fruitless before mid-April.

On the other hand, some areas are practically devoid of morels. Dedicated mycophagists from Long Island, the Gulf Coast, the Great Plains states and much of Saskatchewan, the Southwest desert, and

Black Morel (*Morchella elata*)

other relatively morel-less areas have been known to travel some distance each May to vacation in morel territory.

Generally speaking, it seems that regions with a lot of snow, sandy or limey soils, frequent forest fires, old apple orchards, or lots of dead elm trees have the greatest abundance of morels.

Describing specific morel habitats is not difficult, but the list of characteristic habitats is long. Most species of mushrooms are found only in very specific habitats, but morels are more difficult to pin down. Morel habitats include forests with spruce, Douglas fir, maple and beech, black locust, cottonwood, tulip, or poplar trees; old apple orchards; areas that have been burned over the previous year; land around dead elm trees; and even lawns or old fields. This broad list might lead one to expect morels everywhere, but experience proves otherwise. With rare exceptions, morels are found only in the kinds of habitats listed above. But precisely where and when is another matter. Morels are, in truth, found only in one place: wherever they choose to appear.

Soil saturation, especially in early spring, seems to be an important factor in morel fruiting. Winters with high snowfall levels and springs with abundant rainfall apparently play an important role in strengthening the mycelium. This, in turn, seems to lead to banner morel years. Flood plains, stream banks that go underwater during early spring snowmelts, and the edges of swamp ridges are widely reported to be prime morel-picking spots. Even in upland areas, rounded gullies that are overrun by water during spring snowmelt and rains consistently produce a more abundant crop of morels than higher, drier ground.

It's important to note the difference between well rinsed and soggy ground, though; morels don't fruit *when* the ground is soaked but rather *after* the ground has been soaked.

Half-free Morel (*Morchella semilibera*)

**SIMILAR SPECIES:** The Wrinkled Thimble-cap, or Early Morel (*Verpa bohemica*), which is poisonous (see p. 165) is, at first glance, a dead-ringer for the true morel; however, its cap is not distinctly pitted or honeycombed like a true morel's cap. Rather, its cap surface is composed of vertically wrinkled ridges that only rarely are joined by horizontal ridges. Its cap drapes, but it is attached only at the very top of the stalk; the Half-free Morel's cap is attached about halfway down the cap. If a specimen's cap drapes significantly (some Black Morel caps drape, but only slightly) and seems to conform to the other key identifying characteristics, it must be either an edible Half-free Morel or a poisonous Wrinkled Thimble-cap. Several other differences can help distinguish between these two.

First, the Half-free Morel's stalk usually has vertical perforations near the base; the Wrinkled Thimble-cap's stalk lacks them. Second, the outside of the Half-free Morel's stalk is coated with tiny, granular particles that can be easily rubbed off; the Wrinkled Thimble-cap's stalk has tiny bumps that do not rub off readily. Third, the Half-free Morel's cap typically makes up less than one fourth of the mushroom's overall height; the cap of the Wrinkled Thimble-cap usually makes up at least one fourth of the mushroom's overall height. Also, the Half-free Morel's stalk is invariably hollow, and the Wrinkled Thimble-cap's stalk is normally stuffed with cottony fibers, but slugs often burrow into the mushroom and devour them, leaving no clue that the stalk was originally stuffed.

Poisonous mushrooms of the genus *Gyromitra* (see Conifer False Morel, p. 166) are commonly called "false" morels because at least to some novices they look similar. Upon close inspection, however, there is little similarity. The cap of a *Gyromitra* is slightly to grossly wrinkled and folded but not pitted or honeycombed. A longitudinal section of the cap reveals a multichambered interior, not the single, cylindrical, hollow chamber characteristic of a true morel.

At an autumn group foray in upstate New York, a woman produced a tiny wicker basket. "It's my morel basket," she said, joking but also lamenting. "I found exactly *one* morel this spring."

"I only did twice as well as you did," said another mycophile, "and I went out looking every weekend for two months!"

Everyone in the group whined longingly for the superior morel harvests of previous seasons. Eager to show off, I brought forth a snapshot of a dozen huge specimens. "Guess I had better luck," I boasted.

"This year?" asked one man, drooling.

"Yup, second week in June."

"Where did you find them?" he asked, quickly adding, "I mean, in this county?" He knew full well that there is no better kept secret than the location of a morel patch.

Kindly but cautiously, I gave a few details: about 1,300 feet elevation, mixed maple and beech woods.

I love teaching people about edible wild mushrooms—how to identify them, how to prepare them, even how to find them. But my morel patches are mine alone. I hide my car very carefully when I go morel hunting. I put other species in my basket and stuff the morels inside my jacket. When I spot one, before picking it, I look around like a shoplifter who's about to pocket a watch, making sure that no one is looking. I am very, very quiet.

And if you happen to bump into me as I leave the woods and ask if I have found any morels, the answer will be no. Not yet. Maybe next week.

And I'll show you the pictures later.

—DAVID FISCHER

In addition to the Yellow, Black, and Half-free morels, some mycologists apply a number of other names to some morels found in North America. There is little agreement between professional mycologists over which, if any, of these others are truly distinct species. This debate makes for interesting conversation, but it is of little culinary interest. All morels are eminently edible.

Among the species listed in some field guides are Peck's Morel (*M. angusticeps*), the Conical Morel (*M. conica*), *M. canaliculata*, and *M. crassistipa*. Many consider these to be only variant forms of the Black Morel. The White Morel (*M. deliciosa*) and the Thick-footed Morel (*M. crassipes*) are generally considered to be early and late forms, respectively, of the Yellow Morel.

EDIBILITY: Black Morels frequently cause gastric upset when consumed with or followed by alcoholic beverages, and some individuals have unpleasant reactions to Black Morels even without alcohol. No morels should be eaten raw, undercooked, or in large quantity; eating them so can cause digestive discomfort, also.

These precautions aside, the morel, in its myriad forms, is the clear favorite of most mushroom hunters. The morel reigns supreme among nature's fungal fruits, esteemed by gourmets on both sides of the Atlantic. During morel season, area mushroom clubs gather specifically to scour the woods and orchards for this king of edible mushrooms.

Recently, attempts to cultivate morels have started to pay off. With such tremendous demand for them, morels may be on their way toward large-scale, commercial cultivation. Some longtime morel devotees worry that this will somehow take away the morel's special mystique. Others, less romantic or more pragmatic, anxiously await such progress.

In regions where morels are abundant, it is not unusual to see Posted signs expressly forbidding mushroom picking. In areas not blessed with such abundance, patience and perseverance are essential to finding morels. The best foraging tactic is to look as often as possible in as many of the known types of habitat as possible during morel season.

When the searching pays off and you find your first morel, search around the immediate vicinity for more. Then, note as many specifics about where you found them as you can: What kinds of trees, plants, and soil are present? Is the ground sloping? If so, is it sloping to the east, west, north, or south? With these factors in mind, keep looking in similar habitats. This is the most likely way to fill your basket.

Once you're certain of your identification, cut off the base of the stalk. Then slice the whole morel in half vertically, and gently brush or blow away any insects, dirt, sand, or plant debris.

Morels usually grow in the same place for several years but may skip one or more years between fruitings. Look for them next year wherever you find them this year. If you don't find any there next year, check again the year after that.

If you try and try, but don't find any morels, there is another option—many gourmet shops stock dried morels. Be prepared for "sticker shock": one ounce of dried morels might cost you fifteen dollars or more. That's a rather steep price for something that's free when you can find it, but even the most experienced morel hunters have been known to splurge on a small jar when that's the only way to get some.

Jelly Tooth (*Pseudohydnum gelatinosum*)

## JELLY TOOTH AND APRICOT JELLY

*Pseudohydnum gelatinosum*
*Phlogiotis helvelloides*

### KEY IDENTIFYING CHARACTERISTICS

1. Gelatinous, tongue- to funnel-shaped mushroom, one to four inches long, one-half to three inches wide
2. Flesh translucent, white or gray to brownish; undersurface has tiny soft spines; *or* flesh apricot to rose; undersurface smooth to slightly wrinkled

**DESCRIPTION:** The Jelly Tooth (*Pseudohydnum gelatinosum*) is shoehorn to tongue shaped, with translucent, gelatinous, or rubbery white flesh. It is one to three inches long, including a narrow, lateral, stalklike appendage (sometimes absent); the widest part of the mushroom measures one-half to three inches across. The upper surface is smooth to minutely velvety, white to grayish or brownish; the undersurface is densely coated with tiny, soft, whitish spines.

Apricot Jelly (*Phlogiotis helvelloides*) is very similar in texture and size; however, it is pinkish orange to rose and usually rather funnel shaped but with a split side. It typically stands more erect than the Jelly Tooth and lacks a well-defined stalk. Its upper surface is smooth, and its lower surface is smooth to slightly wrinkled. It also tends to be slightly longer than the Jelly Tooth, standing up to four inches high. Both species produce white spore prints.

JS

Apricot Jelly (*Phlogiotis helvelloides*)

**FRUITING:** Both of these distinctive mushrooms are found throughout most of North America and are associated with coniferous wood. The Jelly Tooth always grows on decaying wood, and Apricot Jelly is more frequently found in moss on logs or on the ground. Both species usually fruit in groups, typically from summer through fall, but either may be found from late spring through midsummer if the weather is cool and rainy.

**SIMILAR SPECIES:** Neither of these mushrooms can reasonably be confused with any other species.

**EDIBILITY:** These beautiful, fascinating mushrooms have the same taste and texture. They are thoroughly bland, rather like firm, unflavored gelatin. Nonetheless, the creative gourmet can use these as a delightful culinary novelty. They can be eaten raw, but the gelatinous flesh will take on flavor if marinated, pickled, or candied. Culinary options are as unlimited as the chef's imagination, and these fungi will certainly be the talk of the table.

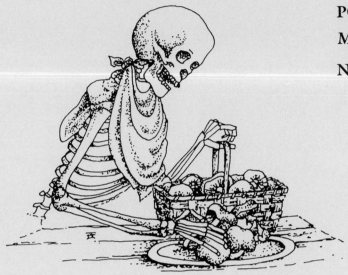

# PART THREE

# Mushroom Poisoning

More than five thousand species of mushrooms have been identified in North America. The edibility or toxicity of most of these is unknown. There is no simple or universal way to tell an edible mushroom from a poisonous one.

The frequency and severity of mushroom poisoning is often exaggerated. To many people, wild mushrooms have a dubious reputation at best. There are some valid reasons for this: poisonous mushrooms, including several of the dozen or so North American species known to be potentially deadly, are quite common. People who are interested in eating wild mushrooms should therefore familiarize themselves with the poisonous species as well as the edible ones. Mushrooms of the genus *Amanita,* in particular, should be avoided. They account for most fatal cases of mushroom poisoning. Before picking any gilled mushroom that you think may be edible, carefully examine the specimen to rule out the presence of a saclike cup, or volva, around the base of the stalk. The single exception to this is the edible Tree Volvariella (*Volvariella bombycina;* see p. 86); it has a volva, but it grows only on wood, has no partial veil, and no ring.

The key identifying characteristics used in this book are expressly designed to rule out all but the target species. Characteristics used to rule out those poisonous mushrooms that might be mistaken for the edible species are given special emphasis. These toxic mushrooms are illustrated and described here as well. Before eating an edible mushroom identified with the aid of this book, carefully examine the illustration and description of any poisonous species mentioned as a similar species.

In the authors' contacts with mycophagists at all levels of knowledge and experience, we have heard many frightful assumptions. Perhaps the most dangerous of these are old wives' tales that suggest that simple rules of thumb will distinguish edible mushrooms from poisonous ones. Among these is the silver coin myth that asserts that any poisonous mushroom will blacken a silver coin or spoon "cooked" along with the mushroom. Many poisonous mushrooms will not be ruled out by this test, but it will rule out some of the best and safest edible species. Another dangerous myth is that no brown mushrooms that grow on wood are poisonous. The Deadly Galerina and several other poisonous mushrooms are brown and grow only on wood. The only way to safely determine whether a wild mushroom is safe for the table is to identify the species and find out whether or not it is edible. There are no simple shortcuts. If there were, there would be no need for this book.

Three factors are responsible for most cases of serious mushroom poisoning. The first factor is explained above—trusting folk myths. The second factor is ignoring the danger of look-alike species. Too many people become vaguely familiar with the overall appearance of

Opposite page:
Jack O'Lantern Mushroom
(*Omphalotus illudens*)

an edible mushroom and then gather "it" for the table without recognizing key characteristics that distinguish it from poisonous species. The third factor, and perhaps the most dangerous one, is uneducated experimentation, the try-it-and-see approach to mycophagy. This, truly, is like playing Russian roulette.

Before discussing the various classes of mushroom toxins, it is important to point out that in some cases the appearance of poisoning symptoms can occur without the ingestion of a poisonous mushroom species. For example, if you identify a wild mushroom as edible, eat it, and then start doubting the accuracy of your identification, you may experience a panic reaction. Such a situation can provoke an elevated pulse rate, sweating, and an overall flushed feeling. However, if mushroom poisoning is suspected, *seek medical attention immediately*.

Follow the guidelines presented on p. 10, under the heading "Inedible Edibles: Yucky Bugs and Contaminants." Ingestion of agricultural sprays can produce severe gastrointestinal symptoms.

Take special care to avoid polluted areas and roadsides when you're picking wild mushrooms. Scientific research has produced evidence that mushrooms concentrate heavy metals present in rain, air, and soil as environmental contaminants.

Mushrooms that are safely eaten by most people but cause gastrointestinal upset or allergic reactions in a few should not be labeled as poisonous. Specific proteins and other organic chemicals present in some mushrooms can cause gastrointestinal irritation, itchy and watery eyes, or hives in susceptible individuals but don't cause any adverse reactions for most people. This is especially true in the case of mushrooms that are not cooked thoroughly. It is important when eating any mushroom—or, for that matter, any kind of food—for the first time to consume only a small portion and to note any unfavorable reaction. One friend of the authors enjoys a variety of edible wild mushrooms but gets very sick from eating any species of the genus *Agaricus,* even the *Agaricus* button mushroom typically sold in grocery stores.

Mushrooms, like many—or most—other foods, can also cause gastrointestinal upset if overeaten. Consumption of large amounts of butter or cooking oil is another known cause of gastrointestinal symptoms. In some instances sufferers mistakenly accuse the mushrooms when the fat was to blame.

When collecting for the table, only gather specimens that are fresh and in prime condition. Some people have been sickened by edible species that were decomposing because of insect larvae or bacteria or were otherwise spoiled.

### Mushroom Toxins

Most authorities presently recognize seven classes of mushroom poisoning based on the toxins involved and the type and onset of symptoms. A brief discussion of each class is presented here.

Amatoxins are cyclopeptides composed of a ring of amino acids that inhibit the production of specific proteins within liver and kidney cells. Without these proteins, cells cease to function. Following ingestion of a mushroom containing amatoxins, five to twenty-four hours (average, twelve hours) pass before nausea, vomiting, abdominal pain, and diarrhea begin. These initial symptoms are followed by a brief period of apparent improvement, but without treatment, severe liver damage and kidney failure often result in coma and death. Several North American mushroom species are known to contain amatoxins. The most common include: *Amanita phalloides*, *A. virosa*, *Galerina autumnalis*, *Lepiota helveola*, and *Conocybe filaris*.

At least one North American species of *Cortinarius*, *C. rainierensis*, contains another deadly toxin, orellanine. The effects are similar to those caused by amatoxins, but symptoms are delayed from three to fourteen days after ingestion.

**CLASS I:**
**AMATOXIN POISONING**

---

Monomethylhydrazine is a substance used as a propellant for rockets. It is produced when gyromitrin (present in some mushroom species) is gently heated. Monomethylhydrazine (MMH) interferes with normal utilization and function of vitamin $B_6$, thus affecting amino acid metabolism.

Following ingestion, seven to ten hours pass before the onset of nausea and vomiting. Victims typically feel bloated and experience abdominal pain and diarrhea. Deaths due to liver damage have been reported in severe cases. Several North American *Gyromitra* species, or false morels, are known to produce these symptoms. Some of the most common include *Gyromitra esculenta*, *G. californica*, *G. caroliniana*, *G. fastigiata*, *G. gigas*, and *G. infula*.

**CLASS II:**
**MONOMETHYLHYDRAZINE**
**POISONING**

---

Coprine poisoning occurs when mushrooms containing coprine, an amino acid, are consumed before, with, or after alcohol. When alcohol is consumed by humans, it is normally broken down by enzymes to acetaldehyde, then to vinegar, and finally to carbon dioxide. Coprine interferes with this process.

Following ingestion, there is a delay of thirty minutes to two hours before the onset of symptoms, including an increased pulse rate, flushing over the upper half of the body, headache, and rapid breathing. After fifteen to thirty minutes of these symptoms, the victim feels weak and dizzy and typically experiences nausea and vomiting.

It is important to note that coprine leaves the body primed for poisoning for several days (even a week by some reports) after eating the mushroom. Therefore, it is not only the consumption of a coprine-containing mushroom and an alcoholic drink *at the same time* that can cause coprine poisoning. Symptoms can also occur if someone drinks wine, for instance, two or more days after the meal or eats a coprine-containing mushroom after consuming alcohol. Mushrooms reported to cause coprine poisoning include *Coprinus atramentarius*, *C. variegatus*, and *Clitocybe clavipes*.

**CLASS III:**
**COPRINE POISONING**

| CLASS IV: MUSCARINE POISONING |
|---|

Muscarine, a chemical present in several mushroom species, affects that part of the nervous system that exerts control over glandular secretions and involuntary muscles. Following ingestion, a delay of fifteen to thirty minutes occurs before the onset of nausea, vomiting, and diarrhea. These symptoms are often accompanied by perspiration, salivation, and excessive secretion of tears. Mushrooms reported to cause muscarine poisoning include *Inocybe fastigiata, Boletus luridus, Clitocybe dealbata, Mycena pura, Omphalotus illudens,* and *O. olivascens.*

**CLASS V: IBOTENIC ACID-MUSCIMOL POISONING**

Ibotenic acid and muscimol are toxins found in several *Amanita* species that interfere with the normal metabolism of some amino acids, adversely affecting the central nervous system. Following ingestion, one-half to one and one-half hours pass before the onset of delirium, apparent inebriation, manic behavior, and a tendency to perceive small objects as very large. Some victims exhibit a desire for intense physical activity; most experience a deep sleep, usually with visions. Nausea and vomiting may also occur. Mushrooms reported to cause ibotenic acid–muscimol poisoning include *Amanita muscaria* and *A. pantherina.*

**CLASS VI: PSILOCYBIN-PSILOCIN POISONING**

Psilocybin and psilocin are alkaloids that interact with the brain, affecting nerve transmission and causing hallucinations. Following ingestion, fifteen to sixty minutes pass before the onset of anxiety, giddiness, hallucinations, perceived motion of stationary objects, impaired time and distance perception, and marked euphoria. Later effects include uncontrolled laughter, color images stimulated by sounds, and tingling sensations of the skin. After several hours, victims typically fall asleep, experience intense colorful dreams, and then awaken with general muscle weakness and fatigue. Mushrooms reported to cause psilocybin-psilocin poisoning include *Gymnopilus spectabilis, G. luteus, Panaeolus subbalteatus, Pluteus salicinus,* and many species of *Psilocybe.* Possession of these species is illegal.

**CLASS VII: GASTROINTESTINAL IRRITATION**

Many species of mushrooms contain chemicals—usually proteins—that irritate the gastrointestinal tract. Some mushrooms produce such adverse reactions only when eaten raw, some only when consumed in large quantities, and others regardless of how they are eaten.

Following ingestion and a delay of fifteen minutes to fourteen hours, nausea, vomiting, abdominal cramps, and diarrhea are typical. *Special note:* These symptoms can be severe enough to warrant hospitalization; in extreme cases, the illness can be life-threatening. If mushroom poisoning is suspected, *seek medical attention immediately.* A few of the common mushrooms known to contain gastrointestinal irritants are *Agaricus xanthodermus, Boletus satanas, B. sensibilis, B. subvelutipes, Chlorophyllum molybdites, Gomphus floccosus, Naematoloma fasciculare, Paxillus involutus, Russula emetica, Scleroderma citrinum,* and *Verpa bohemica.*

# 13.

## *Poisonous Wild Mushrooms*

# SCALY VASE CHANTERELLE

*Gomphus floccosus*

Scaly Vase Chanterelle (*Gomphus floccosus*)

**DESCRIPTION:** This funnel- or vase-shaped mushroom is two to seven inches tall and two to five inches wide at the top. The upper-inner surface is yellowish orange to orangish brown or red, depressed, and covered with coarse scales that are the same color. The outer-undersurface, which is continuous with the "stalk," is wrinkled or veined but smooth to the touch; it is creamy yellow to yellowish brown. The flesh is white. The spore print is brownish yellow.

**FRUITING:** This colorful mushroom is usually found singly or in groups, rarely in clusters of two or three specimens, on the ground in coniferous or mixed deciduous and coniferous woods. It fruits from early summer through midfall, and its range includes most of North America.

**SIMILAR SPECIES:** *G. kauffmanii* (suspected of being poisonous) is similar, but it is much larger, has coarser scales, and is tan to dull orangish brown. It is found in western North America.

**TOXICITY:** The Scaly Vase Chanterelle is collected and eaten by some mushroom hunters, but it should be avoided. It often causes abdominal pain, nausea, vomiting and diarrhea. These symptoms usually appear within four hours after consumption. This is a wonderful photographic subject, though. You'll be better off if you take only pictures and keep your specimens off the dining room table. Even some of those who do eat this species readily admit that it's frequently unpalatable.

# JACK O'LANTERN MUSHROOM

*Omphalotus illudens*

**DESCRIPTION:** The cap is two to seven inches wide, yellowish orange to orange, rounded to flat or sunken at the center. The cap flesh is yellow. The gills are yellowish orange, closely spaced, and sharp edged; they are attached to the stalk and descend it somewhat.

Jack O'Lantern Mushroom (*Omphalotus illudens*), showing cap color and gills

Jack O'Lantern Mushroom (*Omphalotus illudens*), showing fused stalks

The stalk is pale yellow to orange, two to eight inches long, and three-eighths to three-fourths inch thick, narrowing toward the base. The spore print is pale cream.

**FRUITING:** The Jack O'Lantern is found clustered on deciduous stumps and buried wood. It fruits from midsummer through late fall, but also through winter in California. It is found throughout much of eastern North America and also in California and Arizona.

**SIMILAR SPECIES:** The Western Jack O'Lantern (*O. olivascens*) is equally poisonous. It has a darker orange cap, which is often tinted olive green, and a white spore print. It is found from British Columbia to California. *O. illudens* is also known as *O. olearius* and *Clitocybe illudens*.

**TOXICITY:** This species causes gastrointestinal upset, including abdominal pain, nausea, vomiting, and diarrhea. Symptoms typically appear within four hours and may last for up to two days.

# DESTROYING ANGEL

*Amanita virosa*

Destroying Angel (*Amanita virosa*)

**DESCRIPTION:** The cap is white, two to five inches wide, rounded to flat; the cap surface is smooth and dry. The cap flesh is white. The gills are white and free from the stalk or barely attached to it. In young button specimens, the gills are covered by a membranous white veil. The stalk is white, smooth, solid, and fairly slender, 2½–7 inches tall and one-fourth to three-fourths inch thick. There is a membranous white volva around the base of the stalk, and mature specimens have a membranous white ring around the upper part of the stalk. Initially, the entire button is enclosed in a membranous white tissue called a universal veil. These buttons resemble small puffballs, but close examination of a longitudinal section will reveal the enclosed stalk, cap, and gills. The spore print is white.

**FRUITING:** Found under trees singly or in groups from early summer through midautumn throughout most of North America.

**SIMILAR SPECIES:** Several other white *Amanita* species, some of which are equally deadly, occur in North America. All share the characteristic volva and white spore print, and all should be avoided.

**TOXICITY:** The Destroying Angel, like several of its close relatives, contains amatoxins; it is fatally poisonous (see p. 145). Unlike some poisonous mushrooms, the Destroying Angel does not have an unpleasant odor or taste. Some who have been poisoned have even reported that it tastes quite good. This certainly refutes any misguided preconceptions that all poisonous mushrooms have an unpleasant odor, taste, or both.

Death Cap (*Amanita phalloides*)

# DEATH CAP
*Amanita phalloides*

**DESCRIPTION:** The cap surface is yellowish green to yellowish brown; it is smooth overall, but has tiny, dark, flattened hairs over the center. The cap is initially dome shaped, expanding until nearly flat; it is 2½–6 inches wide. The cap flesh is white and has a slightly disagreeable odor. The gills are white, rather closely spaced, free from the stalk or barely attached to it. The gills of young specimens are covered by a white, membranous partial veil. The stalk is white, two to five inches tall, and one-half to three-fourths inch thick; mature specimens have a white, membranous ring around the upper portion of the stalk. The stalk is enlarged downward, and quite bulbous at the base. The base of the stalk is enclosed by a white, membranous, saclike volva. Very young specimens are entirely enclosed by a membranous, white tissue called a universal veil. These buttons resemble small puffballs, but a longitudinal section will reveal the enclosed stalk, cap, and gills. The spore print is white.

**FRUITING:** The Death Cap is found singly or in groups, sometimes in great numbers, on the ground in woods. It fruits primarily in the fall, but frequently as late as January (especially in California). Its range is apparently spreading. A few decades ago, it was known only from California; it has since been found in Oregon and Washington, Ohio, Pennsylvania, New York, and other parts of eastern North America.

**SIMILAR SPECIES:** Several closely related Amanitas are colored differently; many are deadly, and all should be avoided. The most common one is the Destroying Angel (*A. virosa*), which is fatally poisonous (see preceding entry). All of these related species share the characteristic volva and white spore print. The button stage of the Death Cap and several other dangerous Amanitas somewhat resembles an edible puffball. The stern warning to section longitudinally all edible puffballs to make sure that no stalk, cap, or gills are present cannot be overemphasized.

**TOXICITY:** As its common name implies, the Death Cap is fatally poisonous. Since it could appear in areas where it has not yet been reported, everyone gathering mushrooms for the table should be aware of this and other mushrooms that contain amatoxins (see p. 145).

# FLY AGARIC

*Amanita muscaria*

Fly Agaric (*Amanita muscaria* var. *formosa*)

Fly Agaric (*Amanita muscaria* var. *muscaria*)

**DESCRIPTION:** The cap is two to ten inches wide, first dome shaped and then expanding until nearly flat; the cap surface is slightly sticky, yellowish orange to red or creamy white, with white wartlike patches. The cap flesh is white. The gills are white, closely spaced, and free from the stalk or barely attached to it; they are covered by a white, membranous partial veil in young specimens. The stalk is white, sometimes tinted pale yellowish; it is two to seven inches tall and ⅜–1⅛ inches thick, enlarging toward the base. In mature specimens, there is a white, membranous ring around the upper portion of the stalk. The stalk is surrounded at the base by two or three concentric bands of white, cottony tissue. The spore print is white.

**FRUITING:** The Fly Agaric is found throughout much of North America, fruiting on the ground in conifer or mixed woods. It generally appears in summer or fall but is also found in January and February in the southern United States.

**SIMILAR SPECIES:** There are several closely related species in North America. Most often recognized are two varieties: *A. muscaria* var. *muscaria*, with a decidedly red cap, and *A. muscaria* var. *formosa*, with a yellowish orange cap. All the related species are considered poisonous and should be avoided.

**TOXICITY:** This is the North American equivalent of the vision-inducing Fly Agaric of Siberia. Our varieties, however, are more poisonous than hallucinogenic. They typically cause delirium and profuse sweating, sometimes accompanied by violent muscle spasms instead of the psychedelic visions some experimenters expect. While there have been *some* reports that *some* North American specimens have induced altered depth perception and a craving for intense physical activity, typically followed by a very deep sleep (with or without visions), in others these effects were consistently accompanied by the universally undesirable ones. Nausea and vomiting are also a frequent part of this "magical" experience.

We strongly urge adventurous mushroom hunters who may be looking for a mood-altering fungal experience to try the Golden Chanterelle—with a nice white wine.

## YELLOW-FOOT AGARICUS

*Agaricus xanthodermus*

**DESCRIPTION:** The cap is two to seven inches wide, somewhat rounded when young but nearly flat at maturity. The cap surface is smooth and white to pale gray but quickly stains yellow when bruised. The gills are free from the stalk and closely spaced; they are initially white, turning pink and eventually dark brown. As in all species of *Agaricus*, the gills of young button specimens are covered by a white, membranous veil. The stalk is two to six inches tall and one-half to one inch thick; it is thickest near its base. The stalk is dingy white and rapidly stains yellow when cut, especially near the base. There is a white, membranous, often flaring ring on the stalk. The mushroom—the gills and cut flesh, especially—have an unpleasant, creosotelike odor. The spore print is dark chocolate brown.

**FRUITING:** This is a West Coast species, found from British Columbia to California; it fruits from fall through spring. It is typically found scattered or in groups on the ground, especially in urban areas and usually near trees. Closely related poisonous species of this genus may be found throughout North America.

DA            Yellow-foot Agaricus (*Agaricus xanthodermus*)

**SIMILAR SPECIES:** Several *Agaricus* species have an unpleasant, creosotelike odor and/or stain yellow when bruised. Many of these are poisonous and should be avoided. The notable exceptions are the edible Horse Mushroom (*A. arvensis;* see p. 38) and the edible Prince (*A. augustus;* see p. 40). Each of these has a yellow bruising reaction, but neither has an unpleasant odor.

**TOXICITY:** The Yellow-foot Agaricus is just one of the numerous poisonous species of this genus. Fortunately, each has an unpleasant odor, a yellow bruising reaction, or both. Avoid specimens with either or both of these characteristics, except for the Prince and the Horse mushrooms. Symptoms of poisoning by the Yellow-foot Agaricus and its close, toxic relatives include nausea, vomiting, and diarrhea, which typically commence within two hours after eating the culprit species.

# GREEN-SPORED LEPIOTA

*Chlorophyllum molybdites*

**DESCRIPTION:** The cap is two and one-half inches to one foot wide, first shaped somewhat like a partly opened parasol, then expanding until nearly flat; the cap surface is dry and white, with a pale brown center and scales. The cap flesh is white, bruising orange and then reddish brown. The gills are white in young specimens and then become green; they are closely spaced and free from the stalk. In young specimens, the gills are covered by a white, membranous partial veil. The stalk is white to dingy white, bruising reddish brown; it is four to ten inches tall and three-eighths to one inch thick, enlarging slightly toward the base. In mature specimens, there is a white, thick-edged, flaring membranous ring around the stalk. The spore print is pale green.

**FRUITING:** This species is found in many parts of North America, but it's most common in the southern United States. It appears

Green-spored Lepiota (*Chlorophyllum molybdites*)

mostly on lawns or grasslands but also in woodchips and along road-sides, usually fruiting in late summer or early fall. It is particularly frequent on lawns that are watered regularly.

**SIMILAR SPECIES:** This is a dead ringer look-alike for the edible Parasol Mushroom (*Lepiota procera;* see p. 43), especially in young specimens whose gills have not developed their tell-tale greenish coloration. Even in such cases, the Green-spored Lepiota can be distinguished by the bruising reaction of the cap flesh; the Parasol lacks this characteristic. Nonetheless, a spore print should always be made before consuming what you think is an edible *Lepiota.* Other poisonous species in the Lepiota family (some are deadly!) bear little resemblance to the Green-spored Lepiota, which is sometimes called *Lepiota morgani.*

**TOXICITY:** This is a dreadful sickener, frequently mistaken for the Parasol Mushroom in areas where both species occur. Symptoms usually begin within two hours after consumption. They include thirst, nausea, confusion, chills, sweating, abdominal pain, vomiting (often violent) and diarrhea (sometimes bloody). These symptoms have reportedly been suffered by people who ate only a "tiny morsel" of the mushroom. Sickness may last as long as forty-eight hours, sometimes requiring hospitalization to alleviate the symptoms.

# ALCOHOL INKY

*Coprinus atramentarius*

**DESCRIPTION:** Grayish to grayish brown, the entire mushroom stands two to six inches (or slightly more) in height. The cap is 1½–3 inches wide, first oval and then somewhat bell shaped, with or without a central knob, or umbo. The surface of the cap is slightly to distinctly pleated, especially at the edge of the cap, but smooth to the touch. The gills are very crowded and free from the stalk; they are

Alcohol Inky (*Coprinus atramentarius*)

white in young specimens, turning gray and then black as the mushroom matures. Finally, the gills dissolve into a thick, inky black fluid. A cross-section reveals that the interior flesh is pale grayish white. The stalk is white and hollow, 1¼–6 inches tall, and three-eighths to one inch thick; a ringlike zone of fibers can usually be seen on the stalk near the base. The spore print is inky black.

**FRUITING:** The Alcohol Inky is found throughout most of North America, usually in dense clusters, on grass, wood chips, near wood debris or buried wood, and around the bases of tree trunks. It fruits from midspring through early fall in most areas but from midfall through midspring on the Pacific Coast.

**SIMILAR SPECIES:** The Scaly Inky Cap (*C. variegatus*; see next entry) is similar in stature and should also be avoided; it has a distinctly scaly cap that is grayish brown overall, and it usually has an unpleasant odor.

**TOXICITY:** The Alcohol Inky is, technically, edible, and it is enjoyed by some people; however, it can cause coprine poisoning if alcoholic beverages are consumed soon before or within several days after eating the mushroom. For this reason, it should be carefully avoided by all but the strictest teetotalers, lest one should forget about this species' interesting but most unpleasant interaction with alcohol. The typical symptoms—marked flushing, rapid breathing, severe headache, nausea, and vomiting—usually commence within thirty minutes after consumption of alcohol or the mushroom itself.

# SCALY INKY CAP

*Coprinus variegatus*

**DESCRIPTION:** The entire mushroom is two to six inches (or slightly more) high; the cap itself is one to three inches wide, first egg and then bell shaped. It is grayish brown between coarse, white to dingy

Scaly Inky Cap (*Coprinus variegatus*)

yellow scales and patches that wash off easily. The gills are very crowded and free from the stalk; they are white in young specimens, graying and finally turning black before dissolving into a thick, inky black fluid. The stalk is white and hollow, two to six inches tall, and one-fourth to one-half inch thick; brown "threads" are usually evident at the base of the stalk. The mushroom usually has an unpleasant odor. The spore print is inky black.

**FRUITING:** This species of Inky Cap is found occasionally in groups, usually in clusters, on decaying deciduous wood, including buried wood—especially on or about stumps in lawns—throughout summer in northeastern North America. Its range extends west to Minnesota and south to the Carolinas.

**SIMILAR SPECIES:** The Alcohol Inky (*C. atramentarius;* see preceding entry) is similar in stature; it, too, should be avoided. It typically has a gray to grayish tan cap, and it lacks coarse scales; it doesn't have an unpleasant odor.

 *C. americanus* is suspect, though we have no reports of adverse reactions associated with it. It is nearly identical to the Scaly Inky Cap, but it has a silvery gray cap with whitish scales when young, darkening until the mushroom is mature. It has been found in the southeastern United States, and some mycologists classify it as *C. variegatus* var. *americanus*. The Scaly Inky Cap has previously been classified as *C. quadrifidus* and *C. ebulbosus*.

**TOXICITY:** The Scaly Inky Cap has been collected and eaten by some people, but it is best avoided. Like the Alcohol Inky, it may contain chemical compounds that inhibit the human body's metabolism of alcohol, causing—in *some* people—marked flushing, rapid breathing, severe headache, nausea, and vomiting. These symptoms can arise if alcoholic beverages are consumed soon before or within several days after eating the mushroom.

Additionally, some specimens of the Scaly Inky Cap, particularly those with a foul odor, have been known to cause gastric upset even without consumption of alcohol. In either case, symptoms typically appear from thirty minutes to one hour after consumption of alcohol or the mushroom itself.

# SWEATING MUSHROOM

*Clitocybe dealbata*

Sweating Mushroom (*Clitocybe dealbata*)

**DESCRIPTION:** The cap is white to gray when young; it is 1–2¼ inches wide, rounded to nearly flat, dry and smooth, with an incurved edge. Mature caps often develop pinkish tones; they usually have sunken centers, and the cap edge becomes wavy and upturned. The cap flesh is thin, whitish, and mild-tasting. The gills are closely spaced to crowded, attached to the stalk or partially descending it; they are white to pale gray. The stalk is white, smooth, and tough; it is often curved and is typically hollow in age. It is one to two inches tall and one-sixteenth to one-fourth inch thick, and either nearly equal in thickness overall or slightly enlarged near the base. The spore print is white to pale creamy white.

**FRUITING:** The Sweating Mushroom grows scattered or in groups on the ground in grassy areas. It is found throughout most of North America, fruiting during summer and fall.

**SIMILAR SPECIES:** The Crowded White Clitocybe (*C. dilatata*), which is poisonous, is a much larger, white mushroom with a wavy, often split edge. It grows in clusters on the ground in the Pacific Northwest.

The Fairy Ring Mushroom (*Marasmius oreades*), which is edible (see p. 50), has a light tan, slightly velvety cap and stalk; its gills are *barely* attached to the stalk. Also, the Fairy Ring Mushroom's stalk is exceedingly pliable. It can be bent or twisted a great deal without breaking; the Sweating Mushroom's stalk is tough but not pliable.

**TOXICITY:** The Sweating Mushroom causes muscarine poisoning. Symptoms begin about fifteen to thirty minutes after ingestion. They include nausea, vomiting, diarrhea, painful constriction of the muscles at the back of the mouth, painful urination, intense sweating, and profuse secretion of tears and saliva.

Sulphur Tuft (*Naematoloma fasciculare*)

## SULPHUR TUFT

*Naematoloma fasciculare*

**DESCRIPTION:** The cap is one to three inches wide, rounded in young specimens but nearly flat in mature ones. The cap surface is smooth and moist and greenish yellow to yellowish orange. The cap flesh is pale yellow, bruising brown; the taste is very bitter. The gills are greenish yellow to yellow in young specimens, maturing to purple-brown. They are closely spaced and attached to the stalk. In very young specimens, the gills are covered by a white to pale yellow, fibrous partial veil. The stalk is pale yellow to yellowish brown, two to four inches long, one-eighth to three-eighths inch thick, and not noticeably enlarged at the base. A ringlike zone of brown fibers (remnants of the partial veil) may be visible around the stalk near the top, especially in dry weather. The spore print is purple-brown.

**FRUITING:** The Sulphur Tuft is found in dense clusters on deciduous logs and stumps throughout much of North America, fruiting from spring through autumn.

**SIMILAR SPECIES:** The Smoky-gilled Naematoloma and the Brick Cap (*N. capnoides* and *N. sublateritium*), which are both edible (see p. 80), lack the Sulphur Tuft's distinctive (in immature specimens) gill color. The Brick Cap's red cap color makes confusion with its poisonous brother unlikely, but the Smoky-gilled Naematoloma could possibly be confused with the Sulphur Tuft, especially if one is uncertain of whether the substrate (log or stump) is from a coniferous or deciduous tree. However, the Sulphur Tuft will be ruled out by the key identifying characteristics listed for the Smoky-gilled Naematoloma.

**TOXICITY:** This is a decidedly poisonous species. Although fatalities from eating this mushroom have been reported in Europe and Japan, symptoms from ingestion of North American specimens are limited to nausea, vomiting, and abdominal pain. These symptoms are typically delayed until about nine hours after ingestion.

# DEADLY GALERINA

*Galerina autumnalis*

Deadly Galerina (*Galerina autumnalis*)

**DESCRIPTION:** The cap is 1–2½ inches wide, rounded at first but nearly flat in mature specimens. The cap surface is smooth, moist, and sticky; it is yellowish brown to chestnut brown. The cap flesh is pale brown. The gills are yellowish brown to rusty brown, darkening as the mushroom matures; they are closely spaced and attached to the stalk. In young specimens, the gills are covered by a white, thin, membranous partial veil. The stalk is one to four inches long and one-eighth to three-eighths inch thick; it is white near the top but brown on the lower portion. It is not noticeably enlarged toward the base. Mature specimens have a tiny, fibrous white ring on the upper portion of the stalk; this ring is often coated with rusty brown spores. The spore print is rusty brown.

**FRUITING:** This little brown mushroom, or "LBM," is common throughout much of North America; it is found singly or in groups on decaying logs and stumps (coniferous or deciduous). As its scientific name implies, it fruits primarily in the fall, but it can also be found in the spring or at other times under favorable weather conditions.

**SIMILAR SPECIES:** Many other closely related species of *Galerina*, some of which are equally deadly, occur in North America. All should be avoided. The Deadly Galerina was previously classified in the genus *Pholiota*.

**TOXICITY:** This innocent-looking mushroom is fatally poisonous. It is partly responsible for the mycophagist's maxim, "Stay away from LBMs." Like many species of *Galerina, Amanita,* and other genera, the Deadly Galerina contains amatoxins (see p. 145).

Some experienced mycologists have heard an old folk myth claiming that all brown mushrooms that grow on wood are safe edibles. Considering that the Deadly Galerina is invariably brown and grows only on wood, this serves to emphasize the danger of trusting folk wisdom when it comes to selecting wild mushrooms for the table.

# RED-MOUTH BOLETE

*Boletus subvelutipes*

Red-mouth Bolete (*Boletus subvelutipes*)

**DESCRIPTION:** The cap surface varies in color from brownish orange to orangish red or dull red, often a paler orangish yellow near the edge. The cap surface is smooth and dry but often minutely fibrous or velvety; it quickly tints dark blue where bruised. The cap is 2–5½ inches wide, well rounded in small specimens but usually nearly flat in larger ones. The undersurface of the cap bears small, round pores that meet or slightly descend the stalk; this pore surface is orange, orangish red, or dull red. The pore surface, like the cap, quickly turns dark blue where bruised. The stalk is one to four inches tall, three-eighths to three-fourths inch thick, and yellowish but with a varying degree of reddish tints; the base of the stalk is usually streaked with reddish, hairlike fibers. The stalk also quickly turns dark blue where bruised. The flesh is yellow, but—again— it quickly turns dark blue where bruised. The spore print is dark greenish brown.

**FRUITING:** This toxic species is found on the ground scattered or in groups in deciduous forests or mixed conifer and deciduous woods, displaying some preference for beech and hemlock. It appears from early summer through early fall; its range includes eastern North America from eastern Canada south to Virginia and west to Minnesota.

**SIMILAR SPECIES:** Many other *Boletus* species are orange to red on the undersurface of the cap, and/or stain blue (more or less) where bruised. Many of these are poisonous, so either of these characteristics—or *both*—should be viewed as a warning to anyone collecting boletes for the table. The scientific name *subvelutipes* means having a slightly velvety foot, a reference to the typical reddish hairlike fibers on the lower part of the stalk.

**TOXICITY:** The Red-mouth Bolete is just one of many poisonous boletes that have orange to red pore surfaces and/or a blue staining reaction when bruised. Symptoms of toxic bolete poisoning, which may be delayed by as much as four hours or more after consumption, include abdominal pain, nausea, vomiting, and diarrhea. These symptoms can be quite painful.

Boletes are a fairly safe group of mushrooms, as long as the mushroom hunter avoids the "red flags": orange or red pore surfaces under the cap and/or a blue bruising reaction. Some species that exhibit neither of these characteristics may be bitter or otherwise unpalatable, but none are known to be poisonous.

# BRICK-CAP BOLETE

*Boletus sensibilis*

Brick-cap Bolete (*Boletus sensibilis*)

**DESCRIPTION:** The cap is two to eight inches wide; it is dome shaped and dark brick-red to pale brick-red when young, becoming nearly flat and fading to pale rose or dull reddish brown in age. The cap surface is dry, dull, and smooth to minutely velvety. The cap flesh is pale yellow and stains blue instantly when cut. The pore surface is bright yellow, instantly staining blue and then slowly staining reddish brown where bruised. The pores are tiny and round; the pore surface is attached to the stalk. The stalk is bright yellow, usually with dull red streaks on the lower half; it is three to six inches high and ½–1½ inches thick, often somewhat thicker at the base. A very fine pattern of netlike ridges may be present near the top of the stalk, though these are often difficult to see. The spore print is greenish brown.

**FRUITING:** The Brick-cap Bolete is found scattered or in groups on the ground under mixed deciduous trees, especially beech, maple, and oak. It fruits during summer and fall and is widely distributed in eastern North America.

**SIMILAR SPECIES:** The Two-colored Bolete (*B. bicolor*), which is edible (see p. 98), has a rose-red cap and a yellow stalk with red tints on the lower portion. It has a yellow pore surface that bruises blue *slowly*, not immediately.

**TOXICITY:** The Brick-cap Bolete is reportedly poisonous. The symptoms may not begin until four hours or more after the meal. The typical symptoms—abdominal pain, nausea, vomiting, and diarrhea—can be very painful.

Bitter Bolete (*Tylopilus felleus*)

## BITTER BOLETE

*Tylopilus felleus*

**DESCRIPTION:** The cap surface is light to dark brown and nearly smooth but fairly sticky when wet. The cap is two inches to one foot wide and somewhat dome shaped or rounded, especially in small specimens. The undersurface of the cap bears small pores that meet the stalk, though in mature specimens they are sunken into the cap up and away from the stalk. The pore surface is white in young specimens and gradually turns pinkish as the mushroom matures; it slowly turns brownish where bruised. The stalk is one to four inches tall, ⅜–1¼ inches thick, usually thicker near the base; it is pale brown, with darker, netlike ridges usually covering most of the stalk surface. The flesh is soft and white, slowly staining light pink where bruised. The flesh has a distinctly bitter taste. The spore print is pink to pinkish brown.

**FRUITING:** This species is typically found scattered on the ground in woods—deciduous, coniferous, or mixed. It has a long season— early summer through midfall—in its range, which includes much of the eastern half of the continent, extending west to Missouri and Michigan; it has also been found in Arizona.

**SIMILAR SPECIES:** Other bitter *Tylopilus* species are very similar in appearance. The Bitter Bolete has been called a dead ringer for the prized edible King Bolete (*Boletus edulis;* see p. 95). Considering that young specimens of this bitter species have white pore surfaces like the King, the easiest way to distinguish between the two (other than taste) is to note that the Bitter Bolete has dark netlike ridges on most of its stalk, whereas the King Bolete has white netlike ridges on the upper portion of the stalk.

**TOXICITY:** The Bitter Bolete is not toxic. We have included it in this section because its taste is so unpleasant and we wanted to warn the reader who has found some boletes. Even while cooking, it smells terrific, but one taste of the Bitter Bolete would not only disappoint but perhaps depress the novice mushroom hunter. Not all individuals are sensitive to bitter tastes; some mushroom hunters with this genetic peculiarity have apparently eaten and enjoyed this species, and none reportedly has become ill as a result.

## PIGSKIN POISON PUFFBALL

*Scleroderma citrinum*

**DESCRIPTION:** This mushroom closely resembles a true puffball: it is nearly round (somewhat so overall, but especially when viewed from above); one to three inches wide; and one-half to two inches high; yellowish brown; and completely covered with small, dark brown, slightly raised "warts." The outer "skin" is fairly thick, tough, and rubbery; it is not easily broken except in overripe specimens with powdery interiors. The smallest young specimens have white flesh; maturing specimens have purplish black interior flesh with white marbling, which finally becomes grayish black and powdery when the mushroom is fully mature. At maturity, the outer rindlike skin develops a pore on top through which spores are released. The stalk, when a discernible one is present, is very short and thick, whitish to yellowish brown, and irregularly folded.

**FRUITING:** This common "earthball" is found on the ground or on well-decayed wood in a variety of wooded areas throughout much of North America. It usually grows in groups or singly but sometimes in clusters. It fruits from midsummer through midfall. *Special note:* Sometimes the Pigskin Poison Puffball is parasitized by an unusual

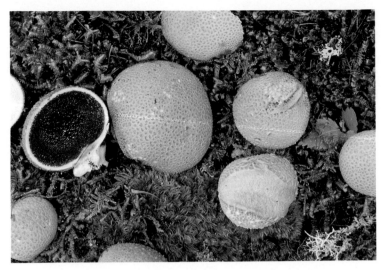

Pigskin Poison Puffball (*Scleroderma citrinum*)

species of bolete, *Boletus parasiticus*. This strange bolete species, whose only known host is the Pigskin Poison Puffball, is reportedly edible, but there is not yet sufficient information to recommend trying it.

**SIMILAR SPECIES:** Several other species of *Scleroderma* with a thick, rubbery skin are known; many are reportedly poisonous. Avoid any "puffball" with a thick rubbery skin. The Pigskin Poison Puffball is sometimes classified as *S. aurantium*.

**TOXICITY:** Although thin, cooked slices of *S. citrinum* are sometimes used as false truffles in Europe, this species cannot be recommended for the table. Signs and symptoms, which typically include abdominal pain, nausea, vomiting, and diarrhea, may occur within four hours after consuming the mushroom.

# WRINKLED THIMBLE-CAP

*Verpa bohemica*

**DESCRIPTION:** The cap is yellowish brown and bell shaped, ¾–1½ inches high and ½–1¼ inches wide, and coarsely wrinkled, draping from its point of attachment at the top of the stalk. The stalk is two to five inches tall and ½–1½ inches wide, not noticeably tapered; it is white to pale yellow, with a smooth to slightly roughened surface. A longitudinal section reveals that the stalk is either hollow or stuffed with soft, cottony tissue.

**FRUITING:** The Wrinkled Thimble-cap grows on the ground in hardwoods and mixed woods singly or scattered during spring. Specimens of *Verpa* are particularly easy to overlook, because they are often covered by leaves. This species is found in many parts of North America, but it is most common in the northern part of the continent.

**SIMILAR SPECIES:** The Smooth Thimble-cap (*V. conica*), which is suspected of being toxic, is much smaller and has a smooth or only

Wrinkled Thimble-cap (*Verpa bohemica*)

slightly wrinkled cap surface. The cap of the Half-free Morel (*Morchella semilibera*), which is edible (see p. 134), like the caps of all true morels, has distinct ridges surrounding pits; the *Verpa* mushrooms do not. The Wrinkled Thimble-cap is sometimes classified as *Ptychoverpa bohemica*.

**TOXICITY:** Some people, calling this species the Early Morel, have gathered and eaten it for years without apparent adverse effects; however, it is now regarded as poisonous—at least for *some* people—especially if it is consumed in quantity. Symptoms include gastrointestinal upset and lack of muscular coordination. We cannot recommend any mushrooms of this genus for the table; they are better regarded as a sure sign that the season for true morels is not far behind.

# CONIFER FALSE MOREL

*Gyromitra esculenta*

**DESCRIPTION:** The cap is reddish brown, so wrinkled and folded that it appears brainlike; it's two to four inches wide, 1½–3½ inches tall, and fairly brittle. In longitudinal section, the cap interior is typically multichambered. The stalk is dull white to pale yellowish brown, one to four inches tall and ½–1½ inches wide, with a smooth to slightly roughened outer surface. The stalk is usually somewhat enlarged near the base, and is hollow, usually with a single chamber but sometimes with multiple chambers.

**FRUITING:** The Conifer False Morel is found on the ground under conifer trees singly or in groups from midspring through early summer. It occurs mostly across northern North America but may be found elsewhere, especially in mountainous areas.

**SIMILAR SPECIES:** Several other species of the genus *Gyromitra* are found in North America; they differ a little in color and require microscopic examination for accurate identification. All species of this

OM

Conifer False Morel (*Gyromitra esculenta*)

genus should be avoided for the table. This and other *Gyromitra* species are sometimes classified as members of the genus *Helvella*. The Conifer False Morel is also commonly called the Brain Mushroom.

**TOXICITY:** This is a potentially deadly mushroom, even though the scientific name *esculenta* means "edible." Symptoms of *Gyromitra* poisoning include abdominal pain, nausea and vomiting, bloody diarrhea, and muscle cramps; fatalities have been reported in some cases.

Some longtime mushroom hunters collect and eat this and other *Gyromitra* species, insisting that either drying or a process of repeated boiling and rinsing will remove all toxins. There is no good evidence to support this view, and there are reported cases in which the person doing the boiling became ill. Regardless, these false morels are also known to contain carcinogens that cause tumors in animals. We advise all mycophagists to steer clear of *Gyromitra* species when gathering mushrooms for the table.

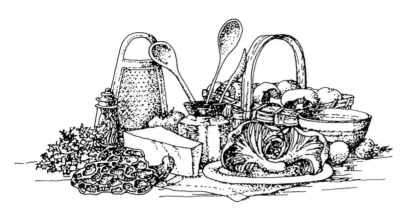

# PART FOUR

# WILD MUSHROOMS
# IN THE KITCHEN

# 14

# Preparing, Preserving, and Cooking Wild Mushrooms

There are edible species in almost every family of mushrooms. The edible species covered by this book are fairly representative of the overall variety of mushrooms found in North America. They range from morels, a type of "cup" fungus (scientifically classified as *Pezizales*) to the more familiar gilled mushrooms (agarics). Perhaps when you first glanced at the color plates in this book, you were surprised to see such diversity of form. It is this very diversity that requires a section such as this. Appropriate ways to clean, preserve, and cook mushrooms are almost as varied as the mushrooms themselves. For example, recipes that work wonderfully well for morels are quite inappropriate for puffballs.

Wild mushrooms provide the gourmet with marvelous opportunities for culinary experimentation; this is part of the joy of eating wild mushrooms. The culinary principles outlined in this chapter will help you make the most of each kind of edible mushroom you find. Additional preparation methods are suggested under "Edibility" in each entry for specific kinds of edible mushrooms.

## Preparing Wild Mushrooms: Basic Culinary Principles

### CHANTERELLES

Among the world's most highly prized gourmet fungi, true chanterelles (*Cantharellus* species) are fairly thin fleshed and contain less water than most other kinds of mushrooms. They also tend to be quite rich in flavor, so a little goes a long way.

Chanterelles can be used fresh, of course, and often require little cleaning. Many gourmets insist that chanterelles, like morels, are even more delicious when they've been dried and reconstituted before cooking. Chanterelles can also be frozen, either fresh or partially cooked. They are also attractive mushrooms, adding a visual elegance to any meal.

The Black Trumpet, Horn of Plenty, and Fragrant Black Trumpet are rich, aromatic mushrooms. They can be used like the true chanterelles; however, a more popular use is as a garnish. Dry them, and then crush or pulverize them. Sprinkle liberally on meats or fish, or in soups, sauces, or gravies. The Fragrant and Clustered Blue Chanterelles can be cooked or preserved in the same manner as the *Cantharellus* species. The Lobster Mushroom has a very firm texture, and is best prepared like a gilled mushroom.

### GILLED MUSHROOMS

Most gilled mushrooms, or agarics, are fleshy with a high water content. Any recipe that calls for the commercially cultivated button mushroom can be used with practically any wild edible gilled mush-

Arleen Rainis Bessette with fresh and dried mushrooms.

room with superior results. This is true for stuffed mushroom caps, casseroles, soups, sauces, gravies, and most other dishes.

Some agarics are not as rich in flavor as others; for such species, avoid using recipes that call for other richly flavored ingredients, for example, strong cheeses or Italian spices. The flavor of mild-tasting agarics can also be enhanced by concentrating the stock. Chop some mushrooms into small pieces, and add a splash of water. Bring the mixture to a boil, and then simmer it in a covered pot for twenty minutes. Next, remove the pot from the stove; let it cool to a moderate temperature; and then strain, pressing the mushroom pieces to get as much of the liquid as possible.

Finally, put the liquid back on the stove over medium heat in an uncovered pot. When half of the liquid has evaporated, you will have doubled the strength of the stock. Either use the stock to reconstitute some dried mushrooms, or simply use it as a base for gravies, sauces, or soups.

If you gather a large quantity of edible agarics, you can preserve enough to last right through winter. Freezing, canning, pickling, and drying are options, depending on the kind of mushroom.

## BOLETES

The King Bolete and its court are quite rich in flavor and not quite so moist as most gilled mushrooms. With this in mind, you can preserve or cook the boletes in the same way as the agarics. Grilling bolete caps is a particularly popular method of cooking them; drying is the most frequently used method of preserving a sizable collection.

For the Slippery Jack and other members of the *Suillus* genus, you should remove the cap cuticle (skin) as well as the spongy layer of tubes beneath the cap. The slimy cuticles cause diarrhea in some people.

## TOOTH MUSHROOMS

The Sweet Tooth and its allies are fleshy mushrooms, very similar to agarics except for the spines, rather than gills, beneath the caps. They can be preserved or prepared in the same manner as gilled mushrooms. The Comb Tooth and other members of the *Hericium* genus, on the other hand, are quite unlike any other mushrooms. For information on cooking and preparing these delicious edibles, we refer you to their specific entries.

## CORAL-SHAPED, CLUB-SHAPED, AND CAULIFLOWER-SHAPED MUSHROOMS

The Crown-tipped Coral Mushroom is best cooked when fresh; drying is the best way to preserve it. (More culinary information is presented at its entry.) The Flat-topped Coral Mushroom, when found in sufficient quantity, can be preserved by canning or pickling. Its substance is fairly fleshy, so recipes that call for agarics or boletes are appropriate.

The Cauliflower mushrooms, the Hen of the Woods, and the Umbrella and Black-staining polypores are all fairly large; one specimen is often more than even a large family can consume at a sitting. They are fairly similar in texture, so a recipe that calls for one of these species will work equally well with the others. If you have enough to preserve some, canning or pickling are preferred, unless you have plenty of freezer space. In all cases, cleaning can be most easily accomplished if you first cut off the base of the mushroom. The Hen of the Woods and the Umbrella and Black-staining polypores sometimes have sticks or other plant debris embedded within their flesh. Clean them carefully to prevent dental injury.

## SHELFLIKE MUSHROOMS, PUFFBALLS, MORELS, AND JELLY FUNGI

Dryad's Saddle is generally too tough to eat whole. Slice off the tender edges of the caps and discard the rest. If you're lucky enough to find a very young, fresh specimen, all but the portion closest to the stalk may be tender enough to be cooked. Dryad's Saddle may also be simmered in water for a long time, the mushroom discarded, and the stock used for soups, sauces, or gravies. This species is also large and common enough that a great quantity can often be collected; in such cases, canning or pickling are recommended.

Like Dryad's Saddle, the Sulphur Shelf has cap edges that are usually far more tender than the part nearest attachment to the log or stump. The Beefsteak Mushroom, on the other hand, is usually tender throughout. Both it and the Sulphur Shelf can be frozen fresh with little loss of quality or, like Dryad's Saddle, they can, in large collections, be canned or pickled. Drying also works fairly well.

All edible puffballs are best cooked when very fresh (or frozen fresh). Slice puffballs with a bread knife, and fry them over low heat. All species of puffballs tend to produce quite a bit of smoke as they cook, especially if the heat is too high. Use the exhaust fan on your range hood, or you're likely to set off the kitchen smoke detector. Raw or partially cooked slices can be frozen for later use if you have more than you can eat within a few days.

Morels are prized mushrooms that deserve special treatment indeed. Most gourmets agree that drying them actually improves their flavor, but few mushroom hunters can wait that long unless they've really gathered a basketful. Pickling is not recommended for these favorites. If you're blessed with enough morels to save some for later, freeze them, can them, or dry them. Morels should be raw and dry before you freeze them; wet ones become mushy when cooked. Their hollow interiors make them natural choices for stuffing. Use mildly flavored ingredients to set off the distinctive morel flavor without risk of overwhelming it.

Apricot Jelly and its pallid cousin, the Jelly Tooth, must be flavored by pickling, marinating, or other methods. They can even be candied—fungi for dessert, anyone?

## When the Basket Overflows: Preserving Wild Mushrooms

Most mushroom hunters soon find themselves with more mushrooms than they can eat right away. It then becomes necessary to find appropriate ways to preserve the haul for later use. There are five basic ways to preserve mushrooms: refrigeration, freezing, canning, pickling, and drying. Each of these techniques has its own advantages and disadvantages; also, techniques suitable for some kinds of mushrooms may be quite unsatisfactory for others.

### REFRIGERATION

Refrigeration is the best method for preserving all kinds of mushrooms: it doesn't damage their flavor or texture, and it is certainly simple. The obvious disadvantage is that refrigeration is strictly a short-term option. Most mushrooms can be refrigerated for about a week; a few, such as puffballs, should be used within a few days, and Inky Caps cannot be kept in the refrigerator.

It is important to clean the mushrooms before refrigerating them. Insect larvae that have invaded part of a mushroom will continue their feast even in the cooler. Many successful mushroom hunters have been heartbroken to discover that the basketful of firm, fresh edibles they put in the refrigerator only a few days earlier has become a mushy mess of larvae-ridden mushrooms unfit for consumption. Eliminating any infested parts first will prevent this unpleasant scenario.

Blot the cleaned mushrooms dry, if necessary, and place them in a rigid, airtight container. If they are quite moist, let them air dry for a day or two. Placing them in the refrigerator on a paper towel, uncovered, is the easiest way to do this. Don't store them in plastic bags, and don't let them soak in excess water; these practices, too, will lead to rapid deterioration.

### FREEZING

Some kinds of mushrooms can be frozen fresh with little or no loss of quality; others should be cooked or blanched first. Some experienced mycophagists prefer to rinse fresh mushrooms in cold water with a dash of lemon juice before freezing them. After blotting the mushrooms dry, arrange them on a cookie sheet so that they're not touching each other, and then place the cookie sheet in the freezer. Once they're thoroughly frozen, quickly transfer the mushrooms to a freezer container—airtight plastic bags are OK now—and return them to the freezer. Mushrooms frozen in this manner will usually remain in good condition for two months or so. Do not use this technique with Inky Caps.

Blanching the mushrooms will lengthen their freezer life a bit. Parboil the chopped or sliced mushrooms for three minutes in water to which a dash of lemon juice has been added. Let the pan cool and then remove the mushrooms, transfer them to an appropriate container, and freeze them. Blanched mushrooms can be kept in the freezer for four or five months before use.

For long-term freezing, the mushrooms should be cooked in a covered pan for a few minutes. Add water, if necessary, to completely cover the mushrooms before placing them in the freezer. Partially cooked mushrooms frozen in liquid will retain their integrity for up to a year.

Regardless of which technique you use to freeze mushrooms, do not thaw them before use; if you do, the mushrooms will become rubbery.

## CANNING

Canning is a very popular method for preserving mushrooms. Although the technique has its critics, canning does preserve mushrooms' flavor and texture fairly well—and for a long time—and the process is fairly easy. The greatest drawback to this technique is the danger of botulism; however, if it is done properly, canning is a safe and practical way to keep wild mushrooms on hand for use when foraging is not an option. Use of a pressure canner is strongly recommended.

## PICKLING

Some people consider pickling to be an excellent way to preserve mushrooms. The process retains flavor and texture, and pickled mushrooms can be kept on hand for a long time without fear of spoilage. Others complain that the characteristic pickled taste doesn't do justice to the flavor of wild mushrooms. In any case, the following method may be used for pickling any edible mushrooms.

Place the cleaned mushrooms in a saucepan, and cover them with water. Add one-fourth cup lemon juice, bring to a boil, reduce heat, and let simmer for five to ten minutes. Drain the mushrooms, discarding the liquid. To prepare the pickling mixture, combine one-half cup olive oil, two teaspoons salt, one teaspoon dried dill weed or basil, one-eighth teaspoon pepper, three cloves crushed garlic, one teaspoon dried oregano, one-half teaspoon mace, and one cup distilled white vinegar. Bring the mixture to a boil, and then place it and the mushrooms in a jar. They will be pickled in two hours. Store them in the refrigerator.

## DRYING

Drying is the world's oldest method for preserving mushrooms and other kinds of food, and it's still as popular among mushroom buffs as it is among squirrels (yes, squirrels put away more than nuts for winter!). The biggest drawback is that most kinds of mushrooms are rather tough and chewy after they've been reconstituted. But for morels, boletes, small species of chanterelles, Graylings, Fairy Ring Mushrooms, and a few other mushrooms whose textures aren't damaged by drying, the technique has two wonderful advantages. First, it's very easy; second, it concentrates the flavor a great deal. Some experienced mycophagists dehydrate a very wide variety of mushrooms. After reconstituting them, they squeeze out the rich extract for use in sauces and such, and discard the mushrooms. Some interesting and delightful culinary treats can be created by reconstituting one kind of dried mushroom in the extract derived from another.

Drying mushrooms is really simple. A food dehydrator is a wonderful tool, especially when you have a lot of mushrooms that you want to save. Either buy a commercial unit or make one yourself, using screens as racks and light bulbs as a convection current heat source. More information on food dehydrators is available through kitchen specialty stores, restaurant suppliers, advertisements in culinary magazines, or local mushroom clubs.

There are also several simpler ways to dry mushrooms. First, cut or slice them into pieces that are no more than an inch thick. Then, you may string them with a heavy-duty sewing needle and thread or spread them out on a screen or paper bag. Place them in direct sunlight or, if the chilly weather of autumn has come, over a heat register. Yet another option is to dry them in a gas oven with only the pilot light on. For some of the daintier species, drying is as easy as leaving them lying around on an unused table and ignoring them for a week or so until the moisture has completely evaporated.

Once the mushrooms are completely dry and crisp—this may take anywhere from one day to a week—they should be stored in clean, dry, airtight containers to keep all moisture out. If they're not thoroughly dried, they may become moldy; storing the dried mushrooms in a freezer will help prevent this. Properly dried and stored mushrooms can be kept for several years.

When you're ready to use the dried mushrooms, reconstitute them by soaking them in warm water for about fifteen minutes, by steaming them briefly, or by simmering them for a few minutes in a covered pan with just a splash of water. Spraying the dried mushrooms with a mist-nozzle spray bottle of the sort used for houseplants is quite effective for morels and small species of chanterelles.

As an alternative to reconstituting mushrooms only in water, we suggest the following: In a pan, cover three ounces of dried mushrooms with cold water. Add one and one-half tablespoons soy sauce, two teaspoons honey, and one crushed clove of garlic. Bring it to a boil, and then reduce the heat and simmer until the mushrooms are tender.

If your recipe calls for wine or cream, you can reconstitute the dried mushrooms in one of these. If you want to use the mushrooms in a soup or sauce, reconstituting them beforehand is unnecessary.

### Cooking Wild Mushrooms

There are many ways to cook mushrooms, and many books on mushroom cookery have been published. Mushrooms can be chilled and added to salads; served with meats; used in soups, stews, sauces or gravies; or even added to cookies. Mushrooms with particularly spicy or strong flavors are often dried and pulverized for use as condiments. Before trying a kind of wild mushroom unfamiliar to you in an expensive or complicated recipe, sample a small amount of the mushroom first. Remember that not everyone likes every kind of mushroom, and not everyone agrees on which mushrooms best complement various foods and wines.

The simplest way to enjoy mushrooms is to sauté them with a bit of butter or margarine. The sliced or chopped mushrooms should be simmered for ten to fifteen minutes until thoroughly cooked but still tender. Remove excess water from the pan to prevent the mushrooms from becoming soggy, but be careful not to let them dry out. As a rule, one should be careful not to overcook mushrooms, because this tends to make many kinds dry or chewy and may ruin their flavor. For some species, though, browning the mushrooms slightly brings out their richest natural flavors.

Baking or broiling is a fine option for many kinds of mushrooms, especially those with large caps. This allows the mushrooms to cook in their own juices, accenting their woodsy flavors. Mushroom sauces are also very popular. Once you know what a given kind of edible mushroom tastes like, decide for yourself whether to try a white wine sauce, a cream sauce, or whatever else appeals to your palate.

For those who enjoy preparing dishes using tried-and-true recipes, we present a variety for you to try. Some of these recipes call for specific kinds of mushrooms, but others simply call for wild mushrooms. Don't hesitate to experiment. No other kind of food is so ideal for culinary creativity as wild mushrooms.

Many of the recipes presented can be converted to strictly vegetarian dishes by substituting vegetable broth or stock for meat broth or stock. Wild mushrooms can also, of course, be substituted in recipes that call for commercially cultivated button mushrooms that are sold in the grocery store, and they will usually yield superior results.

Following pages:
Dryad's Saddle (*Polyporus squamosus*)

# 15.
## *Wild Mushroom Recipes*

*Cantharellus cibarius*

# Cornish Game Hens with Chanterelle Stuffing and Apricot Glaze
ARLEEN RAINIS BESSETTE

½ cup minced onion
¼ cup diced celery
3 cups chopped Golden
    Chanterelles
2 tablespoons plus 1 teaspoon
    butter
¼ teaspoon salt
Dash cinnamon
⅛ teaspoon pepper
¼ scant cup dry white wine
½ cup fresh whole wheat bread
    crumbs (1½ slices)
¼ cup chopped fresh parsley
2 Cornish hens (about 1¼
    pounds each)
1 cup apricot preserves
1 tablespoon brandy
1 tablespoon Triple Sec liqueur
¼ cup honey

Preheat oven to 400°F.

Sauté onions and celery in 2 tablespoons butter until tender. Add Chanterelles and sauté over medium-high heat 3 minutes more. Add salt, cinnamon, pepper, and wine. Cook, stirring constantly, for 2 minutes. Stir in bread crumbs and parsley; remove from heat.

Stuff each hen with about ¾ cup stuffing. Truss and place on rack in shallow pan. Rub each hen with ½ teaspoon butter. Bake at 400°F for about 50 minutes, basting once or twice. Combine preserves, brandy, liqueur, and honey in small bowl; pour over hens. Return to oven for 10 minutes.

Serves 4.

# Curried Cinnabar-red Chanterelle Filo   THERESA REY   *Cantharellus cinnabarinus*

Preheat oven to 350°F.

Melt ½ cup butter. Add mushrooms, onions, and apricots; cook until all liquid is absorbed. Add garam masala (you may add more, to taste) and set aside.

Melt remaining ½ cup butter. Lay a sheet of filo dough in a 9 × 9-inch baking dish, and brush with melted butter. Sprinkle with about 1 tablespoon nuts. Repeat until you have 5 sheets. (Portions of filo dough will hang over edges of pan.) Spread half of chanterelle mixture into pan. Lay 5 more sheets of filo dough, as before; spread remaining chanterelle mixture. Fold filo edges inward. Add 4 more sheets over this—or more. Bake at 350°F until golden brown (about 25 minutes).

Serves 6.

*To make garam masala:* Use a rolling pin or mallet to break 5 3-inch cinnamon sticks into small pieces. Put broken cinnamon sticks into an iron skillet. Add 1½ tablespoons ground nutmeg, ⅓ cup whole cloves, ¼ cup cardamom, 1 cup cumin seed, ½ cup coriander seed, ¼ cup fennel seed, and 1 tablespoon ground ginger. Pan toast all ingredients for about 15 minutes, stirring every 5 minutes or so. Cool.

Put small amounts through spice mill or coffee grinder until reduced to powder. Pass through a sieve. Place in a glass jar, and store in a cool place.

1 cup butter
4 cups chopped Cinnabar-red Chanterelles
1 scant cup chopped onions
1 teaspoon garam masala (see below)
1 package filo dough
1 cup toasted almonds, ground
1 scant cup dried apricots

# Calabrese Mushroom Chili   MARIA GIGLIO

Place meat, garlic, onion, and pepper in oil and brown meat slightly. Add mushrooms, cover, and cook over medium heat about 5 minutes. Add tomatoes, salt, pepper, vinegar, and chili powder. Cover and heat 10 minutes. Add cannelli beans and cover; heat for 5 to 10 minutes, stirring occasionally. Serve over slices of fresh Italian bread. *Buono appetito!*

Serves 4.

1 pound lean ground beef
1 clove garlic, minced
1 onion, chopped
2 sweet peppers, cut into small pieces
½ cup olive oil
1 pound mushrooms, quartered
¾ cup crushed tomatoes
1 teaspoon salt
1 teaspoon black pepper
1 teaspoon vinegar
2 tablespoons chili powder
1 can cannelli beans
Fresh Italian bread

*Cantharellus tubaeformis* **Trumpet Chanterelle Omelet** ARLEEN RAINIS BESSETTE

½ cup chopped green pepper
½ cup minced onion
3 tablespoons butter
2 cups Trumpet Chanterelles
¼ teaspoon ground mace
½ teaspoon salt
¼ teaspoon black pepper
Dash Tabasco sauce
1 tablespoon minced fresh parsley
4 eggs
¼ cup light cream
½ cup grated cheddar cheese

Sauté green pepper and onion in 2 tablespoons butter until tender. Add mushrooms; cook until all liquid is evaporated. Add spices and seasonings.

Butter omelet pan with remaining butter and heat. Whisk together eggs and cream; pour into heated and buttered omelet pan. Cook gently, covered, until eggs are nearly set. Sprinkle with cheese, and top with mushroom mixture. Cook another minute until eggs are set; fold over and serve.

# Black Trumpet Sweet and Sour Salad

*Craterellus fallax*

### ARLEEN RAINIS BESSETTE

Cut bacon into 1-inch pieces, and fry until crisp. Add onion and green pepper, and sauté until tender-crisp. Add mushrooms and cook 3 minutes more; remove from heat.

In saucepan combine water, vinegar, sugar, salt, and mustard. Bring to boil. Add dissolved cornstarch, stirring constantly. Return to boil; cook 2 minutes.

Stir mushroom mixture into sauce. Pour over bean sprouts. Serves 4.

2 strips bacon *or* 2 tablespoons bacon drippings
¼ cup minced onion
½ cup diced green pepper
4 cups Black Trumpets
¼ cup water
½ cup vinegar
¼ cup sugar
¼ teaspoon salt
¼ teaspoon dry mustard
1 teaspoon cornstarch dissolved in 2 teaspoons water
4 cups raw mung bean sprouts

*Craterellus fallax*

# Black Trumpet Trout

THERESA REY

½ ounce dried Black Trumpets
1 pound fresh rainbow trout
   fillets
Butter
¼ cup white wine or more as
   desired

Preheat oven to 350°F.

Crush mushrooms into fine powder with mortar and pestle. Place trout in a buttered baking dish, and pour wine over top. For best results, choose a wine with a fruity character. Sprinkle Black Trumpet powder over fillets. Bake at 350°F until done (about 15 minutes). Season to taste with salt and pepper.

Serves 2.

*Craterellus fallax*

# Black Trumpet Cracker Spread

LIZ KLIPSCH

½ cup dried Black Trumpets
Milk
1 to 2 tablespoons butter
3 tablespoons chopped chives
¼ teaspoon seasoning salt
   (optional)
8 ounces cream cheese, softened

In a small saucepan, cover dried mushrooms with a small amount of milk. Simmer until reconstituted. Remove from heat, drain mushrooms, and reserve milk for later use.

Cut mushrooms into small pieces. Melt butter and sauté mushrooms for approximately 4 minutes.

Using a fork, blend chives, mushroom and butter mixture, and salt into softened cream cheese. Add reserved milk as needed to obtain spreading consistency.

Refrigerate for at least 1 hour before serving.

# Salmon with Black Trumpets and Horseradish Sauce

ARLEEN RAINIS BESSETTE

*Craterellus fallax*

Sauté mushrooms in 1 tablespoon butter over medium-low heat until liquid is absorbed. Season to taste with salt and pepper. In small bowl, mix together mayonnaise, horseradish, parsley, and lemon juice; set aside. Place steaks or fillets in baking dish and dot with remaining butter. Broil 6 inches from heat until barely browned on edges. Spread horseradish sauce over fish; broil until bubbly hot and golden brown. Serve with sautéed mushrooms and lemon wedges.

Serves 2.

2 cups Black Trumpets
2 tablespoons butter
¼ cup mayonnaise
¼ cup prepared horseradish
1 tablespoon minced fresh
  parsley
1 teaspoon fresh lemon juice
2 salmon steaks or fillets
Lemon wedges

*Hypomyces lactifluorum*

# Lobster Mushroom Spinach Salad

ALAN BESSETTE

Fresh spinach, cleaned and with stems removed

1 cup slivered Lobster Mushrooms

*Orange Ginger Dressing:*

1 cup orange juice
¼ cup red wine vinegar
¼ cup oil
1 tablespoon soy sauce
½ teaspoon salt
½ teaspoon dry mustard
2 cloves garlic, crushed
1 teaspoon grated ginger root
1 tablespoon honey

*Marinade:*

2 tablespoons lemon juice
2 cloves garlic, minced
2 tablespoons cooking vermouth
½ teaspoon dried dill
¼ teaspoon salt

Steam mushrooms 5 minutes. Mix together marinade ingredients. Add mushrooms; refrigerate at least one hour. Mix together Orange Ginger Dressing ingredients. Remove mushrooms from marinade; arrange on beds of raw spinach. Serve with Orange Ginger Dressing.
Serves 4.

# Meadow Mushroom Chicken Soup

*Agaricus campestris*

### ARLEEN RAINIS BESSETTE

Heat oil in large saucepan. Stir-fry ginger for 1 minute. Add mushrooms, and stir-fry 2 minutes more. Add chicken and stir-fry 3 minutes more. Stir in corn, then chicken stock. Bring to a boil, reduce heat to low, and simmer for 10 minutes. Stir in dissolved cornstarch; cook until thickened and translucent. Serve immediately.

Serves 2.

3 tablespoons sesame oil
1 teaspoon grated ginger root
1 cup sliced Meadow
  Mushrooms
½ cup diced cooked chicken
1 can (14 ounces) creamed corn
2 cups chicken stock
2 teaspoons cornstarch dissolved in 1 tablespoon water

*Agaricus campestris*

# Meadow Mushroom Pie

YOLA POLIZZI

3 cups sliced Meadow
  Mushrooms
3 tablespoons butter
1 egg, beaten
4 cups mashed potatoes
2 tablespoons chopped fresh dill
1 tablespoon chopped fresh
  parsley
1 tablespoon chopped leeks or
  shallots
¼ cup water
¼ cup seasoned bread crumbs

Preheat oven to 375°F.

Sauté mushrooms in butter for about 5 minutes. In a bowl combine beaten egg and potatoes, and press mixture firmly into the bottom and sides of a 9-inch pie pan. Blend 1 tablespoon dill into the mushrooms. Add parsley, leeks, and water; season to taste with salt and pepper. Place this mixture into the potato pie crust. Top with bread crumbs and remaining dill. Bake for 30 minutes. (Note: Four cups of Shaggy Manes may be substituted for the 3 cups of Meadow Mushrooms.)

Serves 4 to 6.

# Wild Mushroom Gravy

ARLEEN RAINIS BESSETTE

1 ounce dried Meadow Mushrooms, Shaggy Manes, or
  other strong-flavored wild
  mushrooms
3 cups water
2 tablespoons soy sauce
1 teaspoon sugar
¼ cup minced onion
1 clove garlic, minced
¼ cup minced celery
2 tablespoons butter
1 bay leaf
1 tablespoon cornstarch dissolved in 2 tablespoons water

Add dried mushrooms to water, soy sauce, and sugar in saucepan. Bring to boil, reduce heat, and simmer 20 to 40 minutes. Meanwhile, sauté onion, garlic, and celery in butter until translucent. Add sautéed vegetables to mushrooms. Add bay leaf; simmer 5 minutes more and strain. Bring broth to a boil; whisk in dissolved cornstarch. Simmer 2 to 3 minutes until clear. Remove and discard bay leaf. Puree mushrooms and vegetables in food processor, and return to thickened broth. Season to taste with salt and pepper.

Makes approximately 2 cups.

# Arvensis Casino

ARLEEN RAINIS BESSETTE  *Agaricus arvensis*

Remove stems from mushroom caps. Brush caps with lemon juice to prevent discoloration. Chop stems finely. Sauté mushroom stems, onion, garlic, green pepper, and celery in butter until tender. Add clams, seasonings, and vermouth. Mix in enough bread crumbs to form moist stuffing mix. Fill mushroom caps with stuffing mix, rounding tops. Sprinkle with Parmesan cheese. Place on an oiled cookie sheet and broil about 6 inches from heat until heated through and lightly browned. Brush with additional butter and sprinkle with more vermouth before serving, if desired.

Serves 2.

2 large Horse Mushrooms
Lemon juice
¼ cup minced onion
4 cloves minced garlic
¼ cup diced green pepper
¼ cup diced celery
1 can (6½ ounces) minced clams
1 tablespoon parsley
3 tablespoons butter
1 teaspoon Tabasco sauce
1 tablespoon Worcestershire sauce
¼ cup cooking vermouth
Pinch dried thyme
Seasoned bread crumbs
Grated Parmesan cheese

*Stropharia rugosoannulata*

# Stropharia Cheese Muffins

ARLEEN RAINIS BESSETTE

½ ounce dried Wine-cap
  Stropharia
½ cup butter
½ cup milk
¼ cup warm water
1 teaspoon honey
1½ teaspoons salt
1 package active dry yeast
1 cup unbleached white flour
3 eggs
2 cups (about 8 ounces) grated
  medium sharp cheddar cheese
1 cup whole wheat flour

Process mushrooms in food processor or blender, or grind with mortar and pestle until a fine powder. Heat butter, milk, and water until butter is just melted. Add mushroom powder. Cool to luke-warm. Add honey, salt, and yeast; mix well. Add white flour, eggs, and cheese. Beat 3 minutes at medium speed. Stir in wheat flour by hand, mixing well. Cover and let rise in warm place for 45 to 60 minutes. (Note: Batter does not double in size.) Preheat oven to 350°F. Grease muffin tins generously, and fill ⅔ with batter. Bake until light brown (about 15 to 20 minutes). These are excellent served with soup or salad.

Makes 1 dozen.

# Wine-cap Stropharia with Madeira

BOB HOSH  *Stropharia rugosoannulata*

Sauté mushrooms in butter over medium heat for about 4 minutes. Add onion and fennel seed. Sauté another 3 minutes; stir in flour, and cook 1 minute. Add stock and Madeira, and simmer until sauce is medium thick. Add boiled potato and salt and freshly ground pepper to taste. Simmer a few minutes more.

Serves 4 to 6.

*To make neutral stock:* Put 3 pounds of veal bones, 1 pound of chicken backs, and 1 pound of pork neck bones in a shallow pan. Roast bones and backs in oven at 400°F until brown (about 1 hour). Drain off fat and place bones in a stock pot. Add 1 quart of dry red wine and 1 quart water to completely cover bones. Bring to a boil (remove scum) and simmer for 1 hour. Add 1 large onion, 1 leek, 2 carrots, 2 bay leaves, 6 to 8 sprigs of parsley, and 1 small bunch (bouquet garni) of rosemary and sage. Simmer for 4 to 5 hours, and then strain through cheesecloth or fine strainer. Use in Wine-cap Stropharia with Madeira, and freeze remainder in 1- to 2-cup batches.

¾ **pound Wine-cap Stropharias, sliced**
3 **tablespoons butter**
2 **tablespoons minced onion**
1 **teaspoon fennel seed**
3 **tablespoons flour**
½ **cup neutral stock (see below)**
¼ **cup Madeira**
½ **cup cubed boiled potato**
**Freshly ground pepper**
**Salt**

# Reddening Lepiota Fritatta

YOLA POLIZZI  *Lepiota americana*

Melt 3 tablespoons butter in a nonstick skillet; add mushrooms and lemon juice, and season to taste with salt and pepper. Cook 2 to 3 minutes, stirring briskly. Set aside. Beat eggs, water, and Tabasco sauce. Add remaining butter to mushrooms, heat pan to high, and pour egg mixture over. Cook, shaking pan occasionally, until eggs are set. Turn onto a heated serving dish.

Serves 4.

6 **tablespoons butter**
1 **cup sliced Reddening Lepiotas**
1 **teaspoon lemon juice**
6 **large or 8 medium eggs**
3 **teaspoons water**
3 **drops Tabasco sauce**

*Lepiota rachodes*

# Kasha and Shaggy Parasols

ARLEEN RAINIS BESSETTE

1 medium butternut squash
2 cups chopped Shaggy Parasols
1 small sweet red pepper,
 chopped
1 small onion, minced
3 tablespoons butter
1 large egg
1 cup kasha (buckwheat groats)
1 cup vegetable stock
1 cup boiling water
½ teaspoon salt

Peel squash and remove seeds; cut into 1-inch cubes. Cook in water until barely tender; drain and set aside. Sauté mushrooms, pepper, and onion in 2 tablespoons butter until tender; remove from pan. Beat egg in small bowl. Add kasha, and mix until well coated. Cook kasha in additional 1 tablespoon butter, stirring constantly, until grains become dry and separate. Add mushroom mixture, vegetable stock, boiling water, and salt. Bring to a boil; reduce heat to low, cover, and then simmer until kasha is tender (about 10 minutes). Stir in cooked squash and heat through. May be used to stuff baked vegetables or poultry or served as a side dish.

Serves 4 to 6.

## Breaded Parasol Mushroom Caps

BOB HOSH    *Lepiota procera*

Mix dry ingredients and herbs in a large bowl, reserving ¼ teaspoon salt. Beat eggs, milk, Tabasco sauce, and remaining salt together in another bowl. Heat 1 inch of vegetable oil in a 10- or 12-inch skillet for deep-frying. Cut Parasol Mushroom caps into pie-slice quarters. Dip in egg wash and then in flour and bread crumb mixture, coating thoroughly. Place in hot oil, and fry each side until golden brown (about 2 minutes). Drain on paper towels before serving.

Serves 2 to 4.

¾ cup bread crumbs
¾ cup flour
1¼ teaspoons salt
1 teaspoon Hungarian paprika
2 teaspoons minced fresh thyme
2 teaspoons minced fresh
  parsley
¼ teaspoon freshly ground
  pepper
2 large eggs
1 tablespoon milk
2 drops Tabasco sauce
Vegetable oil
4 to 6 Parasol Mushroom caps,
  each 4 to 6 inches wide

## Snow Pea Pods and Fairy Ring Mushrooms

*Marasmius oreades*

CISSY WEISS

Slice mushrooms thinly. Sauté in butter until tender (about 3 minutes). Cook snow pea pods in boiling water for 1 minute and then drain. Add snow pea pods to mushrooms; season to taste with salt and pepper, and sauté 1 minute more. Serve alone or over rice or Chinese noodles.

Serves 2.

½ pound (about 3 cups) Fairy
  Ring Mushrooms
3 tablespoons butter
10 ounces fresh snow pea pods,
  trimmed

*Coprinus comatus*

# Shaggy Mane Salad

MARTIE COCHRAN

1½ cups Shaggy Manes,
  shredded lengthwise
1 tablespoon oil
1 tablespoon butter
1 tablespoon soy sauce
1 teaspoon Worcestershire sauce
1 teaspoon vinegar
1 tablespoon wine, white or red
8 cups washed spinach
  without stems
Ripe olives

Place shredded Shaggy Manes into a large pot. Sauté 2 minutes in oil and butter. Pour off liquid. Add rest of ingredients except spinach and olives; swirl to blend. Add spinach and cover. Shake as if making popcorn, over medium heat, until spinach is just wilted, about 2 or 3 minutes. Serve hot, garnished with ripe olives.

Serves 2 to 4.

---

*Lactarius volemus* or *L. corrugis*

# Pasta with Lactarius Provençal Sauce

PAT AND JERRY BRENDLE

¼ cup olive, peanut, or saf-
  flower oil
8 medium Voluminous-latex or
  Corrugated-cap Milkies,
  thinly sliced
3 to 4 medium tomatoes
1 generous dash lemon juice
2 cloves garlic, minced
1 handful freshly minced Italian
  parsley
Spaghetti or vermicelli
Grated Parmesan cheese

Heat oil in large skillet over medium heat. Add mushrooms and cook for 10 minutes, stirring frequently. Dip tomatoes into boiling water for 10 seconds. Slip off skins; core, chop, and add to mushrooms. Add lemon juice; season to taste with salt and pepper. Add garlic and parsley. Cook pasta until tender; drain well. Serve topped with sauce and generously sprinkled with Parmesan cheese.

Serves 2 to 4.

# Shaggy Mane Sauce

ARLEEN RAINIS BESSETTE   *Coprinus comatus*

Sauté chopped mushrooms in bacon drippings until tender; remove and set aside. Add spinach and garlic to the skillet; steam-fry until spinach is wilted and soft. Puree spinach, garlic, and yogurt or sour cream in blender. Return to pan. Stir in mushrooms and horseradish. Season to taste with salt and freshly ground black pepper. Heat gently. Use to top baked potatoes, steamed vegetables, or fish.

Makes approximately 2 cups.

**2 cups chopped Shaggy Manes**
**2 tablespoons bacon drippings or butter**
**1 cup (packed) chopped raw spinach, washed, without stems**
**1 large clove garlic, minced**
**1 cup plain yogurt or sour cream (or ½ cup each)**
**1 tablespoon prepared horseradish**
**Freshly ground black pepper**

*Laccaria ochropurpurea*

# Pork with Purple Laccaria and Plum Sauce

ARLEEN RAINIS BESSETTE

**4 trimmed pork chops, ¾ inch thick**
**Vegetable shortening**
**1 cup apple juice**
**3 cups coarsely chopped Purple-gilled Laccarias**
**2 cups small red plums**
**½ cup brown sugar**
**½ cup granulated sugar**
**1 teaspoon brandy**

Preheat oven to 325°F.

Sear chops in lightly greased skillet. Remove and place chops and ½ cup apple juice in baking dish; cover and bake 30 minutes. Add mushrooms; cover and bake another 30 minutes. While chops are baking, halve plums and remove pits. Place in heavy saucepan with remaining apple juice and sugars. Gently bring to boil, stirring frequently. Simmer until fruit is very tender; remove from heat and mix in brandy. When chops are tender, remove to serving plate and serve with plum sauce.

Serves 4.

# Laccaria Stir-fry

ARLEEN RAINIS BESSETTE   *Laccaria laccata*

Combine cornstarch, water, and soy sauce; set aside. Heat wok at medium-high for 2 minutes. Add oil; stir-fry mushrooms, onion, and garlic for 5 minutes. Add carrot and celery; stir-fry 3 minutes more. Add bean sprouts, bok choy, snow peas, and peanuts; stir-fry 2 minutes more. Remove vegetables and set aside. Add shrimp to wok; stir-fry until pink (about 2 to 3 minutes). Return vegetables to wok. Add ginger root and soy sauce mixture; stir-fry until thickened. Serve over brown rice.

Serves 4.

2 tablespoons cornstarch
½ cup water
½ cup soy sauce or tamari
2 tablespoons peanut oil
3 cups Common Laccarias
1 medium onion, quartered and separated
1 large clove garlic, minced
1 medium carrot, sliced in rounds
1 stalk celery, sliced diagonally into ¼-inch slices
1 cup fresh mung bean sprouts
1 to 2 cups chopped bok choy
1 cup fresh snow pea pods
¼ cup unsalted peanuts
½ pound shrimp, shelled and deveined
1 teaspoon grated fresh ginger root
Cooked brown rice

*Chroogomphus rutilus*

# Chroogomphus and Dungeness Crab Cakes

JAN WILSON

1 cup finely chopped Brownish
  Chroogomphus
2 tablespoons minced onion
½ cup butter
1 pound (about 2 cups)
  Dungeness crab meat,
  coarsely shredded
¼ cup cracker meal or more as
  needed
¼ cup mayonnaise
1 egg, lightly beaten
2 tablespoons chopped fresh
  parsley
¼ teaspoon Worcestershire
  sauce
¼ teaspoon dry mustard
Dash Old Bay Seasoning
½ cup bread crumbs or flour

Sauté mushrooms and onion in 2 tablespoons butter until tender. Mix with all remaining ingredients except bread crumbs or flour. Add more cracker meal if needed to absorb excess moisture. Chill 1 to 2 hours.

Shape into patties and roll in bread crumbs or flour. Melt remaining butter in large skillet. Quickly brown patties on both sides; reduce heat and cook slowly for 6 minutes more.

Serves 2 to 4.

# Curried Cashew Chicken and Grayling Salad

*Cantharellula umbonata*

ARLEEN RAINIS BESSETTE

Sauté mushrooms in butter over medium-high heat until tender and lightly browned. Combine all ingredients, including mushrooms, adding mayonnaise to desired consistency. Serve on beds of spinach and lettuce, on crisply toasted bread, or in halved avocado as filling.
Serves 2.

1 cup chopped Graylings
1 tablespoon butter
1 cup minced cooked chicken
1 teaspoon curry powder
¼ cup finely chopped toasted cashews
¼ cup chopped pimentos
Mayonnaise
Fresh spinach and lettuce

*Clitocybe nuda*

# Blewit Cream Sauce

DAVID FISCHER

½ pound chopped fresh Blewits
½ cup dry white wine
2 tablespoons butter
1 small onion, finely chopped
1 clove garlic, minced
¼ teaspoon black pepper
1 cup heavy cream
¼ teaspoon salt
1 tablespoon flour
Toast

In a large, covered frying pan, simmer chopped Blewits in wine over low heat for 10 minutes. Add butter, onion, garlic, and pepper; sauté for 5 minutes. Add cream, salt, and flour; cook until slightly thickened, stirring frequently. Serve over toast or pasta.

Serves 2.

---

*Lactarius thyinos*

# Hunter's Stew

A. J. WROBLEWSKI

2 cups coarsely chopped Orange
  Bog Milkies
2 cloves garlic, crushed
Several sprigs of fresh parsley
Several sprigs of fresh dill weed
1 tablespoon vinegar

*Vegetables: use a combination
  from below*

Potatoes
Celery
Tomatoes
Turnips
Onion, diced and sautéed lightly
½ cup barley
½ cup dry beans, cooked until
  soft

*Meat: use a combination from
  below*

8 to 10 slices kielbasa
8 to 10 slices other smoked
  sausage
¼ to ½ pound beef
¼ to ½ pound pork
Chicken— backs, wings, legs
Liver
Bones from meats

*This recipe was originated by European hunters, before common household refrigeration, to use foods hunted and gathered from surrounding fields and meadows. The meat was typically deer, boar, and wildfowl. The recipe has been modified to use foods common in today's marketplace.*

Cut meat into bite-size pieces. Add all ingredients except vegetables and mushrooms to a very large pot with approximately 3 quarts of water. (Add more liquid as necessary during cooking.) Bring to a boil for 20 minutes. Reduce heat and simmer very slowly for 18 to 24 hours, adding vegetables and mushrooms 30 minutes before serving.

*Happy hunting!*
Serves 6 to 8.

# Cordon Blewit

ARLEEN RAINIS BESSETTE          *Clitocybe nuda*

Cut veal into four equal pieces. Sauté both sides of each briefly in butter; remove and drain on paper towels. Sauté mushroom caps briefly in the same butter until just wilted. Place 2 slices of veal side-by-side. Place a slice of ham on each piece of veal, and place a slice of cheese on top of each slice of ham. Layer mushroom caps on cheese and cover with remaining piece of veal, creating two "sandwiches." Mix flour, bread crumbs, salt, and spices in shallow dish. Gently press into all sides of assembled veal until each "sandwich" is well covered. Let stand 15 minutes. Sauté in same pan until golden on each side (about 3 minutes).

Serves 2.

**2 large, thin veal (scaloppine) cutlets**
**4 tablespoons butter**
**4 large, whole Blewit caps**
**2 thin slices smoked ham**
**2 slices Swiss cheese**
**½ cup flour**
**½ cup dry bread crumbs**
**1 teaspoon salt**
**¼ teaspoon paprika**
**Dash dried rosemary**

*Lactarius deliciosus*

# Orange-latex Milkies with Milkweed Pods

ARLEEN RAINIS BESSETTE

**3 dozen young (1- to 2-inch) milkweed pods or 3 cups asparagus spears cut into 2-inch pieces**
**3 cups coarsely chopped Orange-latex Milkies**
**½ cup chopped onion**
**3 cloves garlic, minced**
**¼ cup butter**
**1 tablespoon minced fresh parsley**
**2 teaspoons lemon juice**

If using asparagus, skip to next paragraph. If not, clean milkweed pods. Bring large kettle of water to boil; add pods and simmer 7 to 10 minutes, mixing frequently. Drain, and repeat boiling and simmering process using fresh water.

Sauté mushrooms, onion, and garlic in butter and oil until all liquid is absorbed. Add pods or asparagus spears, parsley, and lemon juice. Season to taste with salt and pepper. Heat through over medium-low heat.

Serves 4.

# Corrugated-cap Milkies with Spiced Cauliflower

*Lactarius corrugis*

ARLEEN RAINIS BESSETTE

Heat oil in saucepan, add mustard seed, and cover. When seeds stop popping and spattering, add ginger, onion, mushrooms, turmeric, and chili pepper. Sauté 2 to 3 minutes. Add cauliflower, salt, and lemon juice. Mix, cover, and reduce heat to low. Simmer until cauliflower is tender (about 20 minutes). Transfer to serving dish; sprinkle with coriander. Serve with plain yogurt, seasoned with cumin.

Serves 4 to 6.

5 tablespoons vegetable oil
1 teaspoon mustard seed
1 teaspoon minced fresh
  ginger root
1 large onion, chopped
3 cups coarsely chopped
  Corrugated-cap Milkies
1 teaspoon turmeric
1 green chili pepper, minced
1 head cauliflower, separated
  into florets
1 teaspoon salt
Juice of ½ lemon
1 teaspoon coriander

*Tricholoma magnivelare*

# Matsutake Canapes

ARLEEN RAINIS BESSETTE

2 tablespoons butter
2 cups finely diced White
  Matsutakes
2 tablespoons minced onion
1 small clove garlic, minced
¼ teaspoon caraway seeds,
  crushed
Whole wheat crackers

Melt butter in skillet. Add mushrooms, onion, garlic, and caraway; sauté until all liquid is absorbed. Season to taste with salt and pepper. Serve on whole wheat crackers.

Serves 6.

# Steamed Gypsies in Sweet Red Pepper Sauce

*Rozites caperata*

ALAN BESSETTE

Heat oil in saucepan. Sauté onions and garlic until tender. Add chicken stock and peppers. Simmer until tender (about 30 minutes); drain. Puree pepper mixture in food processor and return to saucepan. Slowly add cream, salt, and pepper; heat through. Place mushrooms in vegetable steamer over ½ inch of water; cover and bring water to boil. Reduce heat and steam 5 minutes. Serve steamed mushrooms covered with sauce.

Serves 4.

⅓ cup olive oil
4 medium onions, chopped
4 cloves garlic, chopped
3½ cups chicken stock
4 large sweet red peppers, chopped
½ cup heavy cream
½ teaspoon salt
½ teaspoon pepper
1 dozen medium-large Gypsy mushrooms (3 per person)

*Tricholoma caligatum*

# Marinated Tricholoma and Pasta Delight

SUSAN MITCHELL

2 cups chopped Fragrant
 Tricholomas
2 tablespoons butter
1 6-ounce jar marinated artichoke hearts, sliced and
 liquid reserved
2 tablespoons red wine vinegar
8 tablespoons olive oil
1 cup chopped onion
2 or 3 cloves garlic, minced
10 Greek olives, pitted and
 halved
2 teaspoons minced fresh basil,
 or 1 teaspoon dried basil
1 pound pasta, cooked al dente
½ cup grated Parmesan cheese

Sauté mushrooms in butter until tender. Marinate them for several hours in juice of artichoke hearts, combined with vinegar and 5 tablespoons olive oil, stirring occasionally. Sauté onion and garlic in 3 tablespoons oil until soft. Add mushrooms, marinade, and remaining ingredients; heat through. Serve over hot pasta, and sprinkle with Parmesan cheese as desired.

Serves 4.

---

*Pluteus cervinus*

# Fawn Mushrooms au Gratin

SYLVIA STEIN

3 tablespoons butter
1 pound Fawn Mushrooms,
 thinly sliced
2 teaspoons lemon juice
2 tablespoons minced green
 onion
½ cup milk
½ cup heavy cream
¼ teaspoon nutmeg
2 tablespoons flour
⅓ cup grated Swiss or Parmesan cheese
⅓ cup bread crumbs

Melt half of the butter in a 1-quart saucepan. Add mushrooms and lemon juice; cover and cook until all liquid is absorbed. Add onion, milk, and cream; season to taste with nutmeg, salt, and pepper. Simmer without boiling.

Blend flour with remaining butter by kneading. Add this mixture bit-by-bit to the simmering mushroom mixture. When thickened, pour into a heated baking dish. Sprinkle on top a mixture of the cheese and bread crumbs. Brown under broiler, watching carefully to prevent burning. Serve hot.

Serves 4.

# Orange Roughy with Platterfuls

ALAN BESSETTE  *Tricholomopsis platyphylla*

Preheat oven to 350°F. Place fish fillets in single layer in buttered baking dish. Dot with butter. Add wine, chopped pepper, onions, and mushrooms. Sprinkle with parsley, seasonings, and lemon juice. Cover and then bake until fish is just done (about 20 minutes).

Serves 4.

1½ pounds Orange Roughy fish fillets
1 tablespoon butter
¼ cup dry white wine
1 cup chopped red sweet pepper
3 green onions, chopped
3 cups chopped Platterful Mushrooms
¼ cup chopped fresh parsley
¼ teaspoon celery seed
¼ teaspoon ground coriander
¼ teaspoon chili powder
Juice of 1 lemon

*Entoloma abortivum*

# Entoloma and Pearl Onions in Madeira Sauce

ARLEEN RAINIS BESSETTE

1 cup pearl onions
½ cup butter or margarine
1 pound (6 cups) Abortive
   Entolomas
1 tablespoon dried parsley
1 bay leaf
¼ teaspoon allspice
½ cup water
(1 beef bouillon cube)
2 tablespoons flour
¼ cup Madeira wine
Hot buttered egg noodles

Sauté onions in butter for 5 minutes. Cut mushrooms into large pieces, add to onions, and mix to coat with butter. Add remaining ingredients except Madeira and noodles. Cook until onions are tender. Add Madeira; mix well. Serve over buttered egg noodles.

Serves 4.

# Brick Cap Vegetable Casserole ARLEEN RAINIS BESSETTE *Naematoloma sublateritium*

Preheat oven to 400°F.

Sauté onions and peppers in oil until browned, stirring frequently. Set aside. Pour broth into 9 × 13-inch baking dish. Add barley, vegetables, and mushrooms; layer sautéed onions and peppers on top. Combine lemon juice and garlic, pour over vegetables, and sprinkle with salt and paprika. Bake at 400°F until barley is tender (about 1½ hours).

Serves 6 to 8.

2 large onions, sliced into rings
2 medium green peppers, cut in strips
2 tablespoons oil
1 cup beef broth
½ cup barley
2 large carrots, thickly sliced
2 large tomatoes, quartered
1 medium zucchini, cut in chunks
2 cups halved green beans
1 package (10 ounces) frozen peas
½ small cauliflower head, separated into florets
3 cups Brick Caps, cleaned and trimmed
Juice of 1 lemon
2 cloves garlic, minced
2 teaspoons salt
1 teaspoon paprika

*Armillaria mellea*

# Honey Mushrooms with Fettuccini

JULIE CARRIS

6 to 10 sun-dried tomato pieces
1 to 1½ sticks butter or
    margarine
2 ounces olive oil
2 to 3 cloves garlic, pressed
    or chopped
4 leaves fresh basil, finely
    chopped
Parsley to taste
1 six-ounce can of chopped
    clams, with juice
1½ cups Honey Mushrooms,
    sautéed well
Oregano and pepper to taste
1 ounce cooking sherry
Parmesan cheese to taste
1 pound fettuccini

Begin boiling water for fettuccini. Rehydrate dried tomatoes by dropping them into boiling water and cooking until soft. Remove tomatoes; drain; chop into bite-size pieces.

Melt butter and olive oil in skillet; add garlic, basil, and parsley. Drain clams, reserving juice; add to skillet. Sauté slowly for 4 minutes. Add mushrooms, rehydrated tomatoes, oregano, and pepper. Increase heat and cook 4 minutes. Stir in clam juice; cook over medium heat for 3 minutes, stirring constantly.

Add sherry. Remove from heat. Add Parmesan cheese to taste. Mix with fettuccini and serve.

May be prepared ahead of time and reheated in the microwave. Serves 4 to 6.

---

*Armillaria mellea*

# Pickled Honey Mushrooms

GRETE TURCHICK

4 to 5 cups sliced Honey
    Mushrooms
White vinegar
½ cup olive oil
1 to 2 teaspoons salt
⅛ teaspoon mace
2 pinches oregano
Several pinches dill weed
5 to 10 cloves garlic, crushed
Freshly ground black pepper

Simmer mushrooms in water for 5 to 10 minutes; discard water. Cover mushrooms, using 1 part vinegar to 2 parts water; simmer 5 minutes more. Prepare pickling mixture by combining olive oil, salt, mace, oregano, dill weed, and garlic; add pepper to taste. Drain mushrooms and add to pickling mixture; mix thoroughly. Refrigerate for 2 hours before serving.

Serves 6 to 8.

# Honey-cap and Lamb Stew

ARLEEN RAINIS BESSETTE  *Armillaria mellea*

Quickly sear lamb in oil; remove to plate. Sauté onion and mushrooms 2 to 3 minutes. Place lamb, onion, mushrooms, and all remaining ingredients into large pot. Bring to boil, reduce heat, and simmer until vegetables and barley are tender; season to taste with salt and pepper.

Serves 4 to 6.

1 pound lamb, cut into chunks
2 tablespoons oil
1 cup chopped onion
3 cups Honey Mushrooms, cut into large pieces
2 medium potatoes, peeled and cubed
1 cup parsnips, chopped
2 carrots, thickly sliced
½ cup barley
1 bay leaf
2 to 3 cups water or stock
2 tablespoons minced fresh parsley
1 teaspoon dried rosemary

*Pleurotus ostreatus*

# Oriental Oyster Mushrooms and Steak

ALAN BESSETTE

1 teaspoon grated ginger root
½ cup soy sauce
¼ cup cooking sherry
6 tablespoons vegetable oil
4 cloves garlic, crushed
2 tablespoons brown sugar
1 pound flank steak, cut into
   2-inch strips
3 green onions, chopped
½ cup chopped onion
1 cup chopped green pepper
3 cups coarsely chopped Oyster
   Mushrooms
2 teaspoons cornstarch dissolved in 1 teaspoon water
Hot cooked rice

Combine ginger, soy sauce, sherry, 2 tablespoons oil, garlic, and sugar in nonmetallic bowl. Marinate beef strips in this mixture unrefrigerated for 3 hours or refrigerated for 4 to 12 hours (add ¼ cup water to marinade if needed). Sauté onions and pepper in 2 tablespoons oil until tender-crisp. Add mushrooms and cook 3 minutes more on medium-high heat, stirring constantly. Remove to plate. Stir-fry beef strips in remaining 2 tablespoons oil over high heat for about 3 minutes. Add marinade and bring to boil. Add dissolved cornstarch, mixing constantly, until clear and thickened. Add vegetable and mushroom mixture. Bring to boil until heated through. Serve over rice.

Serves 2.

# Oyster Mushrooms Mornay

ARLEEN RAINIS BESSETTE

*Pleurotus ostreatus*

Sauté mushrooms and garlic in 2 tablespoons butter for 3 minutes. Add shrimp and pea pods; simmer until shrimp are pink. In separate pan, melt remaining butter and whisk in flour. Cook over low heat for 3 minutes. Slowly whisk in broth. Add cream and wine; heat without boiling, stirring constantly until thickened. Mix cream sauce with cooked pasta, and stir in mushroom mixture. Season to taste with salt and pepper. Heat through; serve sprinkled with Parmesan cheese.

Serves 2 to 4.

4 cups coarsely chopped Oyster Mushrooms
2 large cloves garlic, minced
4 tablespoons butter
½ pound shrimp, shelled and deveined
1 cup fresh pea pods, halved
2 tablespoons flour
2 cups chicken broth
1 cup heavy cream
¼ cup dry white wine
Cooked and buttered pasta
Freshly ground black pepper
Grated Parmesan cheese

*Pleurocybella porrigens*

# Angel Wings and Scallop Crepes

ARLEEN RAINIS BESSETTE

*Filling:*

3 tablespoons butter
½ cup minced onion
2 cloves garlic, minced
½ cup minced fresh parsley
5 cups Angel Wings, cut into
   2-inch pieces
1 teaspoon dried basil
½ teaspoon dried oregano
½ teaspoon salt
¼ teaspoon nutmeg
¼ teaspoon red pepper flakes,
   crushed
½ cup dry white wine
2 tablespoons flour
1 cup chicken broth
½ pound scallops
3 ounces cream cheese
½ cup grated Parmesan cheese

*Crepe batter:*

2 eggs
⅛ teaspoon salt
1 cup flour
1 cup milk
2 tablespoons butter, melted

One hour ahead combine crepe batter ingredients. Beat well, and then refrigerate at least 1 hour. To cook crepes, heat nonstick skillet over medium-high heat for 2 minutes. Pour 2 to 3 tablespoons batter in pan and swirl. Cook until golden brown; turn crepe and cook another minute. Remove to plate. Repeat with rest of batter. Melt 3 tablespoons butter; sauté onion, garlic, parsley, and mushrooms until all liquid is absorbed. Add remaining spices and wine; cook until most liquid evaporates. Stir in flour, and cook one minute. Add chicken broth and bring to boil; simmer until thickened (about 10 minutes). Add scallops; return to boil, simmer 5 minutes, and remove from heat. Stir in cream cheese and Parmesan cheese; mix until well blended. Fill crepes with mushroom and scallop mixture.

Serves 4.

# Late Fall Oyster Mushroom Pie

*Panellus serotinus*

ARLEEN RAINIS BESSETTE

*Crust:*

1 package active dry yeast
¾ cup warm water
1 tablespoon olive oil
½ teaspoon salt
2 cups flour

*Filling:*

3 medium onions, chopped
1 green pepper, chopped
2 cloves garlic, minced
½ cup olive oil
1 large can crushed tomatoes
½ cup minced fresh parsley
1 cup dry red wine
1 cup water
2 tablespoons vinegar
1 tablespoon sugar
¼ teaspoon cumin
¼ teaspoon basil
¼ teaspoon thyme
¼ teaspoon red pepper flakes, crushed
2 cups coarsely chopped Late Fall Oyster Mushrooms
1 cup grated mozzarella cheese
1 cup highly seasoned meat (cooked sweet sausage, beef, salami), cut in bite-size pieces

Dissolve yeast in warm water. Stir in 1 tablespoon olive oil, salt, and flour. Knead 10 minutes; cover and let rise about 2 hours. While dough is rising, sauté onion, pepper, and garlic in ½ cup olive oil until soft. Add tomatoes, parsley, wine, 1 cup water, vinegar, sugar, and spices. Bring to boil; reduce heat and simmer 1 to 2 hours, stirring occasionally. Season to taste with salt and pepper.

Place mushrooms in saucepan; cover with water and bring to boil. Reduce heat; simmer uncovered for 10 minutes. Drain and rinse mushrooms. Preheat oven to 400°F. Oil an 8 × 8-inch baking dish with olive oil; stretch dough in pan, forming an edge to hold in filling. Prick dough with fork; brush lightly with oil. Spread in cheese; cover with meat, mushrooms, and then sauce. Sprinkle with Parmesan cheese, if desired.

Bake at 400°F until light brown (about 25 minutes). Serves 4.

*Boletus edulis*

# Sautéed King Boletes

ALAN BESSETTE

**2 cups sliced King Boletes**
**1 clove garlic, minced**
**2 tablespoons olive oil**
**½ teaspoon dried basil**
**¼ teaspoon salt**
**¼ teaspoon pepper**

Sauté mushrooms and garlic in oil until tender. Add spices, stirring well.

Serves 2.

# King Bolete Thermidor ARLEEN RAINIS BESSETTE *Boletus edulis*

Melt 4 tablespoons butter in skillet. Sauté onion and mushrooms with brandy until mushrooms are tender. Add parsley.

Melt remaining butter in large saucepan. Add flour and mustard, stirring to form a smooth roux. Cook three minutes over medium heat. Gradually add milk, whisking to keep sauce smooth. Add cream, Tabasco, sherry, and mild cheese. Cook, whisking constantly, until thickened. Add seafood and mushroom mixture; cook, without boiling, until heated through (about 2 to 3 minutes more). Season to taste with salt and pepper. Serve on rice, puff pastry shells, or pasta, topping with Parmesan cheese.

Serves 4.

6 tablespoons butter
½ cup finely minced onion
1 cup thickly sliced King Boletes
1 ounce brandy
½ cup minced fresh parsley
3 tablespoons flour
1 tablespoon dry mustard
2 cups milk
1 cup cream
¼ teaspoon Tabasco sauce
½ cup sherry
½ cup grated mild cheese
½ cup crab meat
½ cup cooked and diced lobster meat
1 cup cooked and shelled shrimp
Hot cooked rice, pastry shells, or pasta
Grated Parmesan cheese

## Bolete and Sausage Pizza Roll

DAVID FISCHER

1 package active dry yeast
¾ cup warm water
½ teaspoon salt
1 tablespoon olive oil
2 cups flour
¼ pound Italian sausage
½ pound (3 cups) any edible
 boletes, chopped
2 tablespoons butter
½ cup tomato sauce
Oregano
Thyme
Parsley
Basil
1 clove garlic, minced
¼ pound grated mozzarella
 cheese

Two hours ahead, dissolve yeast in warm water. Stir in salt, olive oil, and flour; knead 10 minutes. Cover and allow to rise about 2 hours. Preheat oven to 350°F. Cook sausage and crumble. Sauté boletes in 1 tablespoon butter until tender (about 5 minutes). Roll dough into long oval and brush with tomato sauce. Sprinkle with herbs and garlic. Mix boletes and sausage together; spread evenly over dough. Cover with mozzarella cheese. Roll dough into a long, narrow roll, and seal with several kebob sticks. Melt remaining 1 tablespoon butter and brush on roll. Bake at 350°F on a greased baking sheet until browned and well done in center (about 20 to 40 minutes). Remove kebob sticks; slice and serve.

Serves 4.

---

*Boletus bicolor*

## Fried Two-colored Boletes

THERESA REY

1 cup pecans
3 tablespoons flour
3 tablespoons plain bread
 crumbs
Equal parts egg white and
 water, beaten together
2 cups sliced Two-colored
 Boletes
Butter

Preheat oven to 350°F.

Grind or process nuts. Place on cookie sheet, and toast in oven until light gold in color. Allow to cool. Mix nuts with flour and bread crumbs. Dip sliced mushrooms in egg and water mixture, and then coat with nut mixture. Fry in butter until golden on both sides. Season to taste with salt and pepper.

Serves 4.

# Swiss Chicken Edulis

ARLEEN RAINIS BESSETTE   *Boletus edulis*

Butter a 9 × 13-inch baking dish. In heavy skillet, melt 2 tablespoons butter in oil. Add chicken; cook 5 minutes on each side. Remove to dish and set aside. Melt additional 2 tablespoons butter; add mushrooms, and cook over medium heat until tender (about 3 to 5 minutes). Set aside.

Layer broccoli and carrots in baking dish. Season chicken with lemon pepper; place over vegetables. Melt remaining 2 tablespoons butter in saucepan over low heat, and whisk in flour. Cook, stirring constantly, for 3 minutes. Add chicken broth and wine; whisk until thoroughly blended. Continue cooking until thickened. Add cheese, and stir until melted. Season to taste with salt and pepper. Pour over chicken and vegetables; arrange mushrooms on top. Broil 6 inches from heat source for 3 to 5 minutes until bubbly and golden. Serve immediately.

Serves 6.

**6 tablespoons butter**
**2 tablespoons oil**
**6 chicken breast fillets**
**3 cups thickly sliced King Boletes**
**1 large bunch broccoli, cooked al dente**
**3 carrots, sliced thickly and cooked al dente**
**Lemon pepper**
**2 tablespoons flour**
**½ cup chicken broth**
**½ cup dry white wine**
**1½ cups shredded Swiss cheese**

*Hydnum repandum*

# Hydnum Hash

ALAN BESSETTE

1 medium green pepper,
  chopped
½ cup chopped scallions
2 cloves garlic, minced
4 tablespoons butter
2 cups coarsely chopped Sweet
  Tooth mushrooms
1 teaspoon fresh basil or ½ teaspoon dried basil
Cayenne pepper
2 medium potatoes, cooked and
  cut into 1-inch cubes

Sauté pepper, scallions, and garlic in 2 tablespoons butter until tender-crisp. Remove to plate. Sauté mushrooms in remaining 2 tablespoons butter until all liquid is absorbed. Add basil and dash of cayenne pepper; add cooked pepper mixture, and season to taste with salt and pepper. Add potatoes, stirring to blend well; heat through.
  Serves 4.

# Cauliflower Mushroom Salad

ALAN BESSETTE · *Sparassis radicata*

Sauté mushroom slices in butter until golden on both sides; sprinkle with salt, and remove with slotted spoon to plate. Add walnuts to butter, stirring over medium-high heat about 3 minutes, until toasted hot. Place mushroom slices on bed of lettuce; pour walnut and butter mixture over top, and sprinkle with lemon juice.

Serves 2.

**4 or 5 slices Cauliflower Mush-**
**rooms (about 8 ounces)**
¼ **cup butter**
¼ **teaspoon salt**
¼ **cup finely chopped walnuts**
**Fresh lettuce**
**Juice of ½ lemon**

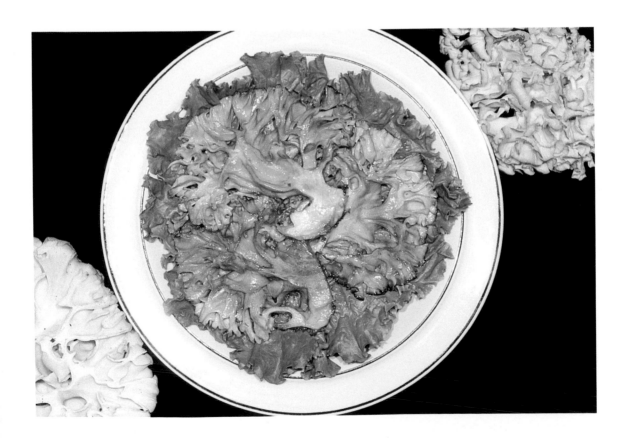

*Grifola frondosa*

# Hen and Lobster with Dill Sauce

ARLEEN RAINIS BESSETTE

4 to 6 slices (½ inch thick) Hen
of the Woods
6 tablespoons butter
2 tablespoons flour
½ cup chicken stock
½ cup light cream
1 teaspoon lemon juice
1 tablespoon minced fresh
dill weed
¼ teaspoon salt
⅛ teaspoon white pepper
1 cup cooked lobster meat, cut
in chunks

Sauté mushroom slices in 4 tablespoons butter until lightly browned on both sides. While mushroom slices are cooking, melt remaining 2 tablespoons butter in separate pan. Whisk in flour, and cook 3 minutes over low heat. Slowly whisk in stock and then cream. Add lemon juice, dill weed, salt, and white pepper. Cook, stirring constantly, until thickened. Add lobster meat and heat through without boiling. Serve over sautéed mushrooms.

Serves 2.

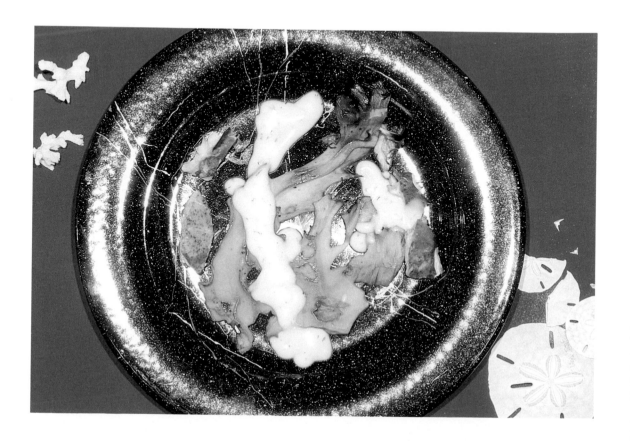

# Pheasant's Back Jambalaya

ARLEEN RAINIS BESSETTE        *Polyporus squamosus*

Melt butter in large pot or Dutch oven. Add vegetables, garlic, parsley, and mushrooms. Cover; cook over medium heat until tender. Add remaining ingredients. Cover and simmer 30 to 40 minutes, until rice is tender and liquid is absorbed to desired consistency.

Serves 2 to 4.

2 tablespoons butter
1 cup chopped onion
½ cup diced celery
½ cup each green and red bell peppers, cut in strips
1 large can (28 ounces) whole tomatoes, cut up
2 cloves garlic, minced
¼ cup fresh parsley
2 cups Dryad's Saddles
2 cups cooked ham, cubed
1 teaspoon sugar
½ teaspoon chili powder
¼ teaspoon black pepper
Dash of Tabasco sauce
1½ cups beef broth
1½ cups water
1 cup long-grain rice, uncooked

*Laetiporus sulphureus*

# Mock Chicken Paprikash

BOB HOSH

2 cups sliced or chopped Sulphur Shelves
½ cup chopped onion
1 medium green bell pepper, chopped
3 to 4 tablespoons oil or butter, or more as needed
2 to 3 tablespoons sweet Hungarian paprika
1 tablespoon finely chopped parsley
1 teaspoon salt
1 medium ripe tomato, peeled, seeded, and chopped
3 cups chicken broth
1 cup sour cream, warmed to room temperature
3 tablespoons flour

In a four-quart skillet or pot, sauté bite-size mushroom pieces, onion, and pepper in oil or butter for 6 to 8 minutes. Remove from heat; add paprika and all remaining ingredients except sour cream and flour. Simmer for 10 minutes. Mix flour into sour cream. Add to simmered mixture, stirring well. Simmer for 5 minutes more. Serve with noodles or *spaetzle*.

Serves 4.

---

*Laetiporus sulphureus*

# Mock Chicken Cacciatore

VICKI HAINES

2 tablespoons vegetable oil
2 cups Sulphur Shelves, cut into ¼- to ½-inch strips
1 medium onion, chopped
1 clove garlic, minced
½ green pepper, chopped
1 medium tomato, cut into chunks
½ teaspoon oregano
Dash Tabasco sauce
2 tablespoons tomato puree
¾ cup sliced zucchini
½ teaspoon basil
¼ cup dry red wine
Hot cooked rice
Grated Parmesan cheese

Heat oil in heavy skillet; add mushrooms, and sauté 3 to 4 minutes. Add onion, garlic, and green pepper, and sauté for 5 minutes. Add remaining ingredients except rice and cheese; stir, cover, and simmer over low heat until vegetables are tender (5 to 10 minutes). Season to taste with salt and pepper. Serve over rice, and top with grated Parmesan cheese.

Serves 2 to 4.

# Sulphur Shelf and Mussels

ARLEEN RAINIS BESSETTE  *Laetiporus sulphureus*

Clean mussels; discard any with broken or cracked shells or any that do not close after placing in freezer for 1 to 2 minutes. Sauté shallots, mushrooms, and peas in butter until tender. Add wine, parsley, and mussels. Bring to boil. Cover, reduce heat, and simmer 6 to 8 minutes, mixing once or twice to ensure even cooking. Serve over saffron rice, or serve over pasta and top with Parmesan cheese. Crusty French bread is a good accompaniment.

Serves 2 to 4.

3 quarts live mussels
5 shallots, minced
3 cups Sulphur Shelves, cut in ½-inch strips
1 cup fresh green peas
4 tablespoons butter
1 cup dry white wine
2 tablespoons minced fresh parsley
Hot saffron rice

ARB

*Grifola frondosa*

# Hen of the Woods Salad

CISSY WEISS

3 green onions with tops,
  chopped
1 small tomato, peeled and
  chopped
2 tablespoons olive oil
1 tablespoon butter
8 ounces Hen of the Woods,
  chopped
1 pound cooked, skinned, and
  boned chicken
2 slices bacon, cooked until
  crisp
2 tablespoons red wine
½ cup peanuts or pine nuts
Favorite salad dressing
Lettuce or avocado

Sauté onion and tomato in oil and butter until onion is soft but not browned. Add mushrooms, and cook 4 minutes more.

Cut chicken meat into large chunks. Add to mushroom mixture, along with bacon (crumbled), wine, and nuts. Sauté a few more minutes; cool, and then add your favorite salad dressing. Chill; serve on a bed of lettuce or on avocado halves.

Serves 2 to 4.

---

*Laetiporus sulphureus*

# Sulphur Shelf Casserole

VICKI HAINES

1 can cream of chicken soup or
  1 can creamy chicken mushroom soup
1 cup milk
2 cups Sulphur Shelves, cut in
  1-inch strips
16 ounces frozen broccoli-
  cauliflower mix, thawed
¾ cup grated cheddar cheese
  (about 3 ounces)
1 can Durkee fried onion rings
1 to 2 teaspoons curry powder
  (optional)
1 8-ounce package refrigerator
  crescent rolls

Preheat oven to 375°F.

Combine all ingredients except crescent rolls; mix well. Spread into a greased 8 × 12-inch baking dish. Bake for 20 minutes. Separate rolls to form a rectangle; cut dough lengthwise into ½-inch strips. Weave as a lattice over casserole; bake 20 minutes more.

Serves 4 to 6.

# Puffball Parmesan

ARLEEN RAINIS BESSETTE  *Langermannia gigantea*

Preheat oven to 350°F.

Sauté onion, pepper, and garlic in 1 tablespoon olive oil until tender. Add tomatoes, tomato paste, salt, sugar, and basil. Bring to boil; reduce heat and simmer gently 15 to 20 minutes. Combine 1 cup Parmesan cheese with seasoned bread crumbs. Melt butter with remaining olive oil in large skillet. Dip puffball slices in beaten egg and milk. Dredge in bread crumb mixture, covering all sides. Fry in butter and oil mixture over medium heat until golden on both sides. Drain on paper towels. Place browned puffball slices in single layer in oiled baking dish. Cover with mozzarella cheese slices, then with tomato sauce. Sprinkle with remaining Parmesan cheese. Bake at 350°F until cheese is melted and all is well heated.

Serves 4 to 6.

2 tablespoons minced onion
½ cup chopped green pepper
3 cloves garlic, minced
4 tablespoons olive oil
1 16-ounce can Italian tomatoes
1 3-ounce can tomato paste
½ teaspoon salt
½ teaspoon sugar
1 tablespoon fresh basil
2 cups grated Parmesan cheese
1 cup dry bread crumbs, seasoned with ½ teaspoon savory
4 tablespoons butter
6 ½-inch thick slices Giant Puffball or other large puffball
1 egg, slightly beaten with 1 tablespoon milk
6 slices mozzarella cheese

*Morchella esculenta*

# Baked Stuffed Morels

ARLEEN RAINIS BESSETTE

1 dozen large Yellow Morels
(caps 2 to 3 inches long)
Butter
4 slices bacon
4 wild leeks (ramps), whites
only, minced, or 2 table-
spoons minced onion
1 cup grated Gruyère cheese
2 tablespoons flour
¼ teaspoon salt
2 eggs, beaten
1 cup milk

Preheat oven to 350°F.

Cut stems from morels. Arrange caps, stalk side up, in buttered baking dish, using aluminum foil to stabilize caps as needed. Cook bacon until crisp; drain and crumble. Sauté leeks in bacon fat, and remove with slotted spoon. Combine leeks, crumbled bacon, and remaining ingredients. Fill morel caps with mixture. Bake until firm (15 to 20 minutes).

Serves 2 to 4.

# Creamed Morels and Potatoes

BUNNY RAINIS  *Morchella esculenta*

Simmer potato cubes in water until tender; drain. In a large skillet, sauté onion, pepper, and parsley in butter until tender. Add morels, and sauté until all liquid has evaporated. Add potatoes, and heat through. Before serving, stir in sour cream, heat well, and season to taste with salt and pepper.

Serves 4.

2 medium potatoes, peeled
  and cubed
1 onion, sliced
½ cup diced green pepper
1 tablespoon minced fresh
  parsley
2 tablespoons butter or
  bacon fat
2 cups Yellow Morels, chopped
1 cup sour cream
Freshly ground black pepper
Salt

*Morchella esculenta*

# Fiddlehead-Morel Quiche

YOLA POLIZZI

4 tablespoons butter
2 tablespoons chopped wild
  leeks or green onions
¾ pound morels, sliced
½ teaspoon salt
¼ teaspoon pepper
1 teaspoon lemon juice
4 eggs
1 cup heavy cream or milk
⅛ teaspoon nutmeg
1 8-inch pastry shell
2 ounces Swiss cheese, grated
10 to 16 fiddlehead ferns, stems
  removed, or asparagus spears
Paprika

Preheat oven to 350°F.

Melt butter. Add leeks, and sauté 1 to 2 minutes. Add morels, salt, pepper, and lemon juice. Cover and simmer until liquid is absorbed (about 5 minutes). Beat eggs, cream, and nutmeg; *carefully* stir into morel and leek mixture. Set pastry shell on a cookie sheet, and sprinkle half the Swiss cheese into the shell. Arrange fiddlehead tips over cheese, and pour morel and egg mixture into pastry shell. Sprinkle with remaining cheese, and add paprika to taste. Bake, *watching carefully,* until top is puffed up and browned slightly (about 45 minutes).

Serves 4.

*Morchella esculenta*

# Morel Blender Hollandaise Sauce

JULIE CARRIS

1 stick butter or margarine
7 to 10 two-inch dried Yellow
  Morels
3 egg yolks
2 tablespoons lemon juice
  (more or less to taste)
¼ teaspoon salt (optional)

Melt butter. Add morels and cook slowly until morels are rehydrated.

Blend egg yolks, lemon juice, and salt for 3 seconds on high in a blender. Add butter and morel mixture; blend on high for another 5 seconds.

Serve at once or keep warm in top of double boiler over hot water. Sauce may be frozen. Complements asparagus, broccoli, and roasted meats.

# Glazed Jelly Tooth

ALAN BESSETTE     *Pseudohydnum gelatinosum*

Combine sugar, water, berries, apple, and butter. Bring to boil; continue cooking until mixture reaches jelly stage (220°–222°), when it will fall from the spoon in a single drop. Remove from heat; stir in liqueur and cool. As jelly thickens, dip fungi to cover. Cool on waxed paper. May be dusted with sifted confectioners sugar.

Serves 4 to 6.

1 cup sugar
¼ cup water
1 cup cleaned raspberries
2 medium apples, chopped
1 tablespoon butter
2 teaspoons fruit liqueur
3 cups Jelly Tooth

# Baked Fish with Mushrooms and Garden Vegetables

ARLEEN RAINIS BESSETTE

1½ pounds fish fillets
Butter
2 medium tomatoes, skinned
  and quartered
2 stalks celery, chopped
1 onion, thinly sliced
1 cup sliced mushrooms
1 tablespoon minced fresh
  parsley
1 teaspoon minced fresh
  oregano
1 bay leaf, broken in half
¼ teaspoon salt
¼ teaspoon pepper
¼ cup dry red wine

Preheat oven to 350°F.

Place fish in single layer in buttered baking dish; layer vegetables on top. Sprinkle with seasonings and spices, and then pour wine over gently. Cover and bake until fish is just done (about 20 minutes).

Serves 2 to 4.

# Cream of Mushroom Soup ARLEEN RAINIS BESSETTE

Chop mushrooms finely in food processor; sauté in 2 tablespoons butter until tender. Add celery, onion, parsley, and chicken broth. Bring to boil, reduce heat, and simmer covered for 20 minutes. Drain cooked mushroom and vegetable mixture, retaining broth in separate bowl. Puree mixture in food processor. Melt remaining 2 tablespoons butter in saucepan. Add flour, whisking over low heat for 3 minutes. Slowly whisk in cream; add bay leaf and cook over low heat until thickened. Slowly stir mushroom broth into cream sauce. Heat thoroughly without boiling. Remove bay leaf. Add pureed mushroom mixture; heat through. Before serving, add sour cream and garnish with paprika.

Serves 2.

½ **pound (3 cups) wild mushrooms**
**4 tablespoons butter**
½ **cup minced celery**
¼ **cup chopped onion**
**2 tablespoons snipped fresh parsley**
**2 cups chicken broth**
**2 tablespoons flour**
**1 cup light cream**
**1 bay leaf**
¼ **cup sour cream**
**Paprika**

# Duxelle and Ricotta Stuffed Shells

ARLEEN RAINIS BESSETTE

*Duxelle:*
3 cups mixed mushrooms, finely
    chopped
3 shallots, chopped
5 tablespoons olive oil
2 cloves garlic, minced
¼ teaspoon red pepper flakes,
    crushed
Salt and pepper

2 eggs
1 pound Ricotta cheese
½ cup grated Parmesan cheese
2-inch pasta shells, cooked
    al dente
1 bunch escarole, steamed until
    tender
4 tablespoons butter
2 large cloves garlic, minced

Preheat oven to 350°F.

To make *duxelle*, sauté mushrooms and shallots in oil until all liquid is evaporated; add 2 cloves garlic, and cook 1 minute more. Stir in pepper flakes; season to taste with salt and pepper. In a bowl lightly beat eggs. Mix with Ricotta and Parmesan cheeses. Mix in 4 tablespoons duxelle; spoon filling into cooked shells. Layer escarole in baking dish. Layer stuffed shells on top. Sauté 2 cloves garlic briefly in butter, and brush over shells. Cover and bake until hot (15 to 20 minutes).

Serves 4 to 6.

# Marinated Wild Mushrooms ALAN BESSETTE

Place mushrooms in saucepan and cover with water. Add lemon juice; bring to boil, reduce heat, and simmer 5 to 10 minutes. Drain and discard liquid. Bring remaining ingredients to a boil in separate saucepan; remove from heat. Pour hot marinade over mushrooms; cool to room temperature. Cover and store in refrigerator, mixing occasionally. Serve chilled.

Makes approximately 1 quart.

**2 pounds mushrooms, quartered**
**¼ cup lemon juice**
**1 cup distilled white vinegar**
**½ cup olive oil**
**2 teaspoons salt**
**¼ teaspoon black pepper**
**3 cloves garlic, crushed**
**1 teaspoon dried oregano**
**1 teaspoon dried dill weed or basil**
**½ teaspoon mace**

# Mixed Mushroom Sauté

ALAN BESSETTE

4 tablespoons butter
3 green onions, chopped
6 cups (1 pound) mushrooms, sliced or chopped
1 teaspoon dried tarragon

Melt butter; add onions and sauté 1 minute. Add mushrooms; sauté until all liquid is evaporated. Add tarragon; season to taste with salt and pepper.

Serves 2 to 4.

# Sausage-stuffed Mushroom Caps

ARLEEN RAINIS BESSETTE

Preheat oven to 375°F.

Remove stems from mushroom caps and mince. Coat caps with lemon juice or white wine to prevent discoloration. Mix well: minced stems, sausage, spices, salt, and pepper. Fill caps with stuffing, rounding tops. Place filled caps on greased baking sheet and bake until sausage is cooked (about 15 minutes).

Serves 4.

16 medium-large mushrooms
Lemon juice or dry white wine
½ pound sweet Italian sausage
1 tablespoon minced fresh
  parsley
Dash crushed red pepper flakes
⅛ teaspoon salt
⅛ teaspoon pepper
Shortening

# Scrambled Eggs and Wild Mushrooms

ALAN BESSETTE

2 tablespoons butter
½ cup chopped wild
    mushrooms
½ cup chopped sweet red
    pepper
½ cup slivered onion
1 small tomato, diced
4 eggs, lightly beaten with
    1 tablespoon light cream
Buttered rye toast

Melt butter in skillet; sauté mushrooms, pepper, onion, and tomato until liquid is absorbed. Season to taste with salt and pepper. Pour in beaten eggs, and scramble over medium heat to desired consistency. Serve over buttered rye toast.

Serves 2.

# Seaweed and Wild Mushrooms

ARLEEN RAINIS BESSETTE

Sauté carrots, onion, and mushrooms in oil. Rinse seaweed in water; add to sautéed mushrooms and vegetables. Add enough water to cover. Simmer covered for 5 minutes. Add tofu, soy sauce, sherry, and vinegar; simmer 15 minutes more. Serve over brown rice.

Serves 4.

2 carrots, sliced
1 medium onion, chopped
1 cup sliced wild mushrooms
1 tablespoon oil
1 cup dried Arame seaweed
½ pound tofu, cut into
    1-inch cubes
1 tablespoon soy sauce or
    tamari
1 teaspoon cooking sherry
1 tablespoon vinegar
Hot cooked brown rice

# Peppers and Mushrooms Filadelfia Style

MARIA GIGLIO

5 pounds mushrooms
½ cup olive oil
3 pounds sweet peppers, cut
  into small pieces
1 pound hot peppers, cut into
  small pieces
1 cup tomatoes, whole or
  crushed
1 teaspoon salt

Boil mushrooms until soft; drain water, and pat mushrooms dry. Fry in ¼ cup olive oil until slightly crispy, and then drain. Fry sweet and hot peppers in remaining ¼ cup oil in a second skillet until slightly browned. Add mushrooms, tomatoes, and salt. Serve with steak or chops, or make a sandwich. A glass of red wine is an excellent way to complement this dish.

Serves 8 to 10.

# Stuffed Mushrooms

VICKI HAINES

12 large mushrooms
1 small onion, chopped
1 clove garlic, chopped
2 tablespoons vegetable oil
1 egg, beaten
6 tablespoons bread crumbs
1 tablespoon minced parsley

Remove mushroom stems and chop until they are very fine. Sauté stems, onion, and garlic in oil. Season to taste with salt and pepper. Combine with egg, 4 tablespoons bread crumbs, and parsley. Fill caps with mixture. Sprinkle with remaining bread crumbs. Bake on greased cookie sheet 20 minutes at 400°F. Seasoned bread crumbs may be substituted for extra flavor.

Serves 2 to 4.

# Tortellini in Mushroom Broth

ARLEEN RAINIS BESSETTE

Chop mushrooms finely in food processor or blender; sauté in butter until tender. Add consommé and bring to boil; reduce heat and simmer 15 to 20 minutes. Strain. Return broth to saucepan; save mushrooms for meatloaf, stuffing, or other use. Bring broth to boil, add Tortellini and cook until done. Add Madeira; remove from heat and serve piping hot.

Serves 4.

**4 cups mixed mushrooms**
**4 tablespoons butter**
**6 cups beef consommé**
**1 package Tortellini**
**¼ cup Madeira wine**

# Glossary

AGARIC: A mushroom with gills.

ATTACHED: Connected to the stalk (refers particularly to gills, tubes, or other spore-producing structures).

BASAL: At or of the base of a mushroom stalk.

BASE: The bottom end of a mushroom stalk.

BOLETE: A mushroom with a cap, a stalk, and a detachable layer of tubes with a visible pore surface.

BROAD: Wide, as measured from the edge of the gill to the cap flesh (refers to gills).

BULBOUS: Swollen (refers to the base of a stalk).

BUTTON: An immature mushroom, especially one with a partial or universal veil.

CAP: The top part of some mushrooms, the undersurface of which bears the gills, tubes, or other spore-producing structures.

CLUSTERED: Having several mushroom stalks that are fused at the base.

CONCENTRIC: Arranged in circles, one around another.

CONIFER: A tree, such as pine, spruce, or fir, that produces seeds in cones.

CUTICLE: A layer of tissue on the top surface of a mushroom cap.

DECIDUOUS: A tree, such as a hardwood, that doesn't produce seeds in cones and typically sheds its leaves annually.

DEPRESSED: Sunken at the center (refers to the top surface of a mushroom cap).

DESCENDING: Attached to and extending somewhat down the stalk (usually refers to gills, pores, or other spore-producing structures).

DOME SHAPED: Having a rounded upper surface, like an upside-down mixing bowl (refers to the shape of a mushroom cap).

DUFF: Dead plant matter, especially leaves or conifer needles, on the forest floor.

FLESH: The interior tissue of a mushroom cap (excluding the gills, tubes, or spines) or stalk.

FORAY: A search, especially for gathering edible wild mushrooms, plants, berries, or other food.

FORKED: Branching in a Y pattern.

FREE: Not connected to the stalk (refers to gills, tubes, or other spore-producing structures). (Note: To be sure that a mushroom's gills are truly free from the stalk, examine the top end of the stalk to rule out vertical lines indicating that the gills were attached but have since separated.)

GILLED MUSHROOM: A mushroom with gills.

GILLS: Flat-sided, bladelike radial structures on the undersurface of some mushroom caps.

GLEBA: The interior tissue of a puffball that matures into a powdery mass of spores.

GROUPED: Several specimens quite close to one another, but not clustered.

HABITAT: The kind of environment a specific fungus requires.

HUMUS: Dead organic matter (e.g., plants, leaves, dung) on the forest floor.

HYPHAE: Microscopic threads of fungal cells.

INCURVED: Curled in toward the stalk somewhat (refers to the edge of a mushroom cap).

INROLLED: Curled in and up (refers to the edge of a mushroom cap).

LARVAE: Insects in an immature, wingless stage, typically looking like tiny worms.

LATERAL: Attached directly to and extending out from the edge of a mushroom cap (refers to a mushroom stalk).

LATEX: A fluid leaked by the cut or damaged gills or flesh of some mushrooms.

LONGITUDINAL SECTION: Cutting a mushroom in half lengthwise (from top to bottom) through the cap and stalk.

MYCELIUM: A mass of hyphae, typically hidden in a substrate.

MYCOLOGIST: A person who studies mushrooms and other fungi.

MYCOLOGY: The study of mushrooms and other fungi.

MYCOPHAGIST: A person who eats mushrooms.

MYCOPHAGY: The use of mushrooms as food.

MYCOPHOBIA: The fear of mushrooms, especially the fear of eating them.

MYCORRHIZAL: Having a symbiotic (mutually beneficial) relationship with a tree or other plant.

NARROW: Not wide, typically a measure of the gills from their edge to the cap flesh.

NOTCHED: Distinctly narrower at or near the stalk (refers to attached gills).

OFF CENTER: Attached somewhat away from the center of the cap undersurface but not attached directly to the edge of the cap (refers to a mushroom stalk).

PARASITIC: Deriving nourishment from another organism at the other organism's expense.

PARTIAL VEIL: A layer of fungal tissue that covers the gills or pores of an immature gilled mushroom or bolete.

PERENNIAL: Living for longer than one year (refers to a mycelium).

POLYPORE: A mushroom with a layer of tubes that cannot be easily separated from the cap flesh.

PORES: The open ends of the tubes of a bolete or polypore.

PORE SURFACE: The undersurface of the cap of a bolete or polypore where the open ends of the tubes are visible.

RADIAL: Pointed away from a common central point, like the spokes of a wheel.

RING: Remnant of a partial veil that remains attached to the stalk after the veil ruptures.

SAPROBIC: Deriving nourishment from such dead organic matter as wood or humus.

SCABERS: Small, stiff, granular points on the surface of some boletes' stalks.

SCALY: Having scales (refers to a mushroom stalk or cap surface).

SERRATE: Jagged or "toothed" (refers to gill edge).

SPINE FUNGI: Mushrooms that have spines.

SPINES: Tapered, typically downward-pointing projections on a mushroom cap's undersurface.

SPORE: A microscopic reproductive cell with the ability to germinate and form hyphae.

SPORE PRINT: A deposit of spores from a mushroom's gills, tubes, or other spore-producing structures on a piece of paper.

STAINING: Changing color when bruised or cut, or in age.

STALK: A typically cylindrical structure that arises from the substrate and supports the cap of a mushroom.

STALKLESS: Lacking a stalk.

SUBSTRATE: Organic matter that serves as a food source for a fungal mycelium.

TEETH: Spines that point downward.

TOOTH FUNGI: Spine fungi.

TUBES: Narrow, parallel, spore-producing cylinders on the undersurface of the cap of a bolete or polypore.

UNIVERSAL VEIL: A layer of fungal tissue that completely encloses immature specimens of some mushrooms.

VEIL: A layer of fungal tissue that covers all or part of some immature mushrooms (see *Partial veil* and *Universal veil*).

VOLVA: A typically cuplike sac that remains around the base of a mushroom stalk when the universal veil ruptures.

WARTS: Small patches of tissue that remain on the top of a mushroom cap when the universal veil ruptures.

ZONES: Concentric, circular bands of different colors on the top surface of a mushroom cap.

# Recommended Reading

## Field Guides

Arora, David. *All That the Rain Promises, and More . . . : A Hip Pocket Guide to Western Mushrooms*. Berkeley, Calif.: Ten Speed Press, 1991.

———. *Mushrooms Demystified: A Comprehensive Guide to the Fleshy Fungi*. 2d ed. Berkeley, Calif.: Ten Speed Press, 1986.

Bandoni, R. J., and A. F. Szczawinski. *Guide to Common Mushrooms of British Columbia*. British Columbia Provincial Museum Handbook no. 24. Rev. ed. Victoria, B.C.: A. Sutton, 1976.

Bessette, Alan E. *Guide to Some Edible and Poisonous Mushrooms of New York*. Rome, N.Y.: Canterbury Press, 1985.

———. *Mushrooms of the Adirondacks: A Field Guide*. Utica, N.Y.: North Country Books, 1988.

———, and Walter J. Sundberg. *Mushrooms: A Quick Reference Guide to Mushrooms of North America*. New York: Macmillan, 1987.

Buczacki, Stefan. *New Generation Guide to the Fungi of Britain and Europe*. Austin: University of Texas Press, 1989.

Groves, J. W. *Edible and Poisonous Mushrooms of Canada*. 2d rev. ed. Ottawa: Research Branch, Agriculture Canada, 1979.

Huffman, Don M., Lois H. Tiffany, and George Knaphus. *Mushrooms and Other Fungi of the Midcontinental United States*. Ames: Iowa State University Press, 1989.

Katsaros, Peter. *Familiar Mushrooms*. New York: Knopf, 1990.

Lincoff, G. H. *The Audubon Society Field Guide to North American Mushrooms*. New York: Knopf, 1981.

McKenny, Margaret, and Daniel E. Stuntz. *The New Savory Wild Mushroom*. Revised and enlarged by Joseph F. Ammirati. Seattle: University of Washington Press, 1987.

McKnight, Kent H., and Vera B. McKnight. *A Field Guide to Mushrooms of North America*. Boston: Houghton Mifflin, 1987.

Marteka, Vincent. *Mushrooms: Wild and Edible*. New York: Norton, 1980.

Metzler, Susan, and Van Metzler. *Texas Mushrooms: A Field Guide*. Scientific advisor, Orson K. Miller, Jr. Austin: University of Texas Press, 1992.

Miller, O. K., Jr. *Mushrooms of North America*. New York: Dutton, 1979.

———, and Hope H. Miller. *Mushrooms in Color*. New York: Dutton, 1980.

Phillips, Roger. *Mushrooms and Other Fungi of Great Britain and Europe*. London: Pan Books, 1981.

———, assisted by Geoffrey Kibby and Nicky Foy. *Mushrooms of North America*. Boston: Little, Brown, 1991.

Smith, A. H. *A Field Guide to Western Mushrooms*. Ann Arbor: University of Michigan Press, 1975.

————, H. V. Smith, and N. S. Weber. *How to Know the Gilled Mushrooms*. Dubuque, Iowa: William C. Brown, 1979.

————, H. V. Smith, and N. S. Weber. *How to Know the Non-gilled Mushrooms*. 2d ed. Dubuque, Iowa: William C. Brown, 1981.

————, and N. S. Weber. *The Mushroom Hunter's Field Guide*. Ann Arbor: University of Michigan Press, 1980.

States, Jack S. *Mushrooms and Truffles of the Southwest*. Tucson: University of Arizona Press, 1990.

Sundberg, Walter J., and John A. Richardson. *Mushrooms and Other Fungi of the Land between the Lakes*. Knoxville: Tennessee Valley Authority, 1980.

Thiers, Harry. *California Mushrooms: A Field Guide to the Boletes*. New York: Hafner Press, 1975.

Tylutki, Edmond E. *Mushrooms of Idaho and the Pacific Northwest*. Vol. 2, *Non-gilled Hymenomycetes*. Moscow: University of Idaho Press, 1987.

Weber, Nancy Smith. *A Morel Hunter's Companion*. Lansing, Mich.: Two Peninsula Press, 1988.

————, and A. H. Smith. *A Field Guide to Southern Mushrooms*. Ann Arbor: University of Michigan Press, 1985.

## General References

Ammirati, J. F., J. A. Traquir, and P. A. Horgen. *Poisonous Mushrooms of the Northern United States and Canada*. Minneapolis: University of Minnesota Press, 1985.

Brodie, Harold J. *Fungi: Delight of Curiosity*. Toronto: University of Toronto Press, 1978.

Cazort, Mimi, ed. *Mr. Jackson's Mushrooms*. Toronto: National Museum of Canada, 1979.

Dickinson, C., and J. Lucas. *The Encyclopedia of Mushrooms*. New York: Putnam, 1979.

Findlay, W. P. K. *Fungi: Folklore, Fiction & Fact*. Richmond, England: Richmond Publishing Co., 1982.

Friedman, Sara Ann. *Celebrating the Wild Mushroom: A Passionate Quest*. New York: Dodd, Mead & Co., 1986.

Hanrahan, J. P., and M. A. Gordon. "Mushroom Poisoning: Case Reports and a Review of Therapy." *Journal of the American Medical Association* 251(1984): 1057–1061.

Harris, Robert. *Growing Wild Mushrooms*. Berkeley, Calif.: Wingbow Press, 1976.

Lincoff, G. H., and D. H. Mitchell. *Toxic and Hallucinogenic Mushroom Poisoning*. New York: Van Nostrand Reinhold, 1977.

Rumack, B. H., and E. Salzman, eds. *Mushroom Poisoning: Diagnosis and Treatment*. West Palm Beach, Fla.: CRC Press, 1978.

Seymour, Jacqueline. *Mushrooms and Toadstools*. London: Crown Publishers, 1978.

Stamets, Paul, and J. S. Chilton. *The Mushroom Cultivator*. Olympia, Wash.: Agarikon Press, 1983.

## *Cooking with Mushrooms*

Carluccio, Antonio. *A Passion for Mushrooms*. Topsfield, Mass.: Salem House, 1989.

Czarnecki, Jack. *Joe's Book of Mushroom Cookery*. New York: Atheneum, 1986.

Leibenstein, Margaret. *The Edible Mushroom: A Gourmet Cook's Guide*. New York: Ballantine Books, 1986.

Phillips, Roger. *Wild Food*. Boston: Little, Brown, 1986.

Puget Sound Mycological Society. *Wild Mushroom Recipes*. Seattle: Pacific Search Press, 1973.

# Index of Common
# and Scientific Names

Boldfaced page numbers refer to photographs
and/or descriptions.
*Italicized page numbers refer to recipes.*